ISLAMIC ☪
BANKING & FINANCE
IN SOUTH-EAST ASIA

Its Development & Future

2nd Edition

Asia-Pacific Business Series – Vol. 3

ISLAMI☪

BANKING & FINANCE

IN SOUTH-EAST ASIA

Its Development & Future

2nd Edition

Angelo M Venardos

World Scientific

NEW JERSEY · LONDON · SINGAPORE · BEIJING · SHANGHAI · HONG KONG · TAIPEI · CHENNAI

Published by

World Scientific Publishing Co. Pte. Ltd.

5 Toh Tuck Link, Singapore 596224

USA office: 27 Warren Street, Suite 401-402, Hackensack, NJ 07601

UK office: 57 Shelton Street, Covent Garden, London WC2H 9HE

Library of Congress Cataloging-in-Publication Data
Venardos, Angelo M.
  Islamic banking and finance in South-east Asia : Its development and future (2nd ed.) / by
Angelo M. Venardos.
   p. cm.
  Includes bibliographical references and index.
  ISBN-13 978-981-256-888-5 (pbk) -- ISBN-10 981-256-888-3 (alk. paper)
   1. Banks and banking--Southeast Asia 2. Banks and banking--Islamic countries.
3. Banks and banking--Religious aspects--Islam. 4. Islamic law--Southeast Asia.
5. Southeast Asia--Economic conditions. I. Title.

HG3.V46 2006
332.1'0959--dc22

                                              2006048289

First Published 2006
Reprinted 2007

British Library Cataloguing-in-Publication Data
A catalogue record for this book is available from the British Library.

Inhouse Editor: Juliet Lee Ley Chin

Typeset by Stallion Press
Email: enquiries@stallionpress.com

Printed by FuIsland Offset Printing (S) Pte Ltd, Singapore

This book is dedicated to Mona, without whose support this book would not have been possible and who continues to remind me of the virtues of humility, persistence and patience.

Contents

Foreword

The title *Islamic Banking and Finance in South-east Asia* modestly understates the achievements of this scholarly yet reader-friendly work. In fact the author, himself a non-Muslim, examines Islamic History, Jurisprudence, Commercial Law, Financing, Issues and Challenges of Sharia'ah Jurisprudence, the challenges to Accounting and Regulatory methodologies and the Impact of English-based Law on Islamic financial beliefs and practices. Yet he achieves immensely more that is both timely and invaluable.

Being a Muslim myself, I have long welcomed for such work, particularly issues touching on Muslim community's sensitivity in business and finance for it to be shared with the rest of the world. We believe that Islam is a religion which is complete in every aspect of life, both in present and hereafter. Since over one thousand and four hundred years, Islam has laid the foundation for a global system of financial administration which encompasses all economic aspects.

Discussions relating to Islamic finance invariably draw comparisons between "Islamic" and "conventional" financial practices. There is a comfortable sound to "conventional" and a slight pejorative ring to "unconventional". Yet the OED defines "conventional" as "... accepting social conventions; in accordance with accepted (artificial) standards or models; orthodox; lacking originality, spontaneity or realism..." and "unconventional" as "... diverging from accepted standards or models...". This can be expressed more simply, it has become "conventional" to be greedy. What if we could eradicate greed? How much stupidity and criminality could be fore-stalled? How much further would we progress towards good gover-nance? How much better off would we all be? And isn't it interesting that for centuries English-based law has needed access to the law of equity to correct the wrongs otherwise wrought by the common law?

Islamic financial methodologies spring from an aversion from greed, and embrace concepts of sharing both profit and loss, of mutual support, the restriction of risk and of reasonable reward. And because no Muslim should be penalized for his or her way of life and beliefs, there is a need for Islamic solutions that are com-petitive with (acceptable) "conventional" products. The author very readably does a fine job of leading us to a better understanding of Islamic thought that treasures what might be cynically dismissed by the uninitiated as "the old standards". Dr. Venardos has worked hard and has produced a gem.

Mr. Khairul A. Khairuddin, LL B(Hons)
Director of HMR Trust Ltd, a licensed trust
company in Brunei Darussalam
Brunei, June 2004

Preface to 2nd Edition

This second edition contains updates of statistics and dates in regards to the development of Islamic Banking in Malaysia, Labuan, Singapore, Indonesia and Brunei.

The chapter on Singapore details significant developments such as the direction which major banks are taking towards Islamic Banking and the increase in Islamic Banking products offered in Singapore.

This book serves as an overview of the development of Islamic Banking in South-east Asia specifically and is not meant to be a practitioner's guide to the aspects of Islamic Banking per se. It offers a more accessible and less exhaustive alternative to other more philosophical and technical books on Islamic banking.

I am pleased that the rights of this book have been sold to be translated into Arabic by the leading Islamic university King Saud in the Middle East.

Angelo M Venardos

Acknowledgements

The genesis of this book commenced with my attendance, as a banker from the conventional system, at the first International Islamic Finance Forum held in Dubai in March 2002. This then led to a research paper as part of a doctoral degree programme at Bond University Law School, Australia, out of which the present study has grown.

My thanks and sincere appreciation goes to Mr Robert Miller, Head of the Brunei International Financial Centre for his encouragement to write this book; to Ms Geraldine Pang, my assistant, who did much of the research; and to Ms Juliet Lee Ley Chin, my editor at World Scientific Publishing, who has worked tirelessly with me to produce this book.

Every effort has been made to cite and acknowledge all sources of reference materials used. Omissions, if any, are unintentional and the author apologises in advance should this be found to be the case.

The royalties from the sale of this book are to go to religious and educational bodies for the betterment of Muslim/Christian understanding.

Angelo M. Venardos

Introduction

The key feature, or principle, that distinguishes Islamic banks from any other kind of bank is the rejection of interest-based financial transactions. The Quran's ban on giving or receiving interest is known to all devout Muslims. The words from Chapter 2, Verse 278 of the Quran are, in fact, quite specific: "O you who believe! Have fear of Allah and give up what remains of what is due to you of usury.... If you do not, then take notice of war from Allah and His Messenger."

Just how serious a sin is paying or receiving interest? Shaykh Nizam Yaquby, an Islamic scholar who is trained in both economics (at McGill University in Canada) and in Islamic Shari'ah law (in Saudi Arabia, India and Morocco), noted that Christianity and Judaism got over their hangups about it sometime during the Middle Ages — the Old Testament also includes several stern warnings about interest — but Islam never really budged. Back in the days of Muhammad, the reasons for deploring interest were self-evident. Loan-sharking was rampant, and failure to repay a loan could mean slavery. By outlawing interest, Islam advocated an economy based on risk-sharing, fair dealing and equity — in both the financial and social-justice senses of the word.

Islamic scholars believe this system is superior on several counts. It leads to more prudent lending, they say, by encouraging financiers to invest directly in an entrepreneur's ventures. "A financial system without interest is more interested," says Shaykh Yusuf DeLorenzo (a Virginia-based Islamic scholar).

1

Accordingly the scholars believe that interest-free finance would also prevent future Enrons and Argentinas. "One reason for prohibiting interest is to keep everybody spending according to his limit," says Yaquby. "This consumerism society was only created because of the banking system, because it encourages 'buy today, pay tomorrow'. You also have poor economies in debt to rich ones. This is because of borrowing and lending with interest. So this is creating big economic chaos in the world."

Against such a background, there are many who see Islamic finance as a possible way forward to a brighter and more socially responsible future. Today, there are more than 200 Islamic financial institutions spread across the Middle East and beyond. They include banks, mutual funds, mortgage companies, insurance companies — in short, an entire parallel economy in which Allah, not Alan Greenspan, has the final say. Industry growth has averaged 10 to 15 per cent a year and sniffing opportunity, conventional banks like Citibank and Hongkong & Shanghai Banking Corporation (HSBC) have opened Islamic "windows" in the Gulf. And whilst the industry's market share is still modest — about 10 per cent in Bahrain — its very existence challenges the modern assumption that global capitalism flattens all before it. According to Fouad Shaker, secretary general of the Union of Arab Banks, there are over 265 Islamic financial institutions in the world with capitalisation in excess of US$13 billion and assets of over US$262 billion.[1]

At the beginning of the twenty-first century, many Western, Middle Eastern and Asian financial institutions recognise Islamic banking as an important new opportunity for growth and have adopted Islamic practices to serve this expanding market. Islamic mutual funds have also sprung up which invest client monies in ways that do not conflict with the conscience or practical interests

---

[1] "Global role seen for Islamic banking", *Al Jazeera*, Qatar, 7 December 2003.

of Muslims. In this respect they are rather like socially responsible funds in the West.

The prohibition of interest — the ethical core of Islamic banking — derives from Islamic law, which is enshrined in the Shari'ah. The word *shari'ah* literally means a waterway that leads to a main stream, a drinking place, and a road or the right path. It is a term that encapsulates a way of life prescribed by Allah for his servants and it extends to every department of daily life, including commerce and financial activities of every kind. Since the advent of Islam dates back to the seventh century, the application of ethical principles that were first established fourteen centuries ago to modern situations and circumstances can be a complex matter. Naturally, ancient texts are mute on such matters as derivatives and stock options, which means that modern-day Islamic scholars must extrapolate. Currency hedging, for instance, is prohibited on the basis of *gharar*, a principle that says that one should not profit from another's uncertainty. Futures contracts are not allowed, since Muhammad said we should not buy "fish in the sea" or "dates that are still on the tree". As for day trading, it is too much like gambling.

Bonds are an area of divergent thinking. Malaysian scholars have approved the issuance of specially designed "Islamic bonds". But Middle Eastern scholars, who take a harder line than their Far Eastern counterparts, have roundly criticised them. "Playing semantics with God is very dangerous," warns Yaquby. "Calling fornication 'making love' doesn't make it any different."

Everybody can agree on one matter, though: It is okay to buy and sell stocks, since stocks represent real assets. And now they can be traded safely, using the Dow Jones Islamic Index. Launched in 1999 with the help of Yaquby, the index offers a pre-screened universe of stocks for the devout stock picker. One screen removes companies that make more than 5 per cent of their revenues from sinful businesses. That expels such notables as Vivendi (alcohol), Citigroup (interest), Marriott (pork served in hotel restaurants), and FOR-TUNE's parent company, AOL Time Warner (unwholesome music and entertainment). A second screen eliminates companies with too much debt, the cut-off being a debt-to-market-capitalisation ratio of 33 per cent. A third screen applies the same standard to a company's cash and interest-bearing securities, whilst a fourth makes sure that accounts receivable do not exceed 45 per cent of assets. "Islamic investing is low-debt, non-financial, socialethical investing," explains Rushdi Siddiqui, who manages the index at Dow Jones.[2]

Of the 5200 stocks in the Dow Jones global index, 1400 make the cut — yet even those may not be entirely pure. If a company makes, say, 2 per cent of its money from selling pork rinds, an investor must give away 2 per cent of his dividends to charity, a process known as "portfolio purification". At the same time, he should urge management to exit the pork-rind business.

But demand for Islamic mutual funds is booming. There are now more than 100 funds worldwide, including three based in the United States, while a clutch of Internet companies position themselves as the Muslim E*Trade (iHilal.com), the Muslim Morningstar (Failaka.com), and the Muslim Yahoo Finance (IslamiQ). The latter offers members a feature called "Ask the Scholars".

The first Muslim-owned banks were established in the 1920s and 1930s, but they adopted similar practices to conventional banks. Then in the 1940s and the 1950s, several experiments with small Islamic banks were undertaken in Malaysia and Pakistan. The first significant success was in the Egyptian village of Mit Ghamr, which set up a bank that conducted business according to Islamic principles in 1963. Other successes include the establishment of the Inter-Government Islamic Development Bank in Jeddah in 1975, and a number of commercial Islamic banks such as the Dubai Islamic

---

[2]Cited in Useem, Jerry, "Devout Muslims don't pay or receive interest. So how can their financial system work?", *Fortune*, 10 June 2002, pp. 61–65.

Bank, the Kuwait Finance House and the Bahrain Islamic Bank in the 1970s and 1980s. Commercial banks have also realised the potential of this new field, and a number of major worldwide institutions have grasped Islamic banking as a significant mechanism for more diversified growth.[3]

The dramatic growth of Islamic finance over the last two decades is one of the more striking phenomena in international banking. Twenty years ago there were a handful of Islamic financial institutions; today there are over 187 Islamic banks worldwide, and major international banks such as Citibank have established their own Islamic finance arms.[4] In 1997, the total assets of Islamic financial institutions were estimated at over US$100 billion,[5] compared with US$5 billion in 1985,[6] and currently the total assets in the global Islamic banking industry stand at over US$260 billion, with an annual growth rate of 23.5 per cent.[7] Moreover, this growth is not limited to Islamic countries such as Pakistan, Saudi Arabia or the Gulf States. The Islamic banking sector has gained a toehold in the United States and Western Europe, with a number of non-bank Islamic finance service entities presently in operation. At least three Islamic leasing companies are currently operating in the United States and the United Bank of Kuwait has recently begun to offer retail Islamic mortgages in the United States. At the same time, US and foreign-based multinationals, such as General Electric,

---

[3]Al Tamimi & Company, "Islamic finance: A UAE legal perspective", International Islamic Finance Forum, International Institute of Research, Dubai, March 2002, p. 1.

[4]DeLorenzo, Yusuf, *A Compendium of Legal Opinions on the Operations of Islamic Banks*, Institute of Islamic Banking and Insurance, London, 1996.

[5]Khalili, Sarah, "Unlocking Islamic finance", *Infrastructure Finance*, April 1997, p. 19.

[6]Iqbal, Zamir, "Islamic banking gains momentum", *Middle East Executive Reports*, January 1998.

[7]"Assets in Islamic banking industry put at over 260 billion dollars", *ClariNet* (www.clari.net), 25 September 2003.

Exxon Mobil and Royal Dutch Shell have all utilised Islamic financing in recent years.[8] The Muslim Community Co-operative Australia (MCCA), which was established in February 1989, operates from its head office in Burwood, Victoria. MCCA's activities involve financial dealings and transactions based on Islamic finance principles. Transactions that involve interest are completely excluded from MCCA's activities.[9] In late 2003, a US$100 million ($1.44 million) Islamic equity fund was launched to invest in private Australian and New Zealand companies with products compatible with Muslim Shari'ah laws.[10]

Although Islam is traditionally associated with the Middle East, North Africa, Pakistan and India, the countries of South-east Asia also make up an important component in the Islamic community worldwide. In 2003, it was estimated that there were 221.16 million Muslims in South-east Asia, which represents some 15 per cent of Muslims worldwide. Malaysia, Indonesia and Brunei Darussalam, though constitutionally secular states, are the principal Islamic countries in the region, but there is also a sizeable Muslim population in the Philippines and significant Muslim representation in Thailand. Indonesia, which has a Muslim majority of 194.04 million, is the most populous Muslim country in the world.[11]

The introduction and implementation of Islamic banking in South-east Asia is not as far advanced as in the Middle East, but the potential of this as yet untapped market is immense, making it an extremely attractive proposition to every kind of investor, including both Islamic bankers and conventional bankers alike. Malaysia was

---

[8]Martin, Josh, "Islamic banking raises interest", The International Islamic Financial Forum, International Institute of Research, Dubai, March 2002, p. 25.

[9]"Principles of Islamic banking", *Nida'ul Islam Magazine* (www.islam.org.au), November–December 1995.

[10]Taylor, Lenore, "Muslim fund for Australia", *Australian Financial Review*, 20 October 2003.

[11]Muslim Population Worldwide (www.islamicpopulation.com).

the first South-east Asian country to develop an Islamic banking sector with the introduction of an Islamic Banking Act and the simultaneous establishment of the Bank Islam Malaysia Bhd in 1983. As of 30 June 2003, Islamic banking assets accounted for 9.4 per cent (RM75.5 billion) of the banking sector in Malaysia and the government wants that share to rise to 20 per cent by 2010 with the aim of putting Kuala Lumpur on the map as a regional hub for Islamic finance in South-east Asia.[12]

Islamic banking in Indonesia is not nearly as well developed as it is in Malaysia with Islamic banks holding only a 0.12 per cent share of the assets in the banking system. However, as mentioned, Indonesia is the world's most populous Muslim nation and in this respect the country represents a potentially huge market with enormous scope for growth and expansion. In order to accommodate the public need for the existence of a new banking system, the Indonesian Government introduced legislation in 1992 which implicitly allowed the development of Shari'ah-compliant banking operations as an adjunct to the conventional banking system — in effect a dual banking system. Subsequent legislation in 1998 and 1999 gave authority to Bank Indonesia to conduct its operations according to Shari'ah principles.[13]

Islamic financial institutions in Indonesia include the Bank Muamalat Indonesia, which has been operating since 1992, several new Islamic branches of regular commercial banks and at least one bank that has just converted from conventional interest-based banking to Shari'ah-compliant banking activities. There are also a large number of smaller banks and savings and loan cooperatives, which also conduct their business according to Shari'ah law.[14]

---

[12] "Malaysia to accept Islamic banks", *The Financial Gazette*, 6 May 2003.

[13] "The blueprint of Islamic banking development in Indonesia", *Bank Indonesia*, September 2002.

[14] Timberg, Thomas A., "Islamic banking in *Indonesia*", *Rural Finance Learning Centre*, Partnership for Economic Growth, June 1999.

The progress of Islamic banking in Indonesia has been impeded by the lack of comprehensive and appropriate framework and instruments for regulation and supervision, limited market coverage, lack of knowledge and understanding on the part of the public, lack of efficient institutional structures supporting efficient Shari'ah banking operations, operational inefficiency, domination of non-share-based financing and limited capability to comply with international Shari'ah financial standards.[15]

Brunei Darussalam is as tiny, as Indonesia is great, in terms of population and geographical extent, but it is politically stable, enormously wealthy and has recently introduced a series of major legislative changes specifically intended to encourage an exciting banking and finance environment. Whilst it is a predominantly Islamic country, it has the infrastructure, legal institutions and government support to recommend itself as a potential modern financial centre, running parallel banking systems to the benefit of both Islamic and traditional investors. In this last respect, Brunei Darussalam represents perhaps the most interesting player in the region in relation to the future development of Islamic banking in South-east Asia.

To do business with Muslim clients, and to engage in cross-border financing, one needs to be familiar with current Islamic financial practices and potential avenues of innovation. Students and scholars of Middle Eastern and Islamic culture will likewise benefit from understanding this important aspect of Islamic life. As a non-Muslim, it has become a timely interest of mine to study and examine the emergence of Islamic Banking and Finance, particularly in regard to its rapid development in South-east Asia. There is a silent financial revolution taking place, and it is spreading to non-muslim countries as well. The importance and potential of Islamic Banking has prompted the International Monetary Fund (IMF) to facilitate the establishment of the Islamic Financial Services Board (IFSB) to

---

[15] *Bank Indonesia*, op. cit.

address the need for a more suitable regulatory framework, new financial instruments and institutional arrangements to provide an enabling operational environment for Islamic finance.[16]

To those who fail to understand the Islamic way of life, it may seem odd a non-Muslim should be involved in the detail of the subject matter of this particular work. However, such an involvement is welcomed by my Muslim friends.

As the reader will learn, Muslims welcome participation in their financial dealings by all who are prepared to abide by the rules. Those rules proscribe usury in the broader sense, and it is this aspect of charging interest, of causing cost without return, that is widely known but imperfectly understood in the "conventional" or non-Muslim world.

---

[16]Sundararajan, V. and Errico, Luca, "Islamic financial institutions and products in the global financial system: Key issues in risk management and challenges ahead", *International Monetary Fund*, November 2002.

Chapter 1

Islamic History

Islam is one of the world's three major monotheistic religions, the other two being Judaism and Christianity. All three share the same historical origins and hold many beliefs in common, a mutual reverence for the Old Testament prophets being among them. As in Judaism, Islam forbids the consumption of pork as well as other meat that has not been ritually killed (*halah*).[17] Muslims recognise Jesus (Isa) as a prophet but reject the belief that he was the Son of God. Nor do they recognise the concept of the Holy Spirit, but insist instead on the unity of God (Allah), disavowing the Christian concept of the Trinity. They also reject the concept of original sin and the notion that there can be any intercessor between a person and God, since in Islam, each person is responsible for his or her own salvation which can be achieved through faith and good deeds, and by striving to keep God's law which is laid down in the Quran.

1.1 The Quran

The Quran is the holy book of Islam, containing revelations received by the Prophet Muhammad from God. It was revealed in the Arabic

---

[17]*Halah* — Islamically permissible, that which is lawful according to the Shari'ah. Although in absolute terms the same thing cannot be *halah* and *haram* (prohibited), an unclear and/or controversial issue in Islamic jurisprudence may end up with it being considered *halah* by some Islamic scholars and *haram* by others (www.iHilal.com).

language. Great importance is placed on the recital of the Quran and it is treated with reverence by all Muslims — one has to be ritually clean (*wudu*) to read the Quran.

1.2   The Five Principles of Islam

The word Islam is derived from the Arabic root *salema*, which means peace, purity, submission and obedience. In the religious sense, Islam means submission to the will of God and obedience to His law. It regulates relations between man and man, thus defining personal and social systems of obligation, and it also regulates relations between man and God and in this respect defines ritual obligation. For the Muslim there is no distinction between these two aspects of obligation; both are equally ordained.

Every solid structure or building is built on firm foundations and Islam is said to stand on "five pillars", which are ordained by God and maintained by all true Muslims. The central tenet of Islam is, of course, belief in Allah as the one God and in Muhammad as His messenger. Regular prayer is also an important part of being a good Muslim and believers are required to pray five times a day — at dawn, midday, mid-way through the afternoon, after sunset and at night. In addition, every Muslim is expected to fast during the month of Ramadan, which is the ninth month of the Islamic calendar (a lunar calendar). At this time, adult Muslims who are in good health, may neither eat nor drink during daylight hours. It is also required that each year, a Muslim should give a defined proportion of his or her accumulated wealth to the poor and needy by way of a compulsory payment known as *zakat*. Finally, each Muslim who can afford it should make a pilgrimage to Mecca at least once in his or her lifetime. This pilgrimage is known as the *Haj* and can only be properly made at the time of *Eidul-Adha*, which comes around once a year according to the Muslim calendar. These are the five pillars of Islam to which every true Muslim subscribes and which constitute the basic tenets of Islam as a religious institution.

1.3   The Mosque

The community mosque, or *masjid*, is the principal focus of Islamic worship. The first mosque was the house of the Prophet Muhammad at Medina. This was a simple rectangular enclosure with rooms for the Prophet and his wives and a shaded area on the south side which could be used for prayer in the direction of Mecca which is the birthplace of both the Prophet and the religion, Islam. Muhammad later built a pulpit or *minbar* from which to deliver his sermons and this basic formula became the archetype for subsequent mosques. The prayer hall or *musalla* is simply a large empty room with an alcove, or *mihrab*, in one wall which serves the purpose of indicating the direction of Mecca, which Muslims face as they pray. Save for the *minbar*, the internal space is kept clear with worshippers sitting on mats spread on the floor. Outside there are facilities for washing, since it is a requirement of Islam that believers be physically and mentally clean before prayer. The first minarets, from which the faithful are called to prayer, were introduced around the middle of the eight century. The mosque is not only a centre of religious worship, but also a place of learning, a community centre, and sometimes even a courtroom.

1.4   Muhammad and the Origins of Islam

According to Muslims, Islam is the original religion of the first prophets, such as Adam and Abraham, which was altered over the years, first by the Jews and then by the Christians, so that their holy books, the Torah and the Bible, no longer reflect the true word of God. For this reason, God sent a final prophet, Muhammad, and a final revelation, the Quran, as a last guidance to all mankind to follow the correct path.

Muhammad was born in Mecca in what is now Saudi Arabia, in AD 570, into a tribe known as the Quraysh who were prominent in the area at that time. Following the death of his father and mother, Muhammad was brought up, first by his grandfather, Abd al-Muttalib, and after his grandfather's death, by his uncle Abu Talib.

Tradition has it that from time to time, Muhammad retreated to a lonely cave on Mount Hira for solitude and contemplation. On one such occasion, during the month of Ramadan, he was shocked suddenly to find himself in the presence of the angel Gabriel who ordered him to recite the words embroidered on a length of green brocade. Fearing he had become possessed, he fled from the cave and reported the experience to his wife, Khadijah. She went to see her cousin, Waraqah, a wise Christian man, who assured him that the vision was genuine and that God had appointed Muhammad to be a prophet to his people. Gabriel began to appear to the Prophet on a regular basis, bringing revelations which Muhammad had to recite aloud. Gradually he began to gather around him a small band of followers, but the Quraysh did not take kindly to this new preacher who urged people to abandon the veneration of idols and worship only the one God, and they persecuted Muhammad and all who followed him — the merchants of Mecca were especially vigorous in their opposition to Muhammad because they objected to the criticism of their practices implicit in the Quran.

Finally, the persecution became so severe that Muhammad and his followers left Mecca and migrated to Medina where they were welcomed by the inhabitants. This was in AD 622 and the year of migration (*hijrah*) marks the first year of the Muslim calendar, which is represented by the letters "AH" (after *hijrah*). In the following years, Muhammad became established in Medina but he and his ever increasing band of followers had to fight many battles before they were able to overcome the opposition of the Quraysh and return to Mecca where the idols in the Ka'bah were destroyed and Islam was victorious.

1.5   The Spread of Islam

After the Prophet's death in AD 632, the leadership of the Muslim community passed to his great friend and companion, Abu Bakr, the first of the four "rightly-guided" Caliphs (successors of the Prophet). At that very moment in time, Islam was threatened with disintegration, but within a year, Abu Bakr was strong enough to attack the Persian Empire to the north-east and the Byzantine Empire in the north-west. In his *History of the Arabs*, Professor P. K. Hitti observes, "If someone in the first third of the seventh Christian century had the audacity to prophesy that within a decade some unheralded, unforeseen power from the hitherto barbarians and little known land of Arabia was to make its appearance, hurl itself against the only two powers of the age, fall heir to the one — the Sassanids, and strip the other, the Byzantine, of its fairest provinces, he would undoubtedly be declared a lunatic. Yet that was what happened."

During Abu Bakr's caliphate, and that of his successor, Omar, many further victories were gained over Byzantium and the Byzantine Empire was considerably reduced in extent by Muslim armies during the seventh and eighth centuries. It was under the next Caliph, Othman, that Islam began to spread southwards through Nubia into sub-Saharan Africa, as well as across the Straits of Gibraltar into the southern part of Spain (Al-Andalus). The Mediterranean islands of Crete, Cyprus and Rhodes were also occupied during this period.

Over the next five hundred years, Islam continued to expand through sub-Saharan Africa and Asia Minor, though the Moors in Spain were on the retreat from the twelfth century. The final defeat of Byzantium came in 1453 when the Greek Orthodox city of Constantinople (known today as Istanbul) fell to Ottoman Turks led by Mehmed II. At this point in time, the Islamic world stretched in a broad swathe across North Africa, through Asia Minor, to Afghanistan and Armenia, with outposts scattered along the maritime trade routes of South-east Asia — Sumatra, Java and the Spice

Islands of Tidore and Ternate. The Moors still had a foothold in southern Spain, but this would only be for another forty years; they were expelled in 1492.

1.6   The Golden Age of Islam

Bernard Lewis, author of *What Went Wrong? Western Impact & Middle Eastern Response*, notes that Islamic power was at its peak from the ninth through to the thirteenth century. At this moment in world history, Islam represented "the greatest military power on earth — its armies were at the same time invading Europe and Africa, India and China. It was the foremost economic power in the world [and] it had achieved the highest level so far in human history in the arts and sciences of civilization". Damascus and Baghdad were the two great centres of learning during this "golden age" of Islam. Here, Muslim scholars assembled Greek manuscripts in large numbers — including the works by Plato, Aristotle, Pythagoras and the other great philosophers and scientists of ancient times — which they studied, translated and provided with illuminating commentaries. They also welcomed other scholars from around the world without distinction of nationality or creed. By the second half of the eighth century, all the best mathematical and astronomical work was done by Muslims, while Muslim cartographers led the way in terms of their knowledge of world geography and methods of cartographic representation.[18] At the same time, schools, colleges, libraries, observatories and hospitals were built throughout the Islamic world.

At this time, the economy of the Islamic world stretched from the western end of the Mediterranean to India, but its influence extended far further as Muslim traders and merchant adventurers pursued their commercial activities to the limits of the known world.

---

[18]Ead, Hamed A., "History of Islamic science", *The Alchemy Web Site* (www.levity.com), based on the book *Introduction to the History of Science* by George Sarton.

Baghdad, the capital, was also the largest city in the Muslim world, and as well as being a great centre of learning, it was famous for its superb craftsmen and artisans, skilled in metalworking, glassware and ceramics (the economy of Baghdad was largely artisan based). Sumptuous textiles of wool, cotton, linen and silk were also produced throughout the Islamic world — the carpet weavers in Persia, Azerbaijan and Bukhara were renowned far and wide, while Egypt was a leading centre for linens and cotton textiles.

This kind of economic specialisation would not have been possible without a high level of trade and commerce. Initially, trading privileges were restricted to Arab (Muslim) merchants, but subsequently other groups such as Jews enjoyed equal trading rights. Commodities were transported from one end of the known world to the other via well-established maritime and overland trade routes with harbours and caravanserai acting as the main centres of exchange and transhipment. The Arabic language and culture facilitated this trade around the Mediterranean and through the Middle East to India, but equally the pursuit of commercial activities beyond the boundaries of the Muslim world encouraged the spread of Islam to other parts of the world including China and South-east Asia. The actual timing and introduction of Islam to South-east Asia is still a matter of considerable academic debate. European historians have tended to argue that Islam was introduced to the region via trading contacts with India, but some South-east Asian Muslim scholars claim it was brought to the region directly from Arabia and the Middle East. A third faction argues that it was Muslim Chinese merchants who were responsible — Chinese ships had been present in Indonesian waters since the beginning of the Han dynasty (206 BC–AD 400) and possibly even earlier.[19]

---

[19]Russell, Susan, "Islam: A worldwide religion and its impact in South-east Asia", www.seasite.niu.edu.

1.7   Decline and Fall

The extraordinary enterprise represented by Muslim scholarship, science, religion and commerce probably reached its highest level of achievement at the end of the fifteenth century; the reversal since that time has been quite remarkable. From around the middle of the sixteenth century, Islamic learning began to be superseded by a dramatic growth of knowledge in the West. In this last respect, the Muslim world was actually a victim of its own success. The fall of Constantinople to the Turks in 1453 prompted a mass exodus of Byzantine scholars to Rome and other European centres of learning. They brought with them the learning of ancient Greece, which had been preserved in the libraries and universities of Byzantium, and thereby set in motion a process of intellectual reawakening which eventually culminated in the Renaissance, and it was the latter which ultimately brought about the eclipse of Islam as a world power.

One consequence of the Renaissance was a broadening of European horizons in terms of world geography; the great voyages of discovery at the end of the fifteenth century quite literally put Asia on the map and enabled Europe to challenge the Muslim hegemony of East-West trade. Vasco da Gama's arrival off the Malabar Coast of India, in 1498, marked the beginning of the end of the long-standing Muslim domination of trade in the Indian Ocean and beyond, though the battle was fiercely fought in the initial years. With the Portuguese conquest of Malacca in 1508, the fight was over. Little by little, Muslims began to lose out to the economic, technological and military advances of the West and the Islamic world entered into a long, slow process of decline, drawn out over centuries, culminating in colonisation by the West and the slicing up of the Ottoman Empire in the aftermath of the First World War.[20]

---

[20]Hussain, Jamila, *Islamic Law and Society*, 1999, pp. 11–23.

1.8   A Revival of Fortunes

The years between the two world wars represent perhaps the lowest point in the history of Islam, but with the conclusion of hostilities at the end of the Second World War marked the beginning of a revival of fortunes in the Islamic world, heralded by the emergence of independence movements in many Muslim countries then under colonial rule. These movements were inspired by the writings of prominent Muslim thinkers from the first half of the twentieth century such as Muhammad Abduh and Rashid Rida in the Middle East, and Maududi in India in the early 1900s. Muhammad Abduh distrusted the Westerners and discouraged parents from sending their children to schools run by missionaries; however, he was not opposed to Western science and technology per se, recognising their essential role in their lives and encouraged mastering such knowledge. A disciple of Muhammad Abduh, Rashid Rida supported the establishment of an Islamic state, emphasising the importance for Muslims to return to the basic principles of Islam, whilst empowering themselves with modern science so as not to fall behind the Western powers. Maududi did not believe that Muslims should be governed by a secular government and so rejected Western Imperialism.

The process of achieving independence was uneven. Egypt, for example, achieved nominal independence from Britain in 1922, but Britain retained enormous influence until the Free Officers' Coup under Gamal Abd al-Nasser deposed King Faruq in 1952. Syria achieved independence from France in 1946, Lebanon was granted the same from France in 1941, whilst Britain unilaterally left Palestine in 1948, leading to the creation of a political division between Israel and the Palestinians in the West Bank and Gaza. Full independence was granted to Jordan by the British in 1946 and Iraq became an independent state from the British in 1932. The Algerian war of independence won independence from France in 1962. The Kingdom of Morocco recovered its political independence from France in 1956 and through subsequent agreements with Spain in 1956 and 1958, certain Spanish-ruled areas were returned to Morocco.

The nationalist regimes that came to power following independence from the Western mandates tended to maintain a tight control over their economies. Using a socialist economic model, countries like Egypt, Iraq, Algeria and Syria agreed to pool national resources and spend them centrally to spur economic development. One strategy adopted in the 1960s was import-substituting industrialisation (ISI). This was an attempt to build local industries that would create jobs, use local resources and allow countries to stop importing Western goods. To achieve this, Governments raised trade barriers and heavily subsidised infant industries (often owning them outright) in order to stimulate rapid economic development. Unfortunately, the ISI scheme failed when these industries became bloated, inefficient enterprises riddled with bureaucracy and corruption; they could not meet local demands and were a drain on national resources.

By the late 1970s, Egypt, under President Anwar Sadat, had abandoned the strategy of ISI in favour of *infitah*, which means opening up the economy to foreign investment. Other Muslim countries decided to follow suit and encourage foreign investment in order to stimulate their economies. Unfortunately the strategy of *infitah* has also been a disappointment. Much of the sought-after foreign investment has been in Western consumer goods and luxuries, like McDonald's and name-brand clothing, rather than in local industry. This importation of Western commodities and associated cultural values has done little to raise the general standard of living in the region. Instead, it tends to increase the cultural and economic gap between a wealthy class that has benefited from Western investment and adopted a more Western lifestyle, and a much larger population of the poor. Furthermore, many Muslims feel that the unrestricted importation of Western goods and cultural values challenges important social traditions and Islamic values. This is one factor in the rise of resentment against the West and the increasing popularity of Islamic opposition groups that promise to restore cultural and economic independence to the region.

1.9   Middle-Eastern Oil

One of the most important factors in the revival of Islamic fortunes in the twentieth century has been the discovery of enormous oil deposits in the Middle East, a serendipitous event which coincided with increasing dependence upon oil in the West. Money from oil has created enormous opportunities for development in those countries where it is concentrated, such as Saudi Arabia, Kuwait, Bahrain, the United Arab Emirates, Qatar, Iraq, Iran and Algeria. States without significant oil resources have also benefited by sending labourers to work in the richer states. The money these workers send home has contributed significantly to the economies of places like the West Bank and Gaza, Egypt and Jordan.

Oil revenues, however, can be a mixed blessing. Iraq, for example, once used its oil wealth to provide a high level of education and health care to its population, among other benefits, but military expenditures during the Iran-Iraq War (1980–88) put a significant strain on Iraq's resources and led to a drastic reduction in social spending. Saddam Hussein's subsequent decision to invade Kuwait in 1990, the US-led bombing and the UN embargo on Iraqi oil that ensued, and the continued use by the government of oil revenues for military purposes have reversed many of the social gains that had been made earlier.

1.10   Islamic Nationhood in the Late Twentieth Century

The new realities of the second half of the twentieth century shifted the concerns of Muslim reformers from the simple issue of how to combat Western influences to the challenges of the setting up and governing a modern Islamic state. In the immediate post-colonial era it was clear that the message of the first generation of Islamic reformers was no longer sufficient to reconstruct an Islamic revival, and the second generation of reformers were obliged to modify their message in order to accommodate the challenges of the home-grown political ideologies, namely nationalism, socialism and to a lesser extent, Western Liberalism. Different Muslim countries have responded in different ways, but throughout the Islamic world there has been a general revival of Islamic sense in the past quarter of a century.

Although the causes of Islam's resurgence vary by country and region, there are several common threads. Among these is a widespread feeling of failure and loss of self-esteem in many Muslim societies. Most Middle Eastern and North African countries achieved independence from colonial rule by the mid-twentieth century, but the expectations that accompanied independence were shattered by failed political systems and economies and the negative effects of modernisation. Overcrowded cities with insufficient social support systems, high unemployment rates, government corruption, and a growing gap between rich and poor characterised many of the newly independent Muslim nations. Modernisation also led to a break-down of traditional family, religious and social values.

Once enthusiastically pursued as symbols of modernity, the Western models of political and economic development increas-ingly came under criticism as sources of moral decline and spiri-tual malaise. Consequently, many countries became disillusioned with the West, and in particular with the United States. The United States' support for authoritarian Muslim rulers who backed West-ernisation, such as Iran's Mohammad Reza Shah Pahlavi, as well as America's pro-Israel policy, have only served to strengthen anti-Western feelings.

Israel's crushing victory over its Muslim neighbours in the 1967 Six-Day War became a symbol of this sense of failure. After defeating the combined forces of several Arab nations, Israel seized conquered territory from Egypt, Syria and Jordan. The loss of Jerusalem, the third holiest city of Islam, was particularly devastating to Muslims around the world.

1.11   The Iranian Revolution and After

A dramatic turning point was reached in 1979, when conservative clerical forces in Iran overthrew the Shah and established a theocratic system of government with ultimate political authority vested in a learned religious scholar, the Ayatollah Khomeini. The so-called Iranian Revolution greatly encouraged Muslim clerics and fundamentalists around the world and Islamic movements everywhere gained new impetus. Several countries, Malaysia among them, began to move towards a "re-Islamisation" of society, including the legal system, whilst still retaining a secular constitution.

The Islamic revival of the last quarter of a century has affected both the private and public lives of Muslims. Many Muslims have recommitted themselves to Islam's basic tenets by attending mosque, fasting, wearing Islamic dress, emphasising family values, and abstaining from alcohol and gambling. Publicly, the revival has manifested itself in the form of Islamic banks, religious programming in the media, a proliferation of religious literature, and the emergence of new Islamic associations dedicated to political and social reform.

As Islamic symbols, slogans, ideology and organisations became prominent fixtures in Muslim politics in the 1980s, Libya's Muammar Qaddafi, Pakistan's General Muhammad Zia ul-Haq, and other government leaders appealed to Islam in order to enhance their legitimacy and authority and to mobilise popular support. Movements in opposition to the government in Afghanistan, Egypt, Iran, Saudi Arabia and other countries did the same. Throughout the 1980s, Iran inspired anti-government protests in Kuwait and Bahrain, and helped create Islamic militias, such as Lebanon's Hezbollah (Party of God) and Islamic Jihad, both of which were involved in hijackings and hostage-takings. These acts, combined with the 1981 assassination of Egypt's president Anwar Sadat by religious extremists, contributed to the image of a monolithic radical Islamic "fundamentalist" threat to governments in the Muslim world and the West.

At the beginning of the twenty-first century, Islam remains a major presence and political force throughout the Muslim world. The question is not whether Islam has a place and role in society, but how best for it to assume that role. Whilst some Muslims wish to pursue a more secular path, others call for a more visible role of Islam in public life. The majority of Islamic activists and movements function and participate within society. A distinct minority are radical extremists who attempt to destabilise or overthrow governments and commit acts of violence and terrorism within their countries.

During the late 1980s and the 1990s Islamic political organisations began to participate in elections, when allowed, and to provide much-needed educational and social services in a number of countries. Headed by educated laity rather than the clergy, these Islamic organisations attracted a broad spectrum of members, from professionals and technocrats to the uneducated and poor. Candidates with an Islamic orientation were elected to high office in several countries. In Turkey, the leader of the Islamist Welfare Party held the office of prime minister from 1996 to 1997. In Malaysia, Anwar Ibrahim, a founder of the Malaysian Islamic Youth Movement (ABIM), served as deputy prime minister from 1993 until his dismissal in a power struggle in 1998. In the first democratic elections in Indonesia, Abdurrahman Wahid, leader of perhaps the largest Islamic movement, the Nahdlatul Ulama, was elected president in 1999. But popular support for him eroded as Indonesia's economic problems worsened, and he was removed from office in 2001.

Although the primary concerns of Islamic movements are domestic or national, international issues have also shaped Muslim politics. Among the more influential issues have been the ongoing Arab-Israeli conflict and Israel's occupation of East Jerusalem; the Soviet occupation of Afghanistan during the 1980s; the devastating impact of United Nations sanctions against Iraq following the Persian Gulf War (1991) and the consequent deaths of an estimated 500,000 Iraqi children; and forceful efforts to suppress Muslims in Bosnia, Chechnya and Kashmir. In addition, countries such as Iran,

Libya and Saudi Arabia have sought to extend their influence internationally by supporting government Islamisation programmes as well as Islamist movements elsewhere.[21]

Contrary to its reputation, Islamism is not a way back; as a contemporary ideology it offers not a means to return to some old-fashioned way of life but a way of navigating the shoals of modernisation. With few exceptions (notably, the Taliban in Afghanistan), Islamists are city dwellers trying to cope with the problems of modern urban life — not people of the countryside.[22]

However, the traditional Islamists have been known to take to violence and the will to use violence does not need much provocation anymore. In 2001, the world saw the most extreme sort of violent Islamism, as Al-Qaeda performed some of the most dramatic non-war attacks on civilian targets the world has ever seen through the September 11 attacks which caused the collapse of the Twin Towers of New York, USA.[23]

1.12   Islamic Banking and Islamic Revival

Nostalgia for this lost golden era of Islam between AD 625 and the early sixteenth century has been a strong impetus for Islamic banking. Another factor has been the imposition of Western-style banking on much of the Islamic world during the period of European colonial domination, which is still a source of resentment to this day. Individual Muslims have responded to the latter in different ways: some open interest-bearing accounts under the principle of *darura*, or overriding necessity; others open accounts but refuse the interest; still others opt for their mattresses. It was mostly this resentment,

---

[21]"Islamic fundamentalism", *Microsoft® Encarta® Online Encyclopaedia 2004*, http://encarta.msn.com ©1997–2004 Microsoft Corporation.

[22]Pipes, Daniel, "Islam and Islamism — faith and ideology", *National Interest*, Spring 2000.

[23]www.wikipedia.org.

which gave rise, in the 1940s, to the quasi-academic field known as Islamic economics — the first thorough studies devoted to the establishment of Islamic financial institutions.

Even with post-September 11 suspicions that Islamic banks may fund terrorist organisations, demand for the services of Islamic financial institutions is on the rise from the towers of Bahrain to the streets of London. Indeed, they represent one of banking's hottest sectors. The total assets managed by Islamic financial institutions are close to US$300 billion, while Islamic equity funds and off-balance-sheet investment accounts are conservatively estimated between US$15 billion and US$30 billion.[24]

Whilst Bahrain's Noriba is operating exclusively under Shari'ah principles, several others — HSBC, Citibank, Commerzbank and BNP Paribas — provide Shari'ah-compliant services along with conventional ones.

Drawing from the success of Islamic financial institutions in Bahrain, Egypt and Dubai, countries such as Malaysia and Indonesia have also identified the advantages in this largely untapped market and demand for Shari'ah-compliant banking and finance. The advantages have clearly outweighed the religious tag as evidenced by the interest of secular countries such as Britain and Australia.

---

[24]Bachmann, Helena, "Banking on faith", *Time Europe*, 16 December 2002.

Chapter 2
Shari'ah Law and Islamic Jurisprudence

Shari'ah is much wider in scope than the concept of law as understood in the West. Shari'ah law encompasses aspects of belief and religious practice, including rules relating to prayer, fasting, the making of the *Haj* and giving *zakat*. It also covers aspects of everyday life such as behaviour towards other people, dietary rules, dress, manners and morals. Lastly, it includes laws relating to crime and evidence, international relations, marriage, divorce and inheritance, commercial transactions and many other subjects that would be included under the Western definition of law.

In this scheme of things, the function of Islamic jurisprudence was the formulation of doctrinal principles elaborate enough, and technically sophisticated enough, to draw these disparate strands together in a consistent and logically coherent manner, integrating the social with the religious in a single, unified system of law. This was achieved by the end of the tenth century. Thereafter, the efforts of medieval Muslim jurists went into an increasingly elaborate series of doctrinal commentaries which constitute the textual authority of the Shari'ah. The Shari'ah is, pre-eminently, a law of the book — a jurists' law — and this of course always implies a certain degree of artificiality.

26

2.1   From the Obligatory to the Forbidden

Every aspect of Islamic society is subject to the lens of Shari'ah scrutiny and can be classified according to five degrees of admissibility ranging from the obligatory to the absolutely forbidden. They are as follows:

(i)   Obligatory (*fard* or *wajib*) — an obligatory duty, the omission of which is punishable.

(ii)   Desirable (*mandub* or *mustahab*) — an action which is rewarded, but the omission of which is not punishable.

(iii)   Indifferent (*jaiz* or *mubah*) — an action which is permitted and to which the law is indifferent.

(iv)   Undesirable (*mukruh*) — an action which is disapproved of, but which is not a punishable offence, though its omission is rewarded.

(v)   Forbidden (*haram*) — an action which is absolutely forbidden and punishable.

Together, these categories define the universe of what is and is not possible in Islamic society and they apply just as much to financial transactions as to any other kind of activity.

2.2   The Quran, the *Sunnah* and the *Hadith*

The key text upon which the Shari'ah is founded is of course the Quran, that is to say, the Revelations of the Prophet Muhammad, which came from God. As Coulson puts it: the Quran is "historically and ideologically the primary expression of the Islamic law".[25] In addition to the Quran, there is the *Sunnah*. The word *Sunnah* literally means "a beaten track" and thus an accepted course of conduct. In Islamic thought, it refers to all the acts and

---

[25]Coulson, Noel J., "Islamic law", 1968, p. 55.

sayings of the prophet as well as everything he approved. The latter are described as *hadith* (plural *ahadith*), which literally means a "narrative" or "communication" but in this context is understood to refer specifically to an account of the life and conduct of the Prophet Muhammad, who is regarded by all Muslims as their ideal role model. The *hadith* was assembled from the recollections of the Companions of the Prophet, and was only put down in writing after some considerable time had elapsed since Muhammad's death.[26]

Only *Sunnah* of a legal nature is held to form part of the Shari'ah and ultimately the Quran takes priority over the *Sunnah* as a source of law; jurists should resort to the *Sunnah* for legal guidance only when no clear directive can be obtained from the Quran.

2.3 The Five Major Schools of Islamic Law

The Quran and the *Sunnah* together constitute the primary sources of Islamic law, after which we have the secondary sources, comprising the various schools of law, or *madhab* (plural *madhabib*), of which there are five. These schools came about as a result of local and historical circumstances in the first two centuries of the Islamic era and they gave rise to the major political and social divisions of the Islamic community today.

After the death of the Prophet in AD 632, his "rightly guided" caliphs became the leaders of the Muslim people or nation (*Ummah*). Unlike the Prophet, they were not the recipients of divine revelation (*wahy*), but they had the full authority to interpret the Shari'ah in their time. Their knowledge, piety and religious authority meant that the people could turn to them for any final decision regarding the

---

[26]There are differences of scholarly opinion concerning how early the *hadith* commenced to be recorded. The earliest systematic collection which has survived was the *Muwatta* of Iman Malik (d. 179 AH). See Daniel Brown, *Rethinking Tradition in Modern Islamic Thought*, 1996, p. 94.

Shari'ah and related matters. The caliphs used to consult the many *sahabah* (companions of the Prophet), but whatever the decision they eventually arrived at, their word was final. In this respect, there was only one school of law (*madhab*) during the time of these early caliphs and it was they who were ultimately responsible for maintaining the unity and uniformity of the *Ummah*. For example, we know that when Muslims differed in their reading of the Quran, the Caliph Uthman sent his authorised copy to every corner of the emerging Muslim world and had all other copies of the Quran removed from circulation and burnt. In this way he was able to preserve the unity of the *Ummah*.[27]

With the emergence of the Umayyad rule (AD 682–754), the situation began to change. The Umayyad caliphs did not have the same religious authority as their predecessors and there was dissension in their ranks. Some of them were regarded as having deviated from the true path of Islam and they were avoided by jurists and scholars, so they left the fold and began to teach independently elsewhere. Many of the companions of the Prophet similarly went to different regions with their followers (*tabiun*) and taught and preached to the local people they found there. There was no central authority that could unite all the opinions at this time, which coincided with the rapid expansion of Islamic state, and this set the stage for the emergence of the different Islamic schools of thought (*madhahib*).

The Umayyad caliphs were followed by the Abbasids (AD 754–1278). They were more supportive of Islamic law and its scholars than their predecessors and during this time scholars were encouraged to write commentaries on Islamic laws. The Abbasid caliphs also patronised the collection of early *fatwahs*, which are legal opinions of jurists and encouraged religious discussion and debate. At the beginning of this period, there were some twenty different schools of Islamic teaching in existence, but by the end of the third century

---

[27] "The authenticity of the Quran", *The Institute of Islamic Information and Education* (www.iiie.net).

of Hijrah (ninth century, Christian era), the majority of these had been eliminated or else had merged with one another resulting in the five major schools of Islamic law that we know today.

(i) Shia

The Shia school, whose followers comprises about 10 per cent of Muslims, came about as a result of early political differences in the Muslim world over whether the leader of the Muslim community should always be a descendent of the family of Ali b. Abu Talib (AD 595–660), the Prophet's nephew and husband of his daughter Fatima. Shias distinguish themselves from other Muslims — who are known as Sunnis — in the following way. The Sunnis are the people of the *Sunnah*. The *Sunnah* of the Prophet is an unerring guide to man in respect to all that is permissible and all that is prohibited in the eyes of God. Without this belief in the Prophet and the Sunnah, belief in God would become a mere theoretical proposition. The Sunni profession of faith is simply: "There is no God but God and Muhammad is the Apostle of God". To this the Shias add: "and Ali the companion of Muhammad is the vicar of God". The elevation of Ali to an almost co-equal position with Muhammad himself, may be stated, popularly, as the great distinctive tenet of the Shias. This school has significant numbers of followers in Iraq, India and the Gulf states.

(ii) Hanafi

The Hanafi school of thought was established by Imam Abu Hanifa (80–150 AH) and his famous pupils, Abu Yusuf and Muhammad. They emphasised the use of reason rather than blind reliance on the *Sunnah*. This is the prevailing school in India and the Middle East.

(iii) Maliki

The Maliki school adheres to the teachings of Imam Malik (96–178 AH) who laid emphasis on the practices of the people of Medina as being the most authentic examples of Islamic practice. The Moors who ruled Spain were followers of the Maliki school, which, today, is found mostly in Africa.

(iv) Hanbali

The Hanbali school was founded by Imam Ahmad Ibn Hanbal (163–240 AH) who had a high reputation as a traditionalist and theologian, and adopted a strict view of the law. The Hanbali school today is predominant in Saudi Arabia.

(v) Shafi'i

The Shafi'i school was founded by Imam As-Shafi'i (149–204 AH) who was a pupil of Imam Malik, and is thought by some to be the most distinguished of all jurists. He was famed for his modernisation and balanced judgement, and although he respected the traditions, he examined them more critically than did Imam Malik. Followers of the Shafi'i school today are found predominantly in South-east Asia and as the focus of this book is on Islamic jurisprudence in that region, it is the Shafi'i school that primarily concerns us here.

2.4 Classical Islamic Jurisprudence and the Processes for Ascertaining the Law

As the emergence of the different Islamic schools reveals, one of the fundamental problems facing the Prophet, and more especially his successors as Islam spread over a wider area, was the need to find a method to define the relationship between the provisions of the Quran and local circumstances and traditions. In essence, this was actually a need to define the provisions of the Quran *itself* and it was not until the accession to power of the Abbasid Dynasty in AD 750 that a systematic approach began to be developed. From this time onwards it was the jurist (*faqih*) who came to occupy the central place in the development of Islamic jurisprudence, while the judge (*qadi*) was charged simply with the application of formulated doctrine.

The English term "Islamic law" is somewhat ambiguous in that it conflates two Arabic terms, Shari'ah (divine law) and *fiqh* (human comprehension of that law). The distinction is an important one. In the first instance, since God is the true and only law-giver, any legal position must ultimately be rooted in the Quran and the *Sunnah*, which are understood to be the revelation of His divine will. However, when it comes to the practical application of this divine law to individual situations and the circumstances of everyday life, the responsibility lies with those who are skilled in interpreting the revealed sources, namely qualified religious scholars or *ulama'*. The first recourse of the *ulama'* is to turn to the primary sources and derive his rulings directly from the Quran and the *Sunnah*. However, it often happens that no clear answer can be found in the primary sources, in which case the *ulama'* must resort to other methods in order to reach a decision.

These methods are collectively described as *ijtihad*, which literally means effort, signifying the use of intellectual exertion by a jurist to derive an answer to a question. *Ijtihad* observes a particular methodology called "the roots of the law" *(usulal-fiqh)*, which includes the following recognised methods of reaching a decision: *ijma, qiyas, istihsan, maslahah mursalah* and *istishab*.

- *Ijma* has been defined as the "consensus of opinion of the Companions of the Prophet (*Sahabah*) and the agreement reached on the decisions taken by the learned Muftis or the Jurists on various Islamic matters".[28]
- *Qiyas* literally means making a comparison between two things with the view of evaluating one in the light of the other. In Shari'ah law it refers to the extension of a Shari'ah ruling from an original case to a new case, on the grounds that the latter has the same effective cause as the former.
- *Istihsan* is similar to the principle of equity as it is understood in the West in the sense that they are both inspired by fairness and good conscience and both allow a departure from a rule of positive

---

[28]Doi, Abdur Rahman I., *Shari'ah: The Islamic Law*, 1989, p. 78.

law when its enforcement will lead to unfair results. The difference is that whereas the notion of equity relies on the concept of natural law as an eternally valid standard apart from the positive law, *istihsan* relies on, and is an integral part of, the Shari'ah and recognises no law superior to it.

- *Maslahah mursalah*, or public interest, is very similar to *istihsan*. If it is evident that a particular course of action will result in public benefit, it may be followed. This is one of the means by which the Shari'ah can be adapted to meet the need to accommodate social change.
- *Istishab* is a legal presumption in Islamic law and is very similar to legal presumptions in English common law.

One further consideration in this scheme of things is the local or customary laws of a particular place (*'urf*). These may be continued under Islamic law so long as they are not contrary to Islamic belief and practices.

2.5   The Concept of *Fatwah*

In Islamic jurisprudence, *fatwah* means the opinion of a scholar (*mufti*) based on that scholar's understanding and interpretation of the intent of the sources of Islam, combined with that scholar's knowledge of the subject in question and the social context that gave rise to the particular issue or question in hand. The scholar's answer, or *fatwah*, is not a binding rule; rather, it is a recommendation. In this respect, a *fatwah* may be opposed, criticised, accepted or rejected, or may even itself become the subject of debate or questioning.

Fatwahs may be asked for by judges or individuals, and are typically required in cases where an issue of *fiqh* is undecided or uncertain. Lawsuits can be settled on the basis of a *fatwah*, so it is vital that the recommendations of a *fatwah* do not involve any personal interests or agenda of the *mufti* or lawyer; rather he should render it in accordance with fixed precedent.

In an egalitarian system such as Islam, a *fatwah* gains acceptance based on the integrity of the *mufti* who offered the *fatwah* and his perceived knowledge of Islamic sources, as well as his understanding of issue itself and the particular circumstances, social, historical or otherwise, surrounding it. His recommendations may be challenged on any of the above accounts — after all a *fatwah* is, ultimately, only an opinion and that opinion may be incorrect. To consider a *fatwah* issued by anyone as binding on all Muslims is a dangerous contemporary trend that merely stifles Islam's rich history of debate and dissent. Moreover, it theoretically allows individuals to claim authority over others by virtue of their supposed knowledge of God's will. The purpose of a *fatwah* is to offer an opinion, not to silence discourse.[29] The Shari'ah is very accommodating here and gives only a principle outline while leaving the matter of details to scholars.[30]

In this last respect, the pluralist approach of Islam is quite clear. Humankind comes in many colours and is divided into different races, tribes and nations; every race is different from the others in terms of their physical appearance and nature, and speaks a different language (Chapter 49: verse 13, Chapter 30: verse 22). This manifest diversity is a reflection of divine wisdom of Allah. The Prophet Muhammad was sent as a mercy on humankind, not to force people to follow his teachings (Chapter 3: verse 164, Chapter 21: verse 107, Chapter 50: verse 45). The very principle of Islam is persuasion — there is no compulsion in Islam (Chapter 2: verse 256). How then can Muslims be intolerant and deny other religious communities the opportunity to live with them peacefully?

Today, *fatwahs* have limited importance in most Muslim societies and are normally resorted to only in cases of marriage, inheritance and divorce. Ultimately, the importance of a *fatwah*

---

[29]Hathout, Maher, "Demystifying the fatwah", The Institute of Islamic Information and Education (www.iiie.net).

[30]Halim, Shah Abdul, "Islam & pluralism: A contemporary approach", www.islamonline.net, 8 May 2003.

depends entirely on its acceptance by the people, and if people do not respect or adhere to it, then it is in reality powerless.

2.6   From Revelation to Codification: Scholasticism and the Formulation of Doctrine

As we have seen, in time, a number of different schools of law began to emerge, each with the avowed aim of formulating an ideal scheme for Islamic law. However, the doctrine expounded by these schools tended to diverge as local conditions and practices exerted their effect. This divergence primarily had to do with the relation between individual or personal reasoning (*ra'y*) and the authority of a given source. In contrast to the Maliki and Hanafi schools, which both permitted a recourse to reason, whether by way of opinion or deduction (*qiyas*), the "supporters of the traditions" (*ahl al-hadith*) maintained the illegitimacy of juristic reasoning. They held that outside the Quran, the only other source of law was the *Sunnah* of the Prophet, which was to be found in the *hadith* books. As in other revealed systems of legal obligations such as Judaism, the key issue is the relation between revelation and reason in law. It is a crucial question, which can admit only one answer: a formal and theoretical limitation on the free use of human reason. The problem, then, was how to organise this limitation so as to turn it into a creative tool that could accommodate the interpretation and application of Islam to the various realities of the Muslim world. This was the achievement of the greatest of all Muslim legal scholars, Shafi'i.

Shafi'i maintained that certain knowledge of the law of Allah could come only from revelation. The material sources of law were thus confined to the Quran and the (divinely inspired) practice (*Sunnah*) of the Prophet. Outside these sources, the need for a disciplined and subsidiary form of reasoning by analogy (*qiyas*) was recognised. In this respect, "the function of jurisprudence was not to make law but simply to discover it from the substance of divine revelation and, where necessary, apply the principles enshrined therein to new problems by analogical reasoning".[31]

The implications of this position for the development of a technical jurisprudence were critical. Muslim scholarship became concerned with the documentation of the *Sunnah* through the classification of *hadith*. Classical jurisprudence was thus largely devoted to the establishment of scholastic canons by means of which the divine law could be ascertained. The concept of *ijma* — the agreement of qualified legal scholars of a given generation — was developed to describe the result of this scholastic endeavour. Once such an agreement had been reached for a particular case, no further development was possible and "the door of *ijtihad* was closed". From the tenth century onwards all that was possible was an 'imitation' (*taqlid*) of established doctrines, which meant detailed commentary and the production of authoritative legal texts for each school of jurisprudence. These texts expounded the divine law for man and his institutions but, because of the multiplicity of *hadith*, variations in doctrine persisted and have long been an accepted feature of the Muslim world. This variation extended not only to doctrine, but also to the science of the principles of law (*usul*) itself, and in this respect, Islamic technical jurisprudence may not unfairly be described as a fragmented scholasticism,[32] although an ideal unity was postulated on the formal grounds described above.

2.7   Closing of the Door of *Ijtihad*

After the beginning of the tenth century, no further schools of law were founded, reflecting an end of scholarly discourse relating to the revision of issues and questions not covered by the Quran and the *hadith*. This phenomenon was later referred to as "the closing of the door of *ijtihad*" (the term *ijtihad*, it will be recalled, refers

[31]Coulson, N.J., "Islamic law", in *An Introduction to legal Systems*, 1968, p. 62.

[32]Burton, John, *The Collection of the Quran*, 1977, pp. 8–45.

Shari'ah Law and Islamic Jurisprudence 37

to the intellectual exertions of Islamic jurists when they applied themselves to an interpretation of the available sources in order to reach a legal verdict or decision in cases which are not specifically dealt with in the Quran or the *hadith*). But there have always been some Islamic scholars who have refused to acknowledge the closing of the door of *ijtihad* and have advocated independent reasoning to find legal solutions. Reformist Muslim theologians of the nineteenth century, for example, attributed the decline of the Islamic world in modern times to the fact that the door of *ijtihad* had been closed since the tenth century and that the majority of Islamic scholars of law considered the most important legal questions resolved. They demanded a "re-opening of the door of *ijtihad*" in order to be able to address the issues of modern life adequately.

After the consolidation of the schools of law and the closing of the door of *ijtihad*, the only method for resolving future legal questions that remained was that of imitation (*taqlid*) — that is the resolution of new legal issues and question by analogy with decisions reached in the past. The secular and spiritual leader of the Sunni Islamic world, the Caliph, who actually was not allowed to formulate laws by himself, unofficially enjoyed the possibility to pass laws by "interpreting" Islamic regulations individually. However, these "interpreted" laws of the ruler had to be in accordance with Islamic jurisprudence.

2.8 Shari'ah and State Law in the Modern Era

The modern era has seen many Islamic countries adopt a codified legal system whereby an existing system of regulations and penalties is set down in writing and fixed as the law of the land. During the colonial era, the authorities were naturally inclined to introduce largely European laws and the only areas where Shari'ah was still applied were in matters of family law, inheritance and religious endowments, as well as cases of retaliatory punishment (*qisas*).[33]

---

[33]In Islam, retaliation should be forgone as an act of charity.

Often Shari'ah courts, dealing with such cases, existed next to secular courts, which dealt with all remaining legal issues.

Today, the application of Islamic jurisprudence in Muslim countries may be divided into three categories:

(i) Those countries where jurisprudence is subordinate to Shari'ah — they include Iran and Saudi Arabia.

(ii) Those countries where the legal system is influenced by Shari'ah. In this instance, Shari'ah is in most cases mentioned in the constitution and typically manifests itself mainly in the area of the status of an individual (such as personal property, marriage and inheritance). However, simply mentioning Shari'ah in the constitution does not necessarily indicate the extent of its application. In Algeria, for example, the Shari'ah is not specifically mentioned as a source of jurisprudence, yet mixed marriages are prohibited. Elsewhere, the Shari'ah is sometimes quoted as one of the sources of jurisprudence (Kuwait, Bahrain), the main source (Qatar, Syria) or the only source (Mauritania).[34]

(iii) Those countries where the legal system is entirely independent of the Shari'ah. Many Muslim (or predominantly Muslim) countries do not mention the Shari'ah at all in their constitution. They are Algeria, Burkina Faso, Cameroon, Chad, Djibouti, Gambia, Guinea, Guinea-Bissau, Iraq, Mali, Morocco, Niger, Senegal, Tunisia and Turkey.

In general, Shari'ah tends to be at least partly in force wherever Islam is the official state religion of a specific country. However, the extent of its application varies from country to country. Shari'ah has been re-introduced in Afghanistan in 2002 and introduced in some northern states of Nigeria, while more Islamicist elements in Malaysia and Indonesia have agitated for the introduction of Shari'ah in those countries, though without success.

---

[34]Schirrmacher, Christine, "Islamic jurisprudence and its sources", www.steinigung.org/artikel/islamic_jurisprudence.htm, 1994.

Shari'ah law in modern Muslim-populated (not Islamic, if it is Islamic countries, then Shari'ah law is part of their law) countries such as Malaysia and Indonesia, are mostly concerned in dealing with the individual (e.g. marriage, inheritance and personal property). There is no relation between international law and Shari'ah law as international law does not incorporate the teachings of the Quran. In Islamic banking, Shari'ah law is abided in the sense of following what the Quran prohibits and allows. The Shari'ah supervisory council board ensures that Islamic banking and finance is carried out in the proper or halah way, for example, no *riba, zakat* is paid, no gambling.

Chapter 3

Islamic Commercial Law

There has always been a close historical connection between Islam and commerce. The Prophet came from the Arabian town of Makkah, or, as it is known today, Mecca. At the time of Muhammad, Makkah had already been a major Middle Eastern commercial centre for over a century. Makkah was home to the Quraysh tribe and during this period the Quraysh had grown quite prosperous, in their desert world, primarily as brokers of trade between the Eastern and Western worlds. The principle reason for their success was a geographical one: Makkah was strategically located on the main commercial artery running from Yemen in Southern Arabia, where goods from the East arrived, northwards to the Mediterranean, where European traders eagerly waited with their own goods or cash. Makkah was also at the centre of another major trading route between the Persian Gulf (another arrival point for Eastern commodities), and the Red Sea Port of Jiddah, where goods from Egypt and other points in Africa entered into the sphere of East-West commerce.[35] Commerce was thus the lifeblood of Makkah and Muhammad, who was of the Quraysh tribe, was himself a successful businessman who after his marriage to his first wife, Khadijah, undertook several trading ventures to various places in Arabia, including Yemen and Bahrain.

Not surprisingly, then, the attitude of Islam towards commercial activities is a generally positive one and there are many verses in

---

[35]Ferrara, Peter J. and Saffuri, Khaled, "Islam and the free market", *Islamic Free Market Institute Foundation* (www.islamicinstitute.org).

the Quran which actually encourage trade and commerce. Morally, the guiding principle here is that there should be no impediment to honest and legitimate trade and business, which enables people to earn a living, support their families and give charity to those less fortunate than themselves. But if Islam does not expect believers to give away all their possessions and live the life of ascetics, it nevertheless requires that all Muslims conduct their business activities in accordance with the requirements of their religion, namely to be fair, honest and just towards others. Nor should Muslims allow their business activities to dominate their lives to the extent that making money becomes a first priority and they neglect their religious duties — it is stipulated in the Quran that all trading must cease during the time of the Friday congregational prayer. And just as the Shari'ah regulates and influences every other sphere of life, so too with business and commercial activities, which are subject to a rigorous code of conduct so that they may conform with Islamic principles.

3.1   Islamic vs. Non-Islamic Commercial Transactions

Perhaps the most important single difference between Islamic commerce and conventional commercial transactions is the Islamic prohibition on paying or receiving interest (*riba*). But there are also other significant divergences, which also need to be taken into account. One of these is the notion that property is God-created and God-given. Clearly, the construction of property here differs radically from the common modern conception of property as a secular value, to be defined and redefined as needed to further utility, or else as the aggregate of whatever property claims the legal system chooses to respect. In Islamic law, by contrast, property is irreducible, sacrosanct and virtually transcendent. The lawfulness of its acquisition and use is grounded in the Quran and the *Sunnah*, whose source lies above reason, and is a matter with which God is minutely concerned.

Ultimately, the aim of the Islamic economic system is to allow people to earn their living in a fair and profitable way, without exploiting others, so that the whole of society may benefit. In this last respect, Islam emphasises the welfare of the community over individual rights. This is in line with recent Western thinking which criticises open-market approaches to economic management because they emphasise economic growth at all cost without regard for quality of life and the widening gap between rich and poor in society.[36] Clearly, Islamic religious precepts are fundamentally opposed to the doctrines of unbridled capitalism, which are seen by Islamic countries as posing a threat to society by undermining Shari'ah values.

3.2   Principal Requirements of the Shari'ah in Relation to Commercial Activities

As we have seen, the most striking difference between Islamic commercial activities and conventional business activities is that Islam expressly forbids the giving or receiving of interest, which in the eyes of the Quran is tantamount to usury (*riba*).

The prohibition of interest in Islam should be seen in the context of the basic characteristics of an Islamic economic system, which may be enumerated as follows:

(i) All persons should have at least the minimum economic resources needed for subsistence.

(ii) Undue concentration of wealth in a few hands should be prevented.

(iii) Hoarding should be discouraged and the use of wealth for productive purposes should be encouraged.

---

[36]Baydoun, Nabil and Blunt, Peter, "Notes on Islam, culture and organisational behaviour". Working Paper, Northern Territory University, p. 2, 1997.

(iv) The economic system should function so that there is no room for idlers; reward should accrue solely as a result of the expending of effort, except in the case of the naturally handicapped and involuntarily unemployed.[37]

Apart from this prohibition regarding receiving and giving interest, there are two other activities prohibited by Shari'ah law that have had a significant impact on Islamic finance. They are a ban on gambling (*maysir*) and the prohibition of uncertainty or risk-taking (*gharar*). The prohibition on *maysir* is often used as grounds for the criticism of conventional financial practices such as speculation, conventional insurance and derivatives, while the prohibition of *gharar* can be applied to various types of uncertainty or contingency in a contract. In the latter instance, the prohibition on *gharar* is used as the basis for criticism of conventional financial practices such as short selling, speculation and derivatives. Obviously generalised prohibitions on increase and risk, if interpreted in the widest possible sense, run contrary to the very core of the concept of commercial gain,[38] but here the legitimacy of gain through trade — a vexed issue at the intersection of ethics, economics and contract law — is resolved in a strikingly liberal fashion.

For example, risk-taking, though normally prohibited by Shari'ah law, when related to a commercial enterprise can be a socially productive economic activity and is consequently entitled to a reward. Second, and a related point, the creation of loans that are intended to finance socially productive economic activities receive a similar endorsement. Third, financial risk is

---

[37]El-Badour, R.I., "The Islamic economic system: A theoretical and empirical analysis of money and banking in the Islamic economic framework", 1984, p. 135. Unpublished PhD dissertation, Utah State University, Logan, UT, USA.

[38]Vogel, Frank E. and Hayes, Samuel L., *Islamic Law and Finance: Religion, Risk and Return*, 1998, pp. 68–69.

acceptable if the risk lies solely with the lenders and not with the managers and agents.

Hence, it can be seen that Islam offers a unique and ideal perspective of business ethics. It regards commercial activities as part of one's religious life, provided that they are conducted in accordance with the commands of Allah, and the moral code of conduct prescribed by Islam. In this context, fundamental Islamic principles such as truthfulness, honesty, trust, sincerity, brotherhood, science and knowledge, and justice, provide a moral and ethical background to the way in which business should be conducted.[39]

3.3   Islam: the Difference between Equity and Debt

The distinction between equity and debt in Islam is the same as in conventional economic systems except that the Shari'ah prohibits any return on a debt and does not consider lending to be a legitimate profitable activity. All wealth creation should result from a partnership between the investor and the user of capital in which rewards and risks are shared. Returns on invested capital should be earned rather than pre-determined.

Equity represents an investment exposed to all kinds of business risks and sharing in the profits of the business. It may be of a permanent nature, that is, redeemable only upon liquidation of the business — or earlier by mutual agreement — but not on demand. Debt on the other hand, is a contractual obligation to pay a specific value, whether in cash or kind, on an agreed date or on demand, for value consideration received, with the important proviso that value at both ends of the transaction must be equal in terms of whatever commodity or currency they are denominated in. Any discount or excess on account of a contractual obligation falls in the category of

---

[39]Elati, Mas, "The ethical responsibility of business: Islamic principles and implications", *OIC Exchange* (www.oicexchange.com), 2 May 2002.

riba (interest or usury), which, of course, is expressly forbidden in the Quran.

3.4   Rationale of the Prohibition of Interest

The representation in the holy Quran of the practice of interest as an act of "war with Allah and his messenger" provides an insight into the philosophy behind the prohibition of interest in Islam. It is a clear pointer that the institution of interest is something which runs counter to the scheme of things which Islam stands for and which Allah wanted to see established on earth. That the words "Allah has blighteth *riba* and made *sadaqat* [gift-giving] fruitful", which occur in verse 276 of *Surah Al-Baqara*, also point towards the fact that the practice of interest militates against the objectives of an Islamic society, while *sadaqat* promotes these objectives. The main points of the rationale for the prohibition of interest in Muslim countries may be listed as follows:

(i) Transactions based on interest violate the equity aspect of economic organisation. The borrower is obliged to pay a pre-determined rate of interest on the sum borrowed even though he may have incurred a loss. To insist on payment of a pre-determined rate of interest irrespective of the economic circumstances of the borrowers of money is against the Islamic norm of justice.

(ii) An interest-based system discourages innovation, particularly on the part of small-scale enterprises. Large industrial firms and big landholders can afford to experiment with new techniques of production as they have reserves of their own to fall back upon in case the adoption of new practices does not yield a good dividend. Small-scale enterprises hesitate to go in for new methods of production with the help of money borrowed from banks because the liability of the banks for the principal sum and interest has to be met, irrespective of what the results might be and the fact that small-scale enterprises usually have little reserves of their own.

(iii) In an interest-based system, banks are only interested in recovering their capital along with interest. Their interest in the ventures they finance is therefore strictly limited to satisfying themselves about the viability and profitability of such ventures from the point of view of the safety of their capital and the ability of the venture to generate a cash flow which can meet the interest liability. Since the return the banks get on the capital sum lent by them is fixed and is not linked in any way to the actual profits of the ventures to whom they lend, there is no incentive for the banks to give priority to ventures with the highest profit potential.

(iv) An interest-based system dampens investment activity because it adds to the costs of investment. If interest rates are raised to contain monetary demand in situations where excessive fiscal deficits are fuelling inflation, private investment receives a severe setback leading to "stagflation". This has actually been the experience of a number of developed countries in recent years.

(v) The interest-based system is security oriented rather than growth oriented. Because of the commitment to pay a pre-determined rate of interest to depositors, banks, in their lending operations, are mostly concerned about the safe return of the principal loan along with the stipulated interest. This leads them to confine their lending to the already well-established, big business houses or such parties as are in a position to pledge sufficient security. If they find that such avenues of lending are not sufficient to absorb all their investable resources, they prefer to invest in government securities with a guaranteed return. This exaggerated security orientation acts as a great impediment to growth because it does not allow a smooth flow of bank resources to a large number of potential entrepreneurs who could add to the gross national product by their productive endeavour, but do not possess sufficient security to pledge to the banks to satisfy their criteria of creditworthiness.

3.5 Conventional Banking and the Prohibition of *Riba* in Islam

In a capitalist market economy, the banks are profit-making institutions. They need to maximise their profit by advancing money at a higher rate than the rate at which they obtain it. The borrowing and lending of money takes place at a price called the interest rate, which is the pivotal point of all banking activity. In this last respect, the practices of the modern commercial banking system are directly in conflict with the principles of Islam, which strictly prohibit *riba* (interest or usury).

Seen from an Islamic perspective, the prevailing banking and finance system strikes at the very root of a fundamental principle of the Shari'ah in that it tends to promote a concentration of wealth in a few hands and thus breeds inequalities in society. Interest, which is the kingpin of the modern banking and financial system, serves as a powerful tool of exploitation of one sector of society by another. From the Islamic viewpoint, it has created "haves" and "have-nots", and acts as a barrier to the achievement of maximum welfare for the maximum number of people. It is in this context that Islam forbids interest and it is with the aim of achieving the egalitarian objectives of Islam that the Muslim world is now embarking on the task of Islamising the financial system by unfettering it from interest;[40] it is to this process of transforming conventional financial arrangements into Shari'ah-approved (halah) alternatives that we now turn to.

---

[40]See Al-Harran, Saad Abdul Sattar, *Islamic Finance: Partnership Financing,* 1993, pp. 4–5.

3.6   Treatment of Deposits with Interest

As stated previously, the most striking difference between Islamic banking and Western-style banking is the Islamic view of interest. Because Shari'ah law prohibits interest, direct loans and other forms of lending such as guaranteed investment certificates, are interest-free. Consequently, Islamic financing must rely instead on a kind of joint venture, or mutual participation, between the customer and the Islamic bank, in order to generate profits. To this end, Islamic banking converts existing deposits into *Islamic* investment deposits, whereby the bank acts as agent or trustee (*mudarib*) instead of borrower. In order to persuade depositors to go along with this, it must be demonstrated that the performance of Islamic banks compares very favourably with that of conventional banks in terms of returns.

In the event of being left with depositors who are not willing to convert to Islamic investment deposits, a ruling is adopted under the Shari'ah necessity principle, which allows the continued payment of interest, as per the contract, till the maturation of the deposit, with the interest payments being sourced from borrowers of the same category.[41]

3.7   Profit and Loss Sharing

Commonly, business ventures start off with a loan. For Muslims, loans cannot be made or accepted according to traditional banking methods because this invariably entails the payment and receipt of interest and therefore is not *halah*. Skipping past the laws of conventional finance and banking, Islamic banking allows prospective clients to borrow money while still adhering to Shari'ah law through a profit- and loss-sharing scheme of financing. Profit-and-loss-sharing (PLS) financing is a form of partnership

---

[41]See Hassan, Hussein Hamed, "Conversion of National Bank of Sharjah into an Islamic bank: A Case Study", The International Islamic Finance Forum, International Institute of Research, Dubai, March 2002.

where partners share profits and losses on the basis of their capital share and effort. Unlike interest-based financing, there is no guaranteed rate of return. Islam supports the view that Muslims do not act as nominal creditors in any investment, but are actual partners in the business. This is an equity-based system of financing, where the justification for the PLS-financier's share in profit rests on their effort and the risk that they carry. In other words, they deserve to be rewarded since this profit would have been impossible without their investment and, furthermore, if the investment were to make a loss, then their money would also be lost.[42]

3.8   Profit-Sharing Enterprises

Islamic law recognises two principal forms of profit-sharing enterprises (PSE) based on PLS partnerships:[43]

(i) *Shirkah al-'inan* or limited partnership. In this kind of partnership, partners contribute capital, property and/or labour. Profits and losses are shared in an agreed manner. The difference between this and other forms of partnership is that each partner is only the agent and not a surety for his co-partners, which means that a partner is not liable for a debt contracted by his co-partners and is only able to sue someone with whom he himself has contracted.[44]

(ii) *Mudarabah* or dormant partnership (also called *qirad*). This is a contract whereby one person (the dormant partner) gives funds or property to another on the basis that the lender will share in the active partner's profits in a *proportion* agreed in advance. They may not agree on a fixed return since this would amount to *riba*. Equally, if there is a loss, they also share this

---

[42]Al Tamimi & Company, op. cit., p. 2.

[43]Doi, op. cit., pp. 365–367.

[44]Saleh, Nabil, *Unlawful Gain and Legitimate Profit in Islamic Law*, 1986, p. 93.

loss proportionally, but the liability of the person who has provided the capital is limited to the amount of that capital. The
dormant partner remains the owner of the capital, but takes
no active part in the enterprise. The trader is responsible only
for negligence or breach of contract. Legitimate expenses of the
venture such as employees' wages and travelling expenses are
deductible from the capital. The contract can be drawn by either
party as long as notice is given to the other.[45]

3.9   Islamic Contract Law

Contracts are drawn to ensure the existence of clearly recognised
guidelines for all parties involved. They state the standings of all
those involved and the condition(s) of the transaction(s) that are to
take place. This occurs in both conventional and Islamic banking.
The general principle of the Islamic law of contract is contained in
the Quranic verse: "O you who believe, fulfil all obligations".[46] The
definition of contract (al-'aqd) in Shari'ah law is similar to that in
English common law, but is wider in that it includes dispositions
which are gratuitous as well as endowments and trusts.

A contract in Islamic law consists of an agreement made
between two or more parties and the basic elements are quite similar
to those of English common law:

(i) Offer and acceptance — a contract requires an offer (ijab) and
acceptance (qabul). The contract can be oral or in writing, made
by signs or gestures, by conduct or through an agent. If the offer
is made in writing it remains in force until received by the other
party who must then reply promptly.
(ii) Consideration — as in English common law, consideration may
consist of money, goods or services. It must be something which

---

[45]Hussain, op. cit., pp. 166–167.
[46]Quran, 5:1.

is capable of being given, or, in the case of a service, capable of being performed, and it must not involve materials or acts which are prohibited according to Islamic law.

(iii) Capacity — the parties entering into a contract must be legally competent. A minor, a person of unsound mind, an insolvent person, a person legally declared a prodigal, an intoxicated person or a person suffering from an illness which leads to his or her death (*mard al-mawt*) cannot enter into a binding contract.

(iv) Legality — the purpose of the contract must be legal in terms of the Shari'ah. A contract to grow grapes for winemaking, for example, would be illegal, as would a contract to sell firearms to criminals or to make a loan with interest.

(v) Absence of duress — the parties must enter into the contract of their own free will. A contract concluded under duress is null and void.

3.10   Types of Contract in Shari'ah

There are seven types of contract recognised by Shari'ah law and they are as follows:

(i) *Al-Tamlikat* (acquiring of ownership)

This kind of contract relates to the acquisition of ownership of properties, or the rights to the benefits of properties. The kinds of contract which fall into this category can be further divided into two subgroups, namely:

(a) *Uqud al-Muawadhat* (contracts of exchange)

In this instance, the acquisition of ownership involves some kind of exchange between two parties involving a sale, hire, money changing, compromise, partition, sale by order and the like.

(b) *Uqad al-Tabarruat* (contracts of charity)

This kind of contract relates to situations where the ownership of a property is acquired without involving an exchange, for example as a gift, alms, endowment, benevolent loan (*al-qard al-hasan*) or the assignment of debt. Sometimes a contract may be initiated as a contract of charity, but then later the receiving party is required to give an exchange. Examples of such a contract are guarantees requested by the debtor and gifts with the condition of an exchange. Contracts such as these commence as contracts of charity at the beginning, ending as contracts of exchange.

(ii) *Al-Isqatat* (releases)

These contracts relate to the dropping of rights against others with or without exchange. If the release is without compensation from the other party, then the release is an absolute release and includes repudiation, remission of the penalty of talion, release from debt and withdrawal from the right to pre-emption. If the release is with compensation from the other party, then it is a release with exchange.

(iii) *Al-Itlaqat* (permissions)

This kind of contract includes giving total responsibility to individuals, firms or agencies in the appointment of governors and judges; giving a person who is dispossessed of the power of administration, permission to administer his property, or giving permission to a minor to carry on trade; and the appointment of a nominee to take care of one's children after death.

(iv) *Al-Taqyidat* (restrictions)

Contracts in this group prevent or terminate the performance of certain functions. They include the dismissal of governors, judges and supervisors; the termination of endowments; the termination of the appointment of nominees and agents; and dispossession of the administration of property because of insanity, mental disorder, prodigality or infancy.

(v) *Al-Tauthiqat* (securities)

This kind of contract is meant to secure debts for their owners and guarantee creditors of debts owing to them. They include guarantees and the assignment of debt and mortgages.

(vi) *Al-Ishtirak* (partnerships)

These contracts relate to sharing in projects and profits. They include *al-mudarabah*, where a person gives an amount of money to another to trade or invest with the condition that they share in the profit while the loss is borne by the owner of the capital. They also include partnerships involving the cultivation of land and taking care of trees.[47]

(vii) *Al-Hifz* (safe custody)

Contracts in this group relate to keeping property safe for its owner and include some of the functions of agency.

3.11   Islamic Financing in a Contemporary Setting

Before the modern era, *mudarabah* partnerships, in which some of the partners contribute only capital and the other partners only labour, worked perfectly well, especially in traditional settings which typically involved simple commercial, agricultural or manufacturing ventures, where the number of investors was usually limited and the size of capital invested relatively small. Today, however, contemporary economic circumstances require a much more flexible institutional framework, whereby a PLS company arrangement is able to accommodate itself to a huge number of investors, enormous financial resources and ever-expanding technological frontiers. The problem here has been one of adapting what are essentially mediaeval financial practices to the modern world of banking and investment. This is a

---

[47]Some financing principles of Islam stem from ancient practices in agricultural which allowed parties to deal in crop-sharing for cultivable land and fruit orchards in accordance with Shari'ah law.

challenge that has been met by modifying present-day financial institutions to the extent that they can embody the principle implicit in the former, whilst still remaining compatible with contemporary practices.

3.12   The Problem of Uncertainty (*gharar*)

Risk-taking and uncertainty are a fact of life in the conventional world of business, even though most people will naturally seek to minimise the chances of something going wrong due to unforeseen circumstances. However, as we have seen, under Islamic law, risk-taking or uncertainty (*gharar*) is expressly forbidden. In legal and business terms, *gharar* means to enter into a commercial venture blindly, without sufficient knowledge, or else to undertake an excessively risky transaction, and it can apply in a number of different circumstances. They include:

- Transactions where the seller is not in a position to hand over the goods to the buyer.
- Transactions where the item or commodity for sale cannot be immediately acquired — for example the sale of fruit which has not yet ripened, or fish or birds not yet caught.
- Speculative investments such as trading in futures or on the stock market.
- Transactions where the purchaser is not given the opportunity of inspecting goods before purchasing item.

However, minor uncertainties may be permitted in situations, provided certain necessary conditions are fulfilled, namely:

- The goods or service of the transaction be in existence.
- The characteristics of the goods or service are known.
- The parties to the contract should have such control over the subject as to be able to ensure that exchange will take place.

- If the transaction or exchange is to take place in future, then the date when it is to take place should be certain.

In Islamic law, the principle underlying most illegal contracts is to prevent benefiting from others for nothing and unfairly. A zero-sum exchange encapsulates precisely what is to be avoided: it is an exchange in which one party gains at the expense of another leading to a win-lose outcome. Naturally, no one of sound mind would enter into a game where losing was an absolute certainty; it is only when the outcome is uncertain that such game is played; uncertainty or risk is what tempts rational agents to engage in exchanges where they know in advance that only one party will gain, whilst the other must surely lose. It is this temptation which is best described by the term *gharar* and it follows that a *gharar* contract is characterised as a zero-sum game with uncertain payoffs.[48]

3.13 Summary

It can thus be seen that there has always been a close historical connection between Islam and commerce. The attitude of Islam towards commercial activities is generally seen as a positive one. Hence, the principles and guidelines regarding Islamic finance, in essence, can be simply summarised as follows:

(i) Any predetermined payment over and above the actual amount of principal is prohibited. Islam allows only one kind of loan and that is *qard-el-hassan* (literally a "good loan") whereby the lender does not charge any interest or additional amount over the money lent. Traditional Muslim jurists have construed this principle so strictly that, according to one commentator, "this prohibition applies to any advantage or benefits that the lender might secure out of the *qard* (loan) such as riding the borrower's

---

[48]Al-Suwailem, Sami, "Towards an objective measure of gharar in exchange", *Islamic Economic Studies*, Vol. 7, Nos. 1 & 2, 2000.

mule, eating at his table, or even taking advantage of the shade of his wall." The principle derived from the quotation emphasises that associated or indirect benefits are also prohibited.

(ii) Lenders must share in the profits or losses arising out of the enterprise for which the money was lent.

Islam encourages Muslims to invest their money and to become partners in order to share profits and risks in the business instead of becoming creditors. As defined in the Shari'ah, or Islamic law, Islamic finance is based on the belief that the provider of capital and the user of capital should equally share the risk of business ventures, whether those are industries, farms, service companies or simple trade deals. Translated into banking terms, the depositor, the bank and the borrower should all share the risks and the rewards of financing business ventures. This is unlike the interest-based commercial banking system, where all the pressure is on the borrower: he must pay back his loan, with the agreed interest, regardless of the success or failure of his venture.

The principle which emerges here is that Islam encourages investment in order that the community as a whole may benefit. It is not willing to allow a loophole for those who do not wish to invest and take risks, but rather are content with hoarding their money or else depositing it in a bank in order to receive an increase on their capital for no risk (other than the bank becoming insolvent). Within Islam, either people invest with risk, or else suffer loss through devaluation by inflation by keeping their money idle. Islam encourages the notion of higher risks and higher returns and promotes it by leaving no other avenue available to investors. The objective is that high-risk investments will act as a stimulus to the economy and encourage entrepreneurs to maximise their efforts.

(iii) Making money from money is not Islamically acceptable. From an Islamic point of view money is only a medium of exchange, a way of defining the value of a thing; it has no value in itself, and therefore should not be allowed to give rise to more money simply by being put in a bank or lent to someone else at a fixed interest rate. The human effort, initiative and risk involved in a productive venture are more important than the money used to finance it. Muslim jurists consider money as potential capital rather than capital, meaning that money becomes capital only when it is invested in business. Accordingly, money advanced to a business as a loan is regarded as a debt of the business and not capital and, as such, it is not entitled to any return (i.e. interest). Muslims are encouraged to purchase and are discouraged from keeping money idle so that, for instance, hoarding money is regarded as being unacceptable. In Islam, money represents purchasing power which is considered to be the only proper use of money. This purchasing power (money) cannot be used to make more purchasing power (money) without undergoing the intermediate step of it being used for the purchase of goods and services.

(iv) *Gharar* (uncertainty, risk or speculation) is also prohibited. Under this prohibition, any transaction entered into should be free from uncertainty, risk and speculation. Contracting parties should have perfect knowledge of the counter values intended to be exchanged as a result of their transactions. At the same time, though, parties cannot pre-determine a guaranteed profit. This is based on the principle of "uncertain gains" which, on a strict interpretation, does not even allow an undertaking from the customer to repay the borrowed principal plus an amount to take into account inflation. The rationale behind the prohibition is the wish to protect the weak from exploitation. Therefore, options and futures are considered as un-Islamic and so are forward foreign exchange transactions because rates are determined by interest differentials.

A number of Islamic scholars disapprove the indexation of indebtedness to inflation and explain this prohibition within the framework of *qard-el-hassan*. According to those scholars, the creditor advances the loan to win the blessings of Allah and expects to obtain the reward from Allah alone. A number of transactions are treated as exceptions to the principle of *gharar*: sales with advanced payment (*bai' bithaman ajil*); contract to manufacture (*istisna*); and hire contract (*ijara*). However, there are legal requirements for the conclusion of these contracts to be organised in a way which minimises risk.

(v) Investments should only support practices or products that are not forbidden — or even discouraged — by Islam. Trade in alcohol, for example would not be financed by an Islamic bank; a real-estate loan could not be made for the construction of a casino; and the bank could not lend money to other banks at interest.[49]

Thus in conclusion, it can be seen that ultimately the aim of the Islamic financial system is to allow individuals to earn a living in a fair and profitable manner, without exploitation of others, so that all society benefits.

---

[49] *Nida'ul Islam Magazine*, op. cit.

Chapter 4

Islamic Financial Products

The main difference between conventional and Islamic financial systems is that the latter is based on keeping in view certain social objectives intended for the benefit of society. This is because Islam is an ethical system which guides man in all his activities including commerce and trade. Whereas a conventional banker need not be concerned with the moral implications of a business venture for which money is lent, the Islamic banker has a much greater responsibility in this respect. This leads one to a very fundamental concept in Islamic banking, namely the relation between investor and the bank. In the case of Islamic banks, this relationship is conceived as a partnership, whereas in conventional banking it is that of creditor-investor.

Islamic finance is based on equity, whereas the conventional banking system is debt-based. Islam is not against the earning of money, but it prohibits the earning of money through unfair trading practices and other activities that are socially harmful in one way or another, which is why predetermined interest or *riba* is forbidden. This edict springs from the Islamic belief that wealth should not be hoarded but put to productive use so that others can share in its benefits. It is also considered wrong to charge for the use of money; essentially, the owners of capital must share in any losses as well as in the profits of any enterprise invested in. At the same time, Islam does not allow uncertainty or *gharar* in contracts. This counts out, for example, a contract in which someone undertakes to insure or indemnify another or allow them the option to sell or buy an asset. Speculation or gambling (*maysir*) is also unacceptable, which weighs against insurance and dabbling in futures and options. Finally, Islamic banks will not finance projects involving products that are *haram*, or forbidden under Shari'ah, most obviously pork and alcohol.

Further, Islamic banks which have committees made up of senior officials and Islamic scholars to decide whether or not projects conform to Shari'ah, will not always respond entirely predictably on what is and what is not suitable for funding. This arises from the fact that the Shari'ah is not a codified body of law, but is open to interpretation and always developing with each new ruling. As we saw in chapter 2, Muslim scholars do not always see eye to eye on what is acceptable and what is not and this debate can, on occasions, touch on the very fundamentals of the system.[50]

Thus, in going forward, we will now see how Islamic banking and products have developed following the conventional financial market and how the challenges have also arisen.

4.1   The Emergence of Islamic Banking

The Islamic financial services industry comprises an increasingly diverse range of institutions, including commercial and investment banks, mutual insurance and investment companies. Banks, however, remain the core of the financial services industry in many countries since they account for the bulk of financial transactions and their soundness is of key concern for systemic stability.

The first Islamic bank[51] was established in Egypt in 1963 and was called the Mit Ghamr Local Savings Bank. The bank operated

---

[50]"What is Islamic banking", *Cairo Times* (www.cairotimes.com), 3 April 1997.

[51]The terms "Islamic banks" and "Islamic financial institutions" are used interchangeably to refer to financial institutions operating in countries where all financial transactions are conducted according to Islamic precepts, as well as specialised institutions and windows of conventional banks that offer Islamic products and instruments in countries where both conventional and Islamic banking coexist.

on the basis of Shari'ah law and prospered because it was able to meet the savings and credit needs of its customers. The success of the Mit Ghamr Local Savings Bank proved that a bank operating according to Islamic principles could flourish. It was followed, in 1967, by the Nasir Social Bank. This was the first social bank[52] to be constituted according to Shari'ah principles. Apart from managing various forms of financial transactions, the bank also granted interest-free loans to its customers.[53]

Following these initial successes, a number of Islamic banks were founded in various other Muslim countries in the Middle East from the mid-1970s onwards. They included:

- The Islamic Development Bank in Saudi Arabia (1975)
- The Dubai Islamic Bank (1975)
- The Faisal Islamic Bank in Egypt (1976)
- The Faisal Islamic Bank of the Sudan (1977)
- The Jordan Islamic Bank (1978)
- The Jordan Financial and Investment Bank (1978)
- The Islamic Investment Company Ltd in The United Arab Emirates (1978)
- Kuwait Finance House (1979)

In order to coordinate Shari'ah rulings between the various Islamic banks in different countries, an International Association of Islamic Banks was established in 1977, with its headquarters located in Saudi Arabia.

More Islamic banks followed in the 1980s, including the first Islamic bank to be established in a non-Muslim country. This was the International Islamic Bank of Investment and Development in Luxembourg, which was founded in 1980. Other Islamic banks

---

[52]The projects financed by a social bank are necessarily for the development of society. Such a bank must add some value to the society besides just earning profits.

[53]International Organisation of Islamic Banks 1402H/1982M 5:106.

established in the 1980s included:

- The Abu Dhabi Islamic Bank (1980)
- The Qatar Islamic Bank (1981)
- Islamic counters in Pakistan banks (1981)
- The Malaysia Islamic Bank Ltd (1983)
- The Mauritania Islamic Bank (1985)
- The Tanzibar Islamic Bank (1985)
- The Iraq Islamic Bank (1985)
- The Turkey Islamic Bank (1986)

With the new generation of wealth creation of the Asian Tigers through the mid-1970s to the mid-1990s, came greater awareness of Islamic finance as an alternative to trading and banking in South-east Asia. Malaysia has been particularly energetic in her efforts to popularise its Shari'ah-compliant products and services to position itself to become the centre of the international Islamic capital market in the region. Securities Commission (SC) market policy and development division director, Dr Nik Ramlah Nik Mahmood, has made it known that the country will continue its efforts to develop innovative and competitive instruments to heighten its profile internationally. The challenges include addressing the lack of awareness of products and services as well as Shari'ah requirements. Shari'ah scholars and jurists are to be involved in the development process and the application of new technologies such as e-commerce. Among the significant progress made to date is the good take-up rate for Malaysia's sovereign US$500 million (US$1 = RM3.80) global Islamic debt securities launched in June 2002. The debt papers, which were twice oversubscribed, signal Malaysia's penetration into the West Asian market and the immense appetite the market has for Islamic-based financial instruments. It was a confirmation that the people there were exposed to the product and they were looking for Shari'ah-compliant investments.[54]

---

[54]"Malaysia to popularize *Shari'ah* compliant products and services", www.islamic-banking.com, 23 August 2002.

Whilst Malaysia promoted Islamic banks as a constructive outlet for religious fervour, Saudi Arabia would not allow Islamic banks in, lest they imply that the kingdom's existing banks were un-Islamic. (The Saudi royal family, not incidentally, subsists largely on income from conventional investments.) The government finally allowed one Islamic bank to open in 1987, though the word "Islam" was nowhere in its name.

Today, in banking centres like Kuwait, Dubai and especially Bahrain, which is known for its strict regulatory measures, Islamic banking is serious business. A respected group known by the acronym AAOIFI (Accounting and Auditing Organisation for Islamic Financial Institutions) has codified Shari'ah rulings into a set of industry standards. The early zealots have given way to more pragmatic professionals. Even the Shari'ah scholars — once recruited from the local mosque and barely fluent in English, much less financial statements — are now armed with advanced degrees in economics.

Since 2000, eight countries consisting of Malaysia, Indonesia, Iran, Saudi Arabia, Pakistan, Sudan, Bahrain and Kuwait have been making efforts to establish a common and harmonious Islamic banking system. In a meeting in Kuala Lumpur on 3 November 2002, these countries inked an agreement to establish the Islamic Financial Services Board to promote Islamic banking.[55] "In the last five years, the industry has accomplished more than it did in its first 20", says Shamil Bank's Jaroudi, in 2002.[56]

4.2   Different Paths, Same Goal

However, there are many similarities between Islamic and conventional finance, since both deal with a common set of operating business realities. In most cases, Islamic and conventional finance,

---

[55] "Govt encouraging Islamic banking in country", *The Nation* (www.nation.com.pk) 8 November 2002.

[56] Cited in Useem, op. cit.

simply travel different paths towards the same goal. Consider these examples:

- Most businesses need long-term financing and in conventional finance this is accomplished through some combination of long-term debt and owners' capital. Interest is the mechanism which makes the wheels turn here, but obviously, this is not an option under Shari'ah law, so one Islamic solution is to have passive partners contracted for a certain share of the profits, with another share going to the entrepreneurs who manage the business. This solution meets the concept of partnership as required by doctrine, yet at the same time it functions in a similar way to a conventional preferred-shareholder contract. And if the business does not want to dilute its ownership by bringing in partners, other options exist, such as leasing. A lease does not involve formal interest or a partnership stake, yet satisfies the business' need for long-term financing of plant and equipment and the investor's need to earn a fair return.
- Inventory financing is another requirement common to both Islamic and conventional commerce. An Islamic business in need of short-term inventory financing can purchase the inventory on credit, that credit being supplied either by the inventory supplier or a bank. The bank can purchase the inventory for the business based on the business' promise to buy the inventory later for cost plus a fair markup.
- Many businesses find it necessary to supply credit to their customers through accounts receivable. An Islamic business can do this but is not permitted — as in conventional finance — to refinance by pledging or selling those receivables because they are not real assets. Under Islamic law, financial assets cannot be sold or used as collateral, so an Islamic business either has to finance its credit extensions from internally generated funds or arrange for a third party to buy the goods on behalf of its customers and resell them to those customers with a markup — just as the Islamic business would finance its own purchases from suppliers.

These are some of the simpler Islamic alternatives to conventional finance. To the outsider, some of these arrangements may seem to be no more than elaborate subterfuges for conventional financial transactions. This conclusion, however, would ignore a number of important subtleties with respect to intentions, the detailed legal incidents of the various transactions, the religious and secular constraints on banking practices, and the limited number of financial contracts currently available to practitioners of Islamic finance.

4.3   What Investment Products are Permissible under Islamic Shari'ah Law

Turning our attention to the range of Shari'ah-compliant financial instruments that are available in global markets today, it is clear that interest-based securities (e.g. bonds, bank deposits, etc.) are not acceptable since these securities provide returns that are pre-determined and unrelated to the underlying performance of the asset that is generating the returns. On the other hand, by the same logic, equity securities (shares) are considered permissible by a consensus of contemporary Muslim scholars, including the Islamic Fiqh Academy,[57] because the profits an investor makes on equity securities are tied to the returns of the underlying company and hence are risk-related. However, in recognition of the sensitivity of the subject, it is recommended that Muslim investors place their money in Islamic mutual funds that are professionally managed

---

[57] The Islamic FiqhAcademy (IFA) is a subsidiary organ of the Organisation of the Islamic Conference (OIC), created by the Third Islamic Summit Conference held in Makkah al-Mukarramah (Saudi Arabia) in Rabiul Awwal 1401 H (January 1981). It is based in Jeddah (Saudi Arabia). Its members and experts are selected from among the best scholars and thinkers available in the Islamic world and Muslim minorities in non-Muslim countries, in every field of knowledge (Islamic Fiqh, science, medicine, economy and culture, etc.).

and have the added guarantee of a qualified Shari'ah Supervisory Board.

Investment in a common stock of companies engaged in permissible activities is also allowed under Shari'ah law, though preferred stocks are prohibited in Islam since they guarantee to holders the amounts paid out as dividends to holders of preferred stock. Also permissible for investment are mutual funds whose holdings consist of shares in companies complying with Islamic screening criteria, both qualitative (permissible activities) and quantitative (financial ratios).

4.4   Shari'ah Investment Principles

When it comes to deciding where to place one's investments, the first set of filters is quite straightforward: exclude all companies whose primary business involves forbidden products (e.g. alcohol, pork, tobacco, financial services, weapon production, and entertainment).[58] The second set of filters, which are based on financial ratios, is a lot more complicated, not to say anomalous. They relate to making certain compromises on three prohibitions, namely, carrying interest-bearing debt, receiving interest or some other form of impure income, and trading in debts at a price other than their face values.

The rules recently adopted by the Dow Jones Islamic Index (DJII) board are as follows:

- Exclude companies with a debt-to-total-asset ratio of 33 per cent or more.
- Exclude companies with "impure-plus-non-operating-interest income" to a revenue ratio of 5 per cent or more.

---

[58]A typical screen given by the Dow Jones Islamic Index (DJII) Shari'ah board can be found on the web (www.dowjones.com/corp/index_products.htm).

- Exclude companies with accounts receivable to a total assets ratio of 45 per cent or more.

The first compromise is based rather loosely on a famous *hadith* where Abu Bark asked the Prophet how much of his wealth to give in charity, and the Prophet said: "One third, and one third is plenty". This is clearly an out-of-context application of the *hadith*, and jurists do not claim that it is used as a legal proof, but rather as a comforting rule of thumb. The second compromise assumes that 5 per cent is a negligible amount, though no sources have been found, so far, which mention the origin of this ruling. The third compromise is based on the view that if the majority of the company's assets are illiquid, then the total assets may inherit the status of that majority.[59]

These Dow Jones rulings are virtually identical to those advocated in earlier years by the Shari'ah boards of fund management companies in Islamic countries. They are also much the same as the guidelines used by other equity indices, such as the FTSE Global Islamic Index Series (GIIS). Initially pioneered in January 1999 by The International Investor (TII) and calculated by FTSE, the FTSE GIIS was the first truly global Islamic index series. It was designed to track the performance of leading publicly traded companies whose activities are consistent with Islamic Shari'ah principles. In the same year, 1999, the GIIS was incorporated into the FTSE family of indices. Using the FTSE World Index as the universe, TII applies Shari'ah principles, following guidelines provided by its Fatwa and Shari'ah Supervisory Committee to rule out those companies whose business activities are incompatible with the Islamic law.[60]

---

[59]El-Gamal, Mahmoud Amin, "Permissible investment vehicles", Islamic-World.net   (http://islamic-world.net/economics/permissible_investment_vehicles.htm).

[60]The International Investor (www.tii.com).

4.5 Equity-Financing and Debt-Financing in Pre-Islamic Arab Society

Having laid out the basic principles for Shari'ah-compliant investment, one can now turn our attention to the actual financing of
investment and debt through Islamic financial instruments. Effective risk-management in Islamic finance deserves priority attention,
but it entails many complex issues, including income recognition,
adequacy of collateral and disclosure standards, which need to be
better understood if they are to be successfully addressed. In order
to do so, one must go back to the very beginning of Islamic financial
institutions, for Islamic banking can only be properly understood in
terms of its historical origins.

In every society, Islamic or non-Islamic, traditional or modern,
business ventures are financed either by the proprietor's own capital
or else by borrowing money. Today's banking and financial system,
and the facilities and services that it provides, have evolved largely
to address the need for financing by others' capital.

There are two types of financing from others' capital, namely
equity-financing and debt-financing. In the particular case of Islamic
banking, the relevant question here is what is the stand of Shari'ah
with regard to these two types of financing? Looking back to the pre-
Islamic era, long before the advent of Islam, the Arabian Peninsula
was already a thriving trading community where Arab traders
already practised both equity- financing and debt-financing. Equity-
financing was effected through two basic types of contract (*uqud
al-ishtirak*), namely trustee profit-sharing (*al-mudharabah*) and joint-
venture profit-sharing (*al-musharakah*). Debt-financing was similarly
effected through two types of contract, in this instance, deferred contracts of exchange and *riba*-based lending. Since *riba* is synonymous
with modern-day interest, one can refer to the latter category as
interest-based lending.

The first type of Arab debt-financing in the pre-Islamic period —
deferred contracts of exchange (*al-bai, al-tijarah* and *al-dayn*) — can

be looked at in the following way. A contract of exchange takes place when a commodity or service is exchanged for another commodity or for money. In commercial dealings, contracts of exchange arise in sale-and-purchase contracts and leasing contracts. The contractual relationship is therefore of the category of seller-buyer or lessor-lessee. Contracts of exchange may either be transacted through immediate cash payments or else deferred. When the settlement from one side of the contract — such as payment in money — is deferred or delayed, the contract becomes a deferred contract of exchange. A deferred contract of exchange is therefore akin to a credit sale-and-purchase. Moreover a deferred contract creates a debt and in this respect features as a debt-financing instrument.

In the pre-Islamic period, there were five basic types of deferred contract exchanges in the Arab financial world:

(i) Deferred instalment sales (*al-bai bithaman ajil*)
(ii) Deferred lump-sum sales (*bai al-murabaha*, also spelled as *murabahah*)
(iii) Leasing (*al-ijara*)
(iv) *Salam* sales (*bai al-salam*, also known as *bei salam*, meaning project or capital financing)
(v) Manufacture sale *(bai al-istisna')*[61]

The second category of debt-financing in the pre-Islamic period was based, not on a contract of exchange, but involved, instead, interest-based lending (*riba al-nasiah*) (in modern terms, money lending). The contractual relationship here was that of debtor-creditor. At the point of lending, the lender lends the money to the borrower. At the point of repayment, the borrower repays the lender the principal amount of money lent, plus an "additional" in the form of interest.

---

[61]Refers to an order made by a purchaser to a manufacturer to produce goods according to description given of an agreed price and on the basis of an agreed mode of payment.

Interest-based lending naturally creates a debt, and is therefore a debt-financing instrument.

4.6 Islamic Equity-Financing and Debt-Financing

With the advent of Islam, Shari'ah law, guided by its primary sources of the Quran and the *Sunnah*, laid down various injunctions that would subsequently form the basis of Islamic banking and finance. With regard to equity-financing, a very notable feature of the Shari'ah is the fact that the Quran does not deal directly with this issue at all; it was left to the *Sunnah* to clarify matters. The *Sunnah* simply affirmed that the *uqud al-ishtirak* (profit-sharing contracts) of *al-mudharabah*, *al-musharakah* and other similar contracts, which had been practiced by the pre-Islamic Arab world, were all allowed, being designated *jaiz* or *mubah* ("indifferent") in relation to Islam.

While the Quran is silent on equity-financing, it comes out strongly on debt-financing, as does the *Sunnah*, which also deals extensively with the subject. In essence, although interest-based lending is forbidden (*haram*) by Islam, deferred contracts of exchange are permitted (*jaiz* or *mubah*). In other words, lending is allowed in Islam, but it has to be without interest. Under Shari'ah law, this type of lending is known as a "benevolent loan" (*al-qard al-hasan*) and it therefore has more relevance in relation to the social-welfare economy, or where there are social ramifications to a transaction as in the case of contracts involving the government, rather than in the private or commercial sectors.

Clearly, debt-financing is one area where there are major differences between Islamic finance and the conventional financial system. Whereas debt-financing in conventional finance is almost entirely built upon interest-based lending, this type of contract is expressly forbidden (*haram*) under Islamic law. Conversely, the Islamic debt-financing instruments of deferred contracts of exchange are not generally known in the conventional financial world. Nevertheless, there are still some similarities between the two systems, even when it comes to debt-financing. The contract of *al-ijara* (leasing), for example, is also employed in conventional debt-financing; likewise, the contract of *bai' al-murabaha* (deferred lump-sum sale), which is practised in credit sale-and-purchase transactions in both Islamic and conventional marketplaces.

4.7   Equity Securities: Profit-Sharing Contracts

As Islamic banking prohibits conventional loan-taking to finance business interests, there are two ways in which one can obtain project financing the *halah* way.

(i) *Al-Mudarabah* (trustee profit-sharing)

A bank may undertake to finance acceptable projects according to the principle of *al-mudarabah*. Here the bank acts as the "provider of capital" and will offer 100 per cent financing for the relevant project, whilst the initiator of the project is the "entrepreneur" who will manage the project. The bank cannot interfere in the management of the project, but has the right to undertake the follow-up and supervision task. In these circumstances, both parties will agree, through negotiation, on the ratio of the distribution of the profits generated from the project, if any; in the event of the project making a loss, then the bank bears all the losses.

Mudarabah is the closest classical analogy to the modern relationship between stockholders and bank management. However, the analogy is not perfect. For example, if management corresponds to the *mudarib*, or trustee, and stockholders to capital investors, then *mudarabah* rules would dictate that both be compensated with a share of profits. But if the manager is merely an employee of the bank, who then is the *mudarib* and who is entitled to a share in the profits? The problems arising from such interpretations have been considered mere practical problems, not moral or religious ones, and are therefore easily surmounted. Scholars seem to conclude that the old rules of partnership should be consulted only in broad essentials.[62] In other words, as Vogel has indicated, the modern company is accepted as a new type of contractual relationship, which owes deference only to the basic principles of Islamic partnership law, not to its every detail.[63]

(ii) *Al-Musharakah* (joint-venture profit-sharing)

Alternatively, a bank may undertake to finance acceptable projects according to the principle of *al-musharakah*. In this instance, the bank, together with the initiator or initiators of the relevant project, will provide the equity-financing for the project in agreed proportions. All parties, including the bank, have the right to participate in the management of the project, but equally, all parties have the option to waive such right. All parties agree through negotiation on the ratio of distribution of the profits generated from the project, if any. This ratio need not coincide with the ratio of participation in the financing of the project. In the event of a loss in the project, all parties bear the loss in proportion to their share in the financing.

In all modern forms of *musharakah*, the partners have equal rights. In the case of limited companies and cooperative societies, the shareholders delegate their powers (rights in respect of administration, etc.) to some amongst them to be called directors or some other appropriate title. In a partnership concern, the partners, by a mutual agreement, distribute amongst themselves their responsibilities, duties and jobs. These arrangements are valid being identified as *'urf*, that is to say, customary practices of the business community.

---

[62]See 'Ali al-Khafif, *al-Sharikat fi al-fiqh al-islami* (Cairo: Arab League, 1962); 'Abd al-'Aziz al-Khayyat, *al-Sharikat* (Beirut: Risala, 1984); and Mustafa al-Zaraqa, *Madkhal*, 3:256–287.

[63]See Vogel and Hayes, op. cit., p. 133.

A distinguishing feature of modern *musharakah* partnerships (the partnership aside) is the limited liability of the
shareholders. They cannot be held liable for more than the
amount of capital they have invested. This requirement makes
it necessary to regard the *musharakah* as an entity separate
from the individuality of the shareholders. This common *'urf*
has given way to safe and stable *musharakah*, resulting in big
commercial organisations and flourishing business.[64]

In the real-world, project financing may involve a combination of *mudarabah* and *musharakah* partnerships, where all
partners contribute to the capital but not necessarily to the
entrepreneurship and management as well. In such instances,
profits need not be shared in accordance with capital contributions. They may be shared in any proportion agreed to by the
partners, depending on their contribution to the success and
profitability of the business.

4.8   Debt-Financing Contracts

As we have seen, conventional, interest-based banking methods of
debt-financing are unacceptable in Islamic banking, but there are
several other financial tools which enable debt-financing to be implemented. Vogel's analysis shows the following:

(i) *Al-Bai Bithaman Ajil* (financing the acquisition of assets through
deferred installment sales)

A bank may finance customers who wish to acquire a given
asset but to defer payment for a specific period, or to pay by
installments under the principle of a*l-bai bithaman ajil*. In such
cases, the bank will first determine the requirements of the customer in relation to his period and manner of repayment. The
bank will then purchase the asset concerned. Subsequently, the

---

[64]See Irfani, A.M., *Musharakah and its Modern Applications*, Islamabad,
December 1984.

bank sells the relevant asset to the customer at an agreed price, which comprises the actual cost of the asset to the bank, and the bank's margin or profit. The agreement will allow the customer to settle the payment by installments within the period and in the manner agreed.

(ii) *Al-Ijara* (financing the use of services of an asset through leasing) Alternatively, a bank may finance its customers to acquire the right to use the services of a given asset under the principle of *al-ijara*. In this instance, the bank first purchases the asset required by the customer. Subsequently, the bank leases the asset to the customer for a fixed period, the lease arrangements and other terms and conditions being agreed to by both parties.

As far as the actual lease agreement is concerned, Islamic laws of leasing pose three sets of problems for modern Islamic finance, all arising from *riba* and *gharar* principles. The first set of problems concerns restrictions on the right of parties to fix the nature of the right sold — the usufruct — under the terms of their agreement. Islamic law understands the usufruct largely as a creature of contract, since only by the *ijara* contract does the usufruct become fixed and known (for example, for how many years does the usufruct continue?). Even so, the law does not give the parties total freedom in this respect. It views some benefits and burdens of the property as belonging naturally and unchangeably to the lessee, and others as belonging to the lessor.

The second set of problems arises from the fact that the usufruct of property is not something extant and tangible, but a stream of use extending into the future, which therefore makes it inherently risky and unstable (*gharar*). What if future events reduce the value of the usufruct to the lessee? Cautious in this issue, Islamic law gives broad scope to the lessee to cancel the lease if events should cause the usufruct to be less valuable to him than expected.

A third set of problems concerns the various types of future sale and option terms that conventional financial leases use to dispose of the residual value of the leased goods at the end of the lease term. Under Islamic law, such terms are invalid as uncertainty, risk and speculation are all prohibited by the Quran.

In the event, Islamic financial practice seems to have sidestepped all three groups of problems. As regards problems of damage or destruction of the leased property, many Islamic leases simply adopt the conventional financial lease provision that the lessee remains liable even in the event of the property's total destruction. Other Islamic lease agreements — for example, those of the Islamic Development Bank — pay heed to Islamic law, acknowledging the lessee's right to cancel in such an event, but often impose on the lessee the obligation to buy casualty insurance naming the lessor as the beneficiary. As regards the second problematic area, namely a lessee's right to rescind due to diminished benefit from the usufruct, the present practice seems simply to ignore the problem, allowing lessees to avoid the lease only for conventional legal reasons such as *force majeure* or a breach of contract or warranty.[65] Finally, on the third issue, namely the unenforceability of terms in lease disposing of the future residual value by options or sales, the solution in practice seems to be to include such terms in the leases, even if unenforceable Islamically, in the expectation that incentives other than the Islamic law will cause the promisor to uphold them.[66]

(iii) *Al-Ujr* (fee-based syndication services)

It should briefly be mentioned here that the above facilities may be organised on a syndication basis, for a fee, if the financial requirements are beyond the capability of a single bank or if it

---

[65]*Force majeure* is a legal term which means that some important and critical event has occurred, as a result, releasing the person directly affected from his or her legal obligations in a particular matter that would otherwise have applied.

[66]See Vogel and Hayes, op. cit., pp. 144–145.

is desirable to spread the risk. Similar syndication services also apply to trade finance facilities.

(iv) *Al-Murabaha* (letters of credit: deferred lump-sum sales or cost plus)

In this instance, the customer informs the bank of his letter of credit requirements and requests the bank to purchase or import the required goods, indicating thereby that he would be willing to purchase the goods from the bank on their arrival on the principal of *al-murabaha*. The bank establishes the letter of credit and pays the proceeds to the negotiating bank utilising its own funds. The bank then sells the goods to the customer at a sale price comprising its cost and a profit margin under the principal of *al-murabaha* for settlement on a deferred term.

(v) *Al-Murabaha* (financing working capital: deferred lump-sum sales or cost plus)

Here, the customer may approach the bank to provide financing for his working capital requirements in order to purchase stocks and inventories, spares and replacements, or semi-finished goods and raw materials. In this instance, the bank first purchases the desired items, or else appoints the customer as its agent to purchase the required goods on its behalf, and then settles the purchase price from its own funds. The bank subsequently sells the goods to the customer at an agreed price comprising its purchase price and a profit margin, and allows the customer to settle this sale price on a deferred term of thirty, sixty, ninety days or any other period as the case may be. On the due date, the customer pays the bank the agreed sale price.[67]

This kind of transaction has many advantages. First, although in ordinary circumstances no bank engages in trading in goods, finding this enterprise too risky and distracting, this commissioned *murabaha* enables the bank to avoid the drawbacks normally associated with trading in that a purchase is

---

[67] Ismail, Abdul Halim HJ., *Overview of Islamic Banking*, 2001.

never made unless the bank already has an assured buyer who, moreover, informs the bank how to obtain the goods desired. Secondly, while the bank's profit (the markup) conceivably derives in part from its services in securing the goods through the first sale, it is far more likely — especially in the present day — to derive from the extension of credit in the second sale. To the extent that the bank's services in carrying out the two sales and the costs and risks of its interim ownership can be minimised, the transaction becomes economically very similar to a conventional commercial loan.[68]

(vi) *Salam* (financing the acquisition of assets in the future: forward purchase)

The contract of *salam* — the forward purchase of generically described goods for full advance payment — has important potential as an Islamic financing device, particularly in relation to agricultural produce, but it is not yet used extensively. However, three major problems reduce the *salam* contract's value as a financing vehicle. The first is the risk of default by the seller, made more severe by the fact of repayment. A partial solution is to obtain some form of security from the seller, whether it be a pledge or a guarantee.[69] The second problem is the bank's need to liquidate the goods after delivery, an inconvenience made more serious by the Islamic legal rule that a *salam* buyer cannot sell the expected goods before actually taking possession of them.[70] To address this problem, the idea has surfaced of a "parallel" or "back-to-back" *salam*. Here, after buying goods

---

[68]Vogel and Hayes, op. cit., pp. 140–141.

[69]This is allowed by most, but not all, scholars. See Ibn Qudama, 4:347–352.

[70]See decision 65/1/d7, *Fiqh Academy Journal 1* (1992): 711, 716. Ibn Rushd, *Bi-dayat*, 2:205–207; Ibn Qudama, 4:343–344; Bahuti, 3:306–307. Under the Maliki school, the buyer may sell his expectation of the goods back to the original seller or to another, as long as the purchased goods are not food. See Ibn Rushd, supra.

of a certain description from a seller and paying the full purchase price (*salam* sale 1), but before the seller is due to deliver on that contract, the bank, in a separate and formally unconnected *salam* contract (*salam* sale 2), sells goods of exactly the same description and with the same due date to a third party, receiving full advance payment from that buyer. The net result is that the bank has reserved its position, fixed the profits it will earn from the two trades, and has an assured a purchaser for its goods. Reportedly, classical authors have mentioned this transaction without disapproval.

The third problem affecting the *salam* contract's utility as a financing vehicle is that according to most scholars, Islamic law requires that if at the time of delivery the seller can neither produce the goods nor obtain them elsewhere, the buyer has only two choices: either withdraw his offer, or wait for the goods to become available later, with no compensation permitted for the delay. In either case, the buyer loses all or much of the profit from the use of his money.

4.9   Debt Securities

Islamic debt securities are debt-based financial instruments. It is therefore pertinent to recall that Islam allows, *inter alia*, the following methods of debt-financing:

(i) Deferred Contracts of Exchange

- *Al-bai bithaman ajil* (deferred sales) — this is usually applied for medium and long-term financing with periodic installment payments.
- *Bai al-murabaha* (deferred sales) — this is usually applied for short-term (trade) financing with lump-sum payments.
- *Al-ijara* (leasing) — this is usually a financial-lease type of contract applied for leasing of assets with periodic lease rental payments and ending with sale of the assets at nominal price.

(ii) Loans

- *Al-qardh al-hasan* (benevolent loans) — these are loans which are returned at the end of an agreed period without any interest or share in the profit or loss of the business. Therefore, it is a kind of gratuitous loan given to the needy people for a fixed period without requiring the payment of interest or profit. The receiver of *qard al-hasan* is only required to repay the original amount of the loan.

(iii) Refinancing of Assets

- *Bai al-inah* — here the owner of the assets requiring financing first sells the assets to the financing party for cash. Subsequently, he buys back the assets under a deferred sale contract.

  In essence, the creation and structuring of the Islamic debt securities is as follows: a debt-financing contract is concluded; the provider of financing, to whom the debt obligations are due, securities the debt in accordance with the relevant regulations and guidelines; the debt instruments are sold down and traded in secondary markets. Trading of the debt instruments is undertaken in the secondary markets under the concept of *bai al-dayn* (debt trading). The price of the debt instruments struck by the buyer and seller in any particular transaction is left to be determined by the market forces of supply and demand for funds.

4.10 Shari'ah Qualifications in Leasing

Not all lease contracts qualify as contracts of *ijara* as defined by Shari'ah and the differences between typical lease contracts and those constituting *ijara* must be taken into account. For example, in a typical equipment lease, the risk of loss or damage to the equipment is usually shifted from the lessor to the lessee and the lessee is required to take out insurance to cover this risk. In contracts of *ijara*, by contrast, Shari'ah boards and other regulatory institutions generally require that the lessor must retain the risk of loss or damage of the equipment. Similarly, whereas in most equipment leases the obligation to maintain the equipment is shifted to the lessee, in contracts of *ijara*, the maintenance obligation is generally retained by the lessor.

In structuring a lease programme, contract arrangements must be developed to bridge these disparities between Islamic and conventional types of leases. For example, it may be possible to arrange lease-servicing contracts whereby the lease servicer agrees to maintain the equipment, repair any damage and replace lost equipment. Here the lessor retains the ultimate liability, not the lessee, but the lease servicer (a party that should be capable of bearing these risks) gives support to the lessor.

It generally seems to be the case that *ijara* contracts, as an Islamic investment vehicle, are becoming an integral part of the rapid expansion of Islamic financial products and a major investment tool offered by Islamic financial institutions. Indeed, one cannot foresee a portfolio of an Islamic financial institution that will not include *ijara* — they will be sought by Islamic institutions as part of their diversification strategy, along side *murabaha*, which is similar to any fixed-interest financing such as a car loan, equity and real estate. Market demand is bound to cause the growth of *ijara* contracts.

4.11   Other Risk-Taking Products

What other financial instruments can substitute for Islamically forbidden interest-bearing debt instruments? The most notable effort has been the so-called *muqarada* bond, which resembles a revenue bond. "*Muqarada* bonds" are bonds where the proceeds are to be used for income-yielding public utility projects such as the construction of bridges and roads. Investors who buy *muqarada* bonds take a share of the profits of the project being financed, but also share the

risk of unexpectedly low profits, or even losses. They have no say
in the management of the project, but act as non-voting shareholders. Then there is a financial arrangement known as *qirad* (which
is sometimes also called *mudarabah*), whereby the financier gets a
share in the output, as similar to the case of *muqarada* bonds.[71]

4.12   Islamic Insurance

One of the most obvious situations where there is a conflict between
Shari'ah law and conventional financial institutions is in the case of
insurance policies; here the concept of *gharar* has led to the condem-
nation of some or all types of insurance by Muslim scholars, since
insurance involves an unknown risk. This has led to the development of *takaful* (co-operative) insurance in some Muslim countries.
Takaful is an Arabic word meaning mutual help and cooperation
and dates back to the early days of Islam. Traditionally it referred to
relationships between family groups, villages or mosques, but in a
modern context it is used to refer to the kind of services offered by
an insurance company. Used in this way, the term *takaful* refers to a
pact or practice among a group of members, called participants, who
agree to jointly guarantee themselves against any loss or damage
that may fall upon any of them as defined in the pact. In the event
of any member, or participant, suffering a loss due to the defined
mishap or disaster, he or she would receive a certain sum of money
or financial benefit from a fund as defined under the terms of the
pact to help meet or mitigate that loss. In short, the basic objective of
takaful is to pay for a defined loss out of a defined fund. The loss will
not be transferred as a liability to any intermediary as the operation
does not fall under the contract of buying and selling whereby the
seller would normally agree to provide the guarantee.

Clearly, the way today's so-called *takaful* companies operate,
with administrative buildings and officers especially appointed to

---

[71]Ariff, Mohamed, "Islamic banking", Islamicity.com, (http://www. islam-
icity.com/finance/IslamicBanking_Evolution.asp).

carry out the job, etc., is a long way removed from the traditional workings of *takaful* and as the world progresses, *takaful* transactions have been increasingly modernised and brought up to date. Today's Shari'ah-compliant *takaful* insurance schemes are guided by the following rules:

   (i) *Riba* is to be avoided. Interest is neither taken nor given. Investments are not made in interest-bearing bonds or other non-*halah* investments.

  (ii) No business participation is made in any commodity or activity prohibited by Shari'ah.

 (iii) The *takaful* contract attempts to determine the terms of the contract as clearly and definitely as possible in order to minimise ignorance and uncertainty.

 (iv) Business is conducted on the basis of a *mudarabah* partnership (see above).

  (v) There is no forfeiture of premiums if the policy lapses or is surrendered.

 (vi) A nominee cannot retain the benefit of the policy for his own use but receives it as an agent on behalf of his heirs.

 (vii) A Shari'ah advisory council oversees the operation of the scheme and advises on Shari'ah law.

(viii) The company pays *zakat* (obligatory payment to the poor and needy) on its profits.[72]

4.13   *Takaful* Insurance in a Contemporary Context

The world has defined *takaful* insurance transactions as a competitive product. The first Islamic insurance company, known simply as the Islamic Insurance Co. Ltd, was established in Sudan in 1979. This company was able to distribute profits to its shareholders at the rate of 5 per cent in 1979, 8 per cent in 1980 and 10 per cent in 1981. Following the success of the Insurance Company in Sudan, other

---

[72]Hussain, op. cit., p. 191.

Islamic insurance (*takaful*) companies were established in Islamic and in non-Islamic countries. They included:

- Islamic Arab Insurance Co. Ltd, Jeddah (1979)
- Dar Al-Mal Al-Islami, Geneva (1979)
- Dar Al-Mal Al-Islami (DMI), Switzerland (1979)
- Islamic Takaful Co., Luxembourg (1983)
- Islamic Takaful, Bahrain (1983)
- Islamic Takaful and Re-Takaful, Bahamas (1983)
- Bait Al-Tamwil, Turkey (1986)
- USA Takaful, United States of America (1990)
- IBB Takaful, Brunei (1995)
- Islamic Takaful Company, (ITC) London

4.14 *Takaful* Compared with Conventional Insurance

Takaful companies take those aspects of insurance that are not considered *halah* in Shari'ah law and adjust them so that they can fulfil the conventional role of insurance whilst at the same time being in accordance with Islamic law.[73] The common features shared by *takaful*-style insurance schemes and conventional insurance is that both feature specified maturity periods whereby the sum that is insured is paid to the policy holder, if he survives, or else benefits are paid to his beneficiaries in the event of his premature death. The calculation of premium is done by actuaries taking the same factors into account. In the case of *takaful*, the *tabarru'*[74] portion is calculated by actuaries who take the same principles into account as in conventional insurance.

---

[73]Rashid, Syed Khalid, "Insurance and Muslims", paper presented at IIU Malaysia on 13 October 1992, quoting Siddiqi, *Insurance in an Islamic Economy*, 1985.

[74]This means "donation; gift; contribution". This one word apparently actually Islamises the insurance contract by removing most of the objectionable elements. This is actually the fundamental difference between insurance that is Shari'ah compliant (*takaful*) and conventional insurance.

The distinguishing features of family *takaful*[75] are that there is no element of forfeiture, no non-profit policies and the contribution/installment is the same since there is no policy which does not share profits. The profit-sharing ratio is clearly stated in *mudarabah* contract and the method of determining profit is clearly known to both parties. Profit is calculated and credited monthly at the annual rate of profit. The insured are regarded as participants and the company does not engage in practices or investments which are disallowed by Shari'ah. In the case of conventional insurance, however, forfeiture usually follows within three years if premiums cease; there are both profit and non-profit forms; premiums are high for part policies; policy holders may not know how profits are determined and what proportion they may receive; the interval of determining the bonus is not known; and the insured are clients, not regarded as participants.[76]

4.15 Summary

It has been seen that the essential feature of Islamic banking is that it is interest-free. Although it is often claimed that there is more to Islamic banking, such as contributions towards a more equitable distribution of income and wealth and an increased equity participation in the economy,[77] Islamic banking as a financial institution nevertheless derives its specific rationale from the fact that there is no place for the concept of interest in the Islamic order.[78]

---

[75]This aim of family *takaful* is similar to that of conventional life insurance, which is to provide for the surviving family members in the event of the death of the policyholder.

[76]Hussain, op. cit., pp. 192–193.

[77]Chapra, M. Umer, "Money and banking in an Islamic economy", in M. Ariff (ed.), *Monetary and Fiscal Economics of Islam*, 1982.

[78]Ariff, Mohamed, "Islamic banking", *Asian-Pacific Economic Literature*, Vol. 2, No. 2, September 1988, pp. 46–62.

Whilst interest-bearing debt instruments are prohibited in Islam, there are some Islamic contracts which result in debt. They include *istisna'*, *murabaha*, and *ijara* financing. However, there are no effective derivatives of Islamic debt contracts which replicate conventional risk-hedging and leveraging contracts such as swaps, futures and options.

Similarly, in the equity security sector, there are no risk-hedging or leveraging contracts in Islamic finance that truly compare with available conventional derivatives. Only recently have favourable Shari'ah rulings made it acceptable to trade equity shares in the secondary market. Previously they had been classified as financial instruments in the primary market where the proceeds of the sale goes to the issuer and were therefore ineligible to be bought and sold. Now a number of Islamic scholars classify them as specific claims on real assets, thus making secondary market trading in them acceptable. This is at least a start towards the future formulation of equity derivatives that are acceptable in the Islamic world.

With respect to commodities and other goods, the *salam* contract is an imperfect Islamic substitute for a conventional forward contract. The related *istisna'* contract for goods being manufactured for a buyer provides another partial Islamic proxy for a forward contract. It is even possible to construct an Islamic contract that partially replicates a conventional futures contract, via back-to-back *salam* contracts.

Third-party guarantees do provide some risk protection in an Islamic context, and one of the characteristics of the *mudaraba* contract provides a *de facto* call option for *mudaribs* who are party to these substitute for a Western call option, but it has a number of qualifications that limit its use in many real-life situations. Conventional financial markets provide ample means — in terms of options — for managing risks such as deterioration in quality or another party's outright default, but in Islamic finance, where default remedies are limited by religious principles (e.g. no interest or penalty can be charged subsequently to a default), the only way to protect against credit risk is a third-party guarantee against such a default.

Currency markets in the West are among the most sophisticated of all financial markets, with a myriad of derivatives to handle all sorts of risk dimensions. Unfortunately, currency is not considered a real asset in Islam and hence there are no generally accepted proxy derivatives in this market to deal with foreign exchange risk.[79]

In Vogel's opinion, there is clearly a need for a modification of existing Islamic financial contracts which could meet at least some of the needs of both investors and capital users in the Islamic sector.[80] And even if useful Islamic financial instruments are devised, and their capacity to be traded assured, problems will remain concerning the shape and function of a market in which these instruments can be traded. Since Islamic institutions and investors are already trading on the conventional markets, why should they not either continue to use conventional markets or set up new ones modelled after them? The reason seems to be that use of these markets is just a measure forced on the industry while it awaits Islamically correct markets of adequate volume to emerge. Establishing such markets is made all the more daunting by the need for the government to cooperate by passing the extensive supportive legislation and regulation required to establish a securities market.[81]

---

[79]However, there are transactions between two countries where the poorer country's central bank guarantees the value of its currency but does not assume any other liability in terms of the traded good. It is considered Islamically acceptable for an intermediary to buy the goods at a fixed price from one country in that country's currency and then sell it to another country for a fixed price in its own currency, thereby assuming the intermediate ownership of the traded good and shouldering the currency exposure as well.

[80]See Vogel and Hayes, op. cit., pp. 231–232.

[81]Ibid, p. 178.

Chapter 5
Issues and Challenges of Islamic Banking Today

It is easy for the uninitiated to underestimate the difficulty of applying classical Islamic law to modern commercial transactions. Some believe that the law's dictates can be summed up in a set of vague and general ethical and moral precepts, which do not entail any precise system of legal procedures. In contrast, others assume that the legal restrictions are relatively few in number, concrete in nature, specific in application, and readily dealt with, leaving the rest of the field free for innovation and development. In either case, the outsider may expect to find Islamic banking easily accommodated by Western financial practices, simply by observing a short list of do's and don'ts. Instead, the uninitiated finds, on closer examination, that classical jurisprudence (*fiqh*) relating to commerce and other financial matters is extraordinarily rich and complex. Moreover, whilst this law is derived from profound general principals, it is not stated in those terms but rather as innumerable detailed rules, which are interconnected at a level rarely made explicit. Furthermore, these rules and principles are not only legal edicts but also possess a moral dimension, which, at times, defeats any hope of a legalistic precision.[82]

---

[82]Ibid, p. 28.

5.1 Obstacles to the Application of Islamic Law to Present Day Banking

The rationalising of those areas of Islamic law which relate to commerce and other financial activities, in order to create a legal framework for Islamic banking is not, according to Vogel's studies, all that simple then. First there is the nominalist or provisional nature of much of Islamic jurisprudence (*fiqh*), which relies as much on the interpretive skills of individual Islamic scholars, extrapolating from both primary and secondary sources, as it does on the principal tenets enshrined in Shari'ah law. Divergences of opinion between the different schools of law complicate the picture further, as do the different methodologies that may be called upon when elaborating on the law. Then there is the particular issue of the pluralism of the *fatwahs*, which again has its origins in the subjective and non-binding nature of many *fiqh* rulings.

What all this means is that Islamic jurisprudence lacks something of the consistency and predictability of a more codified system of laws and edicts — as we noted earlier, modern *fiqh* scholarship should be understood as representing the current state of thinking in terms of tolerance parameters and need not necessarily be regarded as the last word on the subject. Further complications inevitably arise when it comes to accommodating Shari'ah law to the existing legal system of a particular country, which more often than not is based on a European model, chiefly French or English, the legacy of the colonial era. Lastly, there are problems relating to proper accounting standards as well as regulatory challenges to ensure proper *halah* banking.[83] The path towards harmonisation of Islamic banking and conventional banking is fraught with interpretations of the *fiqh* and pluralism of the *fatwahs*. That is coupled by differences in the methods of interpretations and arriving at the *fatwahs*.

---

[83]Ibid, pp. 50–51.

5.2 Derivation from Revealed Sources

As we saw in chapter 2, the English term "Islamic law" conceals an important distinction between Shari'ah (divine law) and *fiqh* (the human comprehension of that law). *Fiqh*, unlike Shari'ah, can be faulty, multiple, uncertain, and changing. Indeed, since the revealed texts are only finite and are often ambiguous, the norm is that *fiqh* rulings are uncertain and merely probable suppositions as to what God's law truly is. Indeed, on most points of doctrine *fiqh* writings record multiple opinions, all from qualified scholars.

This situation is further complicated by the different positions taken by the various schools of law. By way of example one might consider the varying perspectives of the different schools in relation to *salam*, forward-purchasing contracts. The term *salam* refers to a contracted sale whereby the seller undertakes to supply specific goods to the buyer at a future date in exchange for an advanced sum fully paid up on the spot. Here the payment for the good is made up front and in cash, but the supply of the purchased goods is deferred. According to the Hanafi school, it is necessary that the commodity that is being sold remains available in the marketplace from the very day that the contract is initiated right up until the date of actual delivery. If the commodity is not available in the marketplace at the time of the contract, then *salam* cannot be effected in respect of that commodity, even though it may be confidently expected that the commodity *will* be available in the marketplace on the agreed date of delivery. The other three schools of law — Shafi'i, Maliki and Hanbali — differ on this, being of the opinion that the availability of the commodity at the time of the contract is not a condition for the validity of *salam*. What is necessary, according to them, is that it should be available at the time of delivery.

This is but one example, but suffice to say, there can be considerable divergences between what is and is not permissible under Islamic law, depending on which school of law is consulted. Such inconsistencies are not in themselves conceived as some kind of failure on the part of Islamic jurisprudence, but rather as a reflection of the fallibility of man. Ultimately, *fiqh* rulings are taken as truly and certainly God's law only when they are established by a literal, revealed text, or when they have been agreed upon unanimously by all Islamic scholars of a particular age. The latter agreement is called "consensus" or *ijma*.[84]

5.3 Methodological Differences

The legal rulings applied in today's Islamic banking and finance are, generally speaking, arrived at using one or the other of four different techniques: interpretation of the revealed sources (*ijtihad*), choice (*ikhtiyar*), necessity (*darura*) and artifice (*hila*). The selection of one technique over another to get a more favourable decision, according to the circumstances, also affects the consistency and predictability of many *fiqh* rulings.

The first and metaphysically most pristine technique is *ijtihad*, or derivation directly from the revealed texts of the Quran and the Prophet's *Sunnah*. This method is increasingly being used in Islamic banking and finance, particularly when a legal instrument or ruling is considered novel — that is never previously considered by scholars in the past. For example, contemporary scholars have found that the option contract has no counterpart in classical law and so must be evaluated afresh using *ijtihad*. Recourse to *ijtihad* is increasing as scholars move from everyday transactions to more complex and less commonplace exchanges.

A second method by which a ruling may be reached is that of choice, or *ikhtiyar*, which in this context means the selection of an appropriate ruling from views already propounded by scholars in the past. This method has the advantage of aligning the modern

---

[84]Scholars' construction of *ijma* differ. For some, no qualified scholar's view can ever be overridden by a later agreement. This gives more scope for variation than other positions on *ijma* holding than an *ijma* in a later generation disproves all the contradictory views of earlier generations. Ibid, pp. 34–35.

scholar's view with that of a great scholar in history, which at least lends the assurance that nothing about the opinion fundamentally offends the Shari'ah and that no disastrous innovation is afoot.

There are various subcategories of this approach defined according to the criteria by which a decision is reached. One method, the most ambitious, reverts to the Quran and *Sunnah* and to basic *fiqh* principles to decide which view offers the best or strongest interpretation of the revealed texts. A second method evaluates an opinion by the rules of decision internal to the school that espouses it, such as the degree of support from the school's founder or its consistency with the position taken by other schools (e.g. there are "stronger" and "weaker" Hanafi views). A third method examines which view best serves the general welfare or *maslaha* (a concept which includes religious welfare). In the latter instance a particular choice may be made simply because it conforms to prevailing practices or customs (*'urf*). One argument in favour of this last approach is that *fiqh* delegates freedom to act to those responsible for the general welfare as long as they do not offend fundamental principles of Shari'ah.

Vogel notes that conservative legal scholars prefer to avoid *ijtihad* wherever they can justify innovations by appeals to precedent (*ikhtiyar*). In practice, though, the method of choice covers *ijtihad*, notably in contemporary deliberations about options, which are financial instruments critical to any effective future for Islamic finance.

A third method of deriving rulings, still lower in metaphysical status, permits one to adopt any position, even one contravening a categorical Shari'ah rule, when one is compelled to do so by stark necessity (*darura*). This necessity must be of great severity, usually one involving life-or-death situations. The basis for this approach is the Quran's frequent recognition that a person may be driven by necessity to eat otherwise forbidden food (e.g. 2:173) and also the Quran's disavowal of any divine intent to cause mankind hardship or to press human beings beyond their capacities (e.g. 2:286). One version of the doctrine holds that a mere "need" (*haja*), if it affects many, may be treated like a dire necessity affecting only one.

Scholars in Islamic banking and finance have invoked necessity to permit exceptional relaxation of rules. They have issued *fatwahs* (opinions) allowing Islamic banks to deposit funds in interest-bearing accounts, particularly in foreign countries, because these banks have no alternative investments at the necessary maturities. Typically, however, they place conditions on such *fatwahs*. For example, it may be required that the unlawful gains be used for religiously meritorious purposes such as charity, training or research. Such *fatwahs* are particular to the circumstances in which they are issued. If conditions change or if an alternative to the necessary evil arises, the scholars require that the practice end.

Classical Islamic law also indulged in one further method of attaining desired legal outcomes, namely that of legal artifice (*hila*, pl *hiyal*). The foundation of this method is a formalistic approach to contract, in the sense of a concern for the external form of trans-actions instead of the parties' substantive intentions. All classical scholars found *hiyal* acceptable when they were merely clever uses of law to achieve legitimate ends. For example, a landlord, wor-ried about a tenant cancelling unfairly, might stipulate payment in advance in the lease terms.

In the case of Islamic banking, one such instance of legal artifice is the artificial *murabaha*. As we saw in the previous chapter, one of the principal instruments of Islamic banking is *murabaha*, a perfectly legitimate means of financing a sale by charging markups to the cur-rent price at a future time. Because Islam accepts the time value of money but rejects making money from money, the bank financing a *murabaha* sale must actually buy the merchandise and then advance it to buyer. In practice, however, Islamic banks in Pakistan, Malaysia and elsewhere have devised artificial *murabaha*, whereby the credi-tor immediately releases the merchandise to the buyer without ever really possessing it or even fully identifying it.[85] The Fiqh Academy

---

[85] An opinion put forward by Saiful Rosly, a professor of finance at the Islamic University of Malaysia.

of the Organisation of Islamic States has condemned this practice, yet many Islamic banks engage in such *hiyal*, perhaps because they lack the commercial expertise and warehousing capabilities literally to fulfil the conditions of a "real" *murabaha*. The major portion of outstanding credit extended by Islamic banks takes the form of *murabaha* but the proportion of it that is artificial is unknown. Any systematic attack on this particular artifice, however, could place the entire Islamic financial movement in jeopardy. Out of necessity Islamic banks are in need of new financial instruments.[86]

5.4 Pluralism of *Fatwahs*

As explained in chapter 2, a *fatwah* is a non-binding legal opinion of a learned scholar, or *mufti*, issued in response to a request for a legal opinion by one party or another. There is no obligation on the part of the person who asked for the opinion to implement what he is told; it is left to his conscience whether to accept that ruling or to turn from it and he bears the responsibility for that. The pluralism of *fatwahs* relates to differences and disagreements between different applications of law (*furu'*) as distinct from the actual principles of law (*usul*). For example, the prohibition of *riba* (interest) *vis-à-vis* the prohibition of *'inah* sales (double sale by which the borrower and the lender sell and then resell an object between them, once for cash and once for a higher price on credit, the net result being a loan with interest). Whilst pluralism is not accepted in matters of principle such as faith, the basic tenets of Islam and clear-cut principles of law, which are divine in character, Islam must nevertheless confront the problem of legal pluralism in other areas if it seeks to ensure that the rule of law be maintained.[87] The key issue here is how to maintain

---

[86]Henry, Clement M., "Guest editor's introduction", *Thunderbird International Review of Business*, Special Issue on Islamic Finance, July 1999.

[87]Bakar, Mohd. Daud, "Pluralism of fatwas: Bridging the differences and disagreements", The International Islamic Financial Forum, International Institute of Research, Dubai, March 2002.

the rule of law in the face of multiple, but equally authoritative legal interpretations backed by differential levels of power? Some of these disagreements need no harmonisation because the divergences of opinion relate to the choice of contract rather than the issues of "Islamicity".[88]

5.5 The Problem of Applying Islamic Law in a Western Legal Environment

Again, according to Vogel, although parties may agree by contract to abide by Islamic precepts, they cannot alter the surrounding legal system which in the end enforces their agreements. In nearly all Muslim countries today, civil and commercial codes have been greatly influenced by European legal civil systems, most commonly French, followed by English common law. For example, Egyptian law and jurisprudence, which are inspired by French and other continental European legal systems, have been widely emulated in other Arab countries and the same goes for the legal institutions and laws of procedure in most other Muslim countries, including those in South-east Asia, which are also derived from Western models. Only in Saudi Arabia, Oman and a few other countries of the Arabian Peninsula do legal rules and institutions resemble those of the classical era, but even in these countries, Western legal influences have made strong impacts. In Saudi Arabia, for example, which is the world's most traditionally Islamic country, the general civil law is that of the classical Hanbali School and is applied by judges trained in Islamic law using largely Islamic procedures and rules of evidence. However, in areas of the law explicitly involving commercial matters, such as company law, banking and commercial

---

[88]Muslim World Book Review (Leicester), "Legal rationality vs. arbitrary judgement: Re-examining the tradition of Islamic law", (http://www.algonet.se/~pmanzoor/ISL-LAW-MWBR-2000.htm), Vol. 21 No. 1, October–December 2000, pp. 3–12.

paper laws, the laws applied strongly resemble French and Egyptian laws.

Bearing in mind that Islamic banking began with the purpose of benefiting all society, situations such as bankruptcy merely offers delay and immunity from collections, not release, and the creditor's grant of delay is not compensated. European legal systems do not give that much leeway to the debtor as they do not take into account the Quran nor accommodate the Shari'ah.[89] Thus we see the historical reasons for the challenges of integrating Islamic law into these various European legal systems.

5.6   Accounting and Corporate Regulatory Practices

A major problem challenging the growth of Islamic banking was the absence of recognised guidelines on prudential, supervisory, accounting, auditing and other corporate regulatory practices. This resulted in ineffective accounting standards and created considerable difficulties when it came to comparing financial statements issued by Islamic financial institutions and those of conventional financial institutions. Two organisations, namely the Accounting and Auditing Organisation for Islamic Financial Institutions (hereinafter referred to as AAOIFI) and the Islamic Financial Services Board (IFSB), are both involved in addressing these issues with the ultimate aim of harmonising corporate governance with the ethical requirements of Shari'ah law.

AAOIFI is an autonomous, international, non-profit-making corporate body which draws up Shari'ah-compliant accounting procedures, auditing methods, corporate governance frameworks and business ethics for Islamic financial institutions. It was established in accordance with an Agreement of Association, signed by major Islamic financial institutions in Algiers on 26 February 1990 and

---

[89]Vogel and Hayes, op. cit., p. 61.

registered in the State of Bahrain on 27 March 1991.[90] The principal aims of the AAOIFI are to standardise on-balance-sheet accounting; adopt uniform Shari'ah standards for the most popular Islamic finance contracts; lobby national regulators to adopt these standards; and mimic as closely as possible the approach of the Basle Committee on Banking Supervision,[91] whilst accounting for Islamic-contract peculiarities in capital adequacy, risk assessment and asset quality assessment.

There are three main areas of difference between Financial Accounting Standards (FAS) developed for Islamic banks and conventional accounting frameworks. They relate to the treatment of investment accounts, the concept of substance over form and the time value of money.[92]

(i) The Treatment of Investment Accounts
     FAS distinguishes between Unrestricted Investment Accounts (URIA) and Restricted Investment Accounts (RIA) on the basis of *mudarabah* contracts between the bank and investors (*mudarabah* contracts it will be recalled, are a form of partnership to which some of the partners contribute only capital

---

[90] www.aaoifi.com.

[91] Task Force on Accounting Issues was established by the Basle Committee on Banking Supervision in 1996, with the mission to foster effective and comprehensive supervision and safe and sound banking systems. The Task Force carries out this task by identifying accounting issues that are important from the point of view of banking supervisors, contributing to international accounting harmonisation efforts and developing supervisory guidance on sound accounting practices in banks. It consists of supervisory experts on accounting issues from the member institutions of the Basle Committee. The Task Force is chaired by Mr Nick LePan, Deputy Superintendent at the Office of the Superintendent of Financial Institutions, Canada, and a member of the Basle Committee.

[92] Jamall, Ashruff, "Role of western institutions with Islamic windows", The International Islamic Financial Forum, International Institute of Research, Dubai, March 2002.

and the other partners only labour). An unrestricted *mudarabah* agreement permits the Islamic bank to co-mingle its own assets with that of URIA unconditionally and without restrictions. FAS, therefore, requires these assets to be reflected on the balance sheet of an Islamic bank. RIAs, on the other hand, impose investment restrictions on the Islamic bank and, therefore, do not qualify for inclusion in the Islamic bank's balance sheet. Under conventional accounting frameworks, the assets of URIA would not qualify for recognition as assets of the bank because the economic benefits embodied in those assets flow to holders of URIA and not to the bank.

(ii) The Concept of Substance over Form

In conventional banking, accounting for items according to their substance and economic reality and not merely their legal form is one of the key determinants of reliable information. For most transactions there will be no difference, so no issue arises. In some cases however, the two diverge and choosing how to present these transactions can lead to very different results. Differences arise when an asset or liability is not recognised in the accounts, even though benefits or obligations may result from the transaction. The concept of substance over form is one of the fundamental qualitative characteristics of accounting information under conventional accounting frameworks, but this distinction is not recognised by FAS.

(iii) The Time Value of Money

In conventional banking, "net present value" (NPV) is a way of comparing the value of money now with the value of money in future. A dollar today is worth more than a dollar in future, because inflation erodes the buying power of the future money, while money available today can be invested and grown. "Constant dollars" refers to the NPV relative to a fixed date, whilst "current dollars" refers to the unadjusted value of the money. The term "discount rate" refers to a percentage used to calculate the NPV, and reflects the time value of money.

Conventional accounting frameworks recognise NPV as an acceptable basis of measurement — indeed, the Financial Accounting Standards Board (FASB) and International Accounting Standards (IAS) are increasingly moving towards a fair value basis of measurement and encourage the use of NPV as a unit of measurement when market values are not readily available. Unfortunately, this understanding of the relationship between time and money in conventional accounting runs into difficulties when it comes to Islamic banking for the simple reason that in terms of Shari'ah law, money is not a commodity and, therefore, does not have a time value. Consequently, NPV is not admissible as an acceptable basis of measurement under FAS, which recognises only the historical cost basis and the cash equivalent basis for impaired assets.

5.7 Depositors and Regulators

The complete absence of interest in Islamic financial institutions changes the role of depositors and regulators, and the way in which deposits are handled. A depositor places his money in the bank, whilst the regulator is an officially appointed party who is there to ensure proper control and supervision of the banking activities. The difference between conventional and Islamic banks as regards the role of depositors and regulators is that in conventional banks, private or public, regulators act as a proxy for debt-holders and take control away (perhaps through a regulator) from equity holders in bad times. To unsophisticated depositors, just because an Islamic bank seems to hold quasi-equity Profit-Sharing Investment Accounts (PSIAs) instead of debt (guaranteed deposits), they as depositors do not have the shareholders' voting and control privileges and thus, public regulators should act as their representatives.

The following two models of Islamic banking methods, as regards the role of depositors and regulators, are both considered to be fully consistent with Islamic rules and guidelines.

(i) The Two-tier *Mudarabah* Model (Scheme A)

In this scheme of things, the assets and liabilities sides of a bank's balance sheet are fully integrated. On the liabilities side, depositors enter into a *mudarabah* contract with the bank to share the overall profits accruing to the bank's business. Here, the depositors act as financiers by providing funds and the bank acts as an entrepreneur by accepting them. On the assets side, the bank, in turn, enters into *mudarabah* contracts with agent-entrepreneurs who search for investable funds and who agree to share profits with the bank according to a certain percentage stipulated in the contract. In addition to investment deposits, banks are allowed to accept demand deposits that yield no returns and may be subject to a service charge. These deposits are repayable on demand at par value. However, depositors are also aware that banks will be using demand deposits for financing risk-bearing projects. Under this arrangement, banks may grant short-term interest-free loans (*qard al-aasanah*) to the extent of a part of total current deposits. Finally, it should be noted that, although the concept of reserve requirements is recognised in Islamic banking, the two-tier *mudarabah* scheme does not mandate specific reserve requirements on either type of deposits.[93]

(ii) The Two Windows Model (Scheme B)

Under this arrangement, bank liabilities are divided into two windows: one for demand deposits, with 100 per cent reserves being held, and the other for investment accounts, with no reserve being held at the bank. In both cases, the major tool of operation is *mudarabah* or *musharakah*. The choice of the window is left to depositors. Demand deposits are assumed to be placed as *amanat* (safekeeping) and in this respect they are

---

[93]Traditionally, banks operating with the two-tier *Mudarabah* scheme have kept substantial reserves against demand deposits (even if they were not considered *Amanat* or safekeeping) and little (sometimes none) on investment deposits.

considered to belong to depositors at all times. Hence, they cannot be used by the bank as the basis to create money through fractional reserves. Consequently, banks operating according to this arrangement must apply a 100 per cent reserve requirement ratio on demand deposits. By contrast, investment deposits may be used to finance risk-bearing investments projects with depositors' full awareness. These deposits are not guaranteed by the bank and reserve requirements are not applied to them. The bank may charge a service fee for its safekeeping services. Interest-free loans may only be granted from funds specifically deposited for that purpose.

Islamic banks can use all of their deposits (demand and investment) for their financing and investment activities in scheme A, whilst only investment deposits can be utilised for such purposes in scheme B. This makes scheme A, where banks' assets and liabilities are fully integrated, far riskier than scheme B, where banks' liabilities are divided into two windows.[94]

5.8 Regulators' Concerns

Several concerns have been raised by regulators, relating to the accounting standards of Islamic banking and the possibility of a conflict of interest between bankers and their clients. They include the following areas of concern:

(i) Capital Adequacy Ratio
The existence of PSIA raises some fundamental issues in calculating the Capital Adequacy Ratio (CAR) for an Islamic bank. The basic problem has to do with the possibility of including PSIA as a component of capital because they have a risk-absorbing

---

[94]Errico, Luca and Farahbaksh, Mitra, "Islamic banking: Issues in prudential regulations and supervision", International Monetary Fund, Monetary and Exchange Affairs Department, March 1998, pp. 9–11.

capability. In this respect, AAOIFI's Discussion Memorandum on the Calculation of the Capital Adequacy Ratio for Islamic Banks (issued in January 1998) is relevant. This document sets out to try to design a capital adequacy framework for Islamic banks within the Basel's capital adequacy framework. Following this, AAOIFI issued a Statement on the Purpose and Calculation of the Capital Adequacy Ratio for Islamic Banks in March 1999. According to this statement, Islamic banks' own capital is exposed to normal commercial risk, fiduciary risk and displaced commercial risk,[95] the implication here being that these types of risk should underlie the design of the capital regulations. The AAOIFI statement proposed three things. First, that there should be no inclusion of the risk-bearing capital PSIA.[96] Second, that all assets financed by debt-based liabilities and own-equity should be included in the denominator of the CAR. Third, that 50 per cent of PSIA-financed assets should be included in the denominator of the CAR. The last measure is needed to cover possible losses arising from misconduct or negligence in investment activities.[97]

---

[95]Displaced commercial risk expresses the possibility that depositors will withdraw their funds if the return paid to them is lower than that paid by the other banks. As a result, some Islamic banks give minimum guaranteed returns to depositors, although it is prohibited by the Shari'ah principles (AAOIFI, 1999).

[96]$PSIA^R$ — restricted profit-sharing investment deposits; $PSIA^U$ — unrestricted profit-sharing investment deposits. The $PSIA^R$ depositors have the right to determine the investment types chosen; the banks merely provide them with information about feasible investments. Therefore, in $PSIA^R$ the depositors take responsibility for investment risk. In fact, the statement does not distinguish between $PSIA^R$ and $PSIA^U$; arguably, the former should be included in the capital base.

[97]If the bank's management acts in breach of the investment contract, or is guilty of misconduct or negligence in the management of the investors' funds, then the bank may be legally liable in respect of losses sustained on those funds (AAOIFI, 1999).

Taking a closer look at these proposals, one should note that first of all, the existing CAR developed by AAOIFI is only designed to assure a given level of solvency and ignores the agency roles performed by Islamic banks and the principal/agent relationships involved. Second, there has been an inconsistency in defining the restricted-investment deposits. According to the IAS developed by AAOIFI in 1997, the restricted profit-sharing investment deposits (PSIA^R deposits), cannot be recognised as liabilities of Islamic banks and should not be reflected on the banks' statement of financial position. This is because the depositors are highly involved in investment decisions. Thus, it can be argued that PSIA^R-financed assets should be excluded from the risk-weighted assets in the denominator of the CAR. Yet in the CAR, no distinction is drawn between PSIA^R and PSIA^U. A third point raised by the AAOIFI proposals, is the possibility of a bank facing "an abnormal risk" arising from a managerial dispute (i.e. where the PSIA^U depositors consider that a bank has neglected or breached the contract agreed upon). This should be seen as legal risk and should ideally involve a case by case approach (i.e. depending on the terms used in the contract), in which case, the banks should be able to identify the difference between deposits taken on a pure PLS basis and those representing a hybrid contract. Deposits with any potential claim (partly) should be classified as hybrid-based deposits.[98]

Without distinctions between PSIA^R and PSIA^U, the CAR is not a clear representation of the bank, coupled by the exclusion of the liabilities portion in the form of PSIA^R deposits from the bank's balance sheet, the AAOIFI proposals have not adequately provided for the difference in the role of Islamic banks from the conventional banks from the customer's point of view.

---

[98]Muljawan, Dadang, Dar, Humayon A., and Hall, Maximilian J.B., "A capital adequacy framework for Islamic banks: The need to reconcile depositors' risk aversion with managers' risk taking", *Economics Research Paper*, No. 02–13, (http://magpie.lboro.ac.uk/dspace/bitstream/2134/369/1/02–13.pdf), 2002.

Even the AAOIFI/Basle accounting standards (cost-of-acquiring accounting) pushes managers in the direction of gains trading in that risk-cushioned shareholders of the bank encourage excessive risk-taking in bad times and insufficient risk-taking in good times. What this means for PSIA-holders is that while their risks will be amplified during bad periods, equally, too little risk-taking during good times will be reflected in lower returns on their investment. When private rating and auditing agencies raise a flag of warning, they exacerbate the crisis of confidence and increase risk-taking, creating a double moral-hazard problem for Muslim investors. And because AAOIFI standards focus on "bank's own capital" risk measures, this gives managers and shareholders the incentive to shift even more risks onto the PSIA-holders, especially when responding to major downturns in global financial markets.

This is against the spirit of Islamic banking which is not to disadvantage one party for the unfair benefit of another.[99]

It is generally agreed that Islamic banking should go beyond mimicking the Basle solvency-orientated formulas (which were designed to protect debt-holders). The true goals of regulation are to safeguard the interests of small un-represented investors and to protect the financial system against meltdowns. Therefore, a coherent Islamic bank regulatory framework is required to protect PSIA-holders from managers adopting inappropriate strategies (too much or too little risk-taking) in order to cater to interests of the bank's shareholders. One possible framework would include efficiency and risk monitoring of Islamic bank management, and/or alternative Islamic-banking claims structure to reduce the gap between PSIA-holders' rights and that of the debt-holders.[100]

[99]See El-Gamal, Mahmood, "Western regulatory concerns about Islamic banks", International Islamic Financial Forum, International Institute of Research, Dubai, March 2002.
[100]Ibid.

5.9 Legal Challenges

Several legal challenges exist in Islamic finance. They relate to the management of investment risks, consumer protection laws, the lack of legal precedents, situations involving uncertainty, integrating Shari'ah rulings within a conventional banking framework, accommodating Shari'ah references in conventional legal documents and property law issues. In order to provide proper legal foundations for the supervision of Islamic banks, it is necessary that the nature of these banks and their specific operating relationship in relation to a particular country's central bank and other conventional banks, if applicable, be defined in detail by that country's banking laws. Such a legal framework should contain provisions relating to licensing and permissible modes of financing, and state, clearly, legislative powers to address compliance with laws and regulations. In particular, such provisions should determine which enterprises may call themselves Islamic banks, collect deposits and carry out banking practices on the basis of Islamic principles. Moreover, it should be clearly established that the central bank (or a separate supervisory authority) has the authority and all necessary powers to supervise Islamic banks as well as conventional banks, if applicable.[101]

5.10 Developing an Efficient Regulatory Framework

Prudential supervision is just as necessary in Islamic banking as in conventional banking in order to reduce risks to the soundness of the banking system and to enhance the role of banks as active players

---

[101]The above approach has been adopted by the authorities of countries where all banks and financial institutions operate according to Islamic principles (i.e. Iran, Pakistan and Sudan), as well as a number of countries where Islamic banks operate alongside conventional banks (e.g. Jordan, Malaysia, Egypt and United Arab Emirates).

in the development of the economy.[102] This is so for a number of reasons.

First, it is worth keeping in mind that even in a paradigm version of Islamic banking, insolvency risks cannot be ruled out altogether, most notably in cases where banking operations are carried out according to a two-tier *mudarabah* arrangement, that is, when the assets and liabilities sides of a bank's balance sheet are fully integrated.

Second, risks of economic losses, or losses incurred as a result of poor investment decisions, are just as likely whether banks operate the two-tier *mudarabah* system of investment or the two windows framework. Poor investment decisions may derive from a mix of factors, including a volatile operating environment, weak internal governance (notably mismanagement) and limited market discipline. Economic losses here would not only be reflected in the depreciation of the value of depositors' wealth, but also in a decline in banks' profitability. If not corrected, these factors, in due course, could jeopardise a banks' soundness, which in turn, would progressively reduce banks' intermediation role in the market and discourage the mobilisation of private savings towards investment.

Third, weak banks may detract from the achievement of fundamental macroeconomic objectives, such as the efficiency of the payment system or the effectiveness of monetary policy, particularly if the latter is implemented through the use of indirect instruments. Unsound banks may also reduce public confidence in the financial

---

[102]In some Islamic countries a significant portion of the banking sector is state-owned (in the case of Iran, all banks). Prudential supervision of state-owned banks, however, is equally as essential because any deterioration of their financial position would ultimately affect the State budget. Such deterioration could develop progressively, remaining unnoticed for a long period, because there would be no concern about banks' solvency. When finally discovered, such deterioration would materialise in the form of a need for recapitalisation, at the State's budget expenses.

system, thus impeding or delaying necessary structural reforms in this area.

Fourth, a weak banking system is likely to prevent the economy from benefiting from the ongoing process of globalisation and the liberalisation of capital markets, particularly in developing and emerging market countries (which are often the ones where Islamic banking principles are followed) where banks are the major (or even the sole) players in domestic financial markets.

As in the case of conventional banking, an appropriate regulatory framework for an Islamic financial system should aim, therefore, at reinforcing the operating environment of banks, as well as their internal governance, and market discipline. To help develop such a regulatory framework, standards and best practices established by the Basle Committee on Banking Supervision are useful and provide a valuable reference.[103] However, these standards cannot always be applied to Islamic banking in the same way that they are in conventional banking systems.

5.11 Special Requirements of Islamic Banking

According to Errico and Farahbaksh, Islamic banking entails special issues that need to be recognised and addressed to help make the conduct of banking supervision more effective. First, it is most important to recognise the impact of PLS modes of financing on Islamic banks and, in particular, the fact that when Islamic banks provide funds through their PLS facilities, there is no recognisable default on the part of the agent-entrepreneur until PLS contracts expire, barring proved negligence or mismanagement on the part of the agent-entrepreneur. In fact, a "default" of PLS contracts means that the investment project failed to deliver what was

---

[103]Basle Committee on Banking Supervision, "Core principles for effective banking supervision", Bank for International Settlements, (http://www.bis.org/publ/bcbs30a.pdf), September 1997.

expected — that is to say, it came in with a lower profit margin or no profit at all, or even a loss. In such instances, the lower profit or loss is shared between parties according to the stipulated PLS ratios.

For example, in the case of a *mudarabah* contract, the bank is entitled to receive from the entrepreneur the principal of a loan at the end of the period stipulated in the contract, if and only if, profits have been accrued. If, on the contrary, the enterprise's books showed a loss, the bank would not be able to recover its loan.[104] Such a situation would not normally constitute default on the part of the entrepreneur, whose liability is limited to his time and efforts. Moreover, banks have no legal means to control the agent-entrepreneur who manages the business. This individual has complete freedom to run the enterprise according to his best judgement. Banks are contractually entitled only to share with the entrepreneur the profits (or losses) stemming from the enterprise according to the contractually agreed PLS ratio.[105] In *musharakah* and direct investment contracts, banks have better opportunities to monitor the business they invest in. Indeed, in these arrangements, all partners may concur to the management of the enterprise and banks hold direct voting rights.[106]

---

[104]Of course, in the typical case of a restricted *Mudarabah*, the bank seeks to stipulate in the *Madarabah* contract certain conditions that it considers essential for a successful outcome. However, this is done ex-ante and the contract's terms and conditions cannot be altered during the life of the contract except with the mutual consent of the parties.

[105]By contrast, Khan and Mirakhor, 1993, contend that banks have direct and indirect control over the agent-entrepreneur through both explicit and implicit contracts. This is so because banks could refuse further credit or blacklist the agent-entrepreneur and (an important consideration in the Islamic ethos) because the agent-entrepreneur puts at stake his credibility and respectability; therefore, a strong deterrent to irresponsible behaviour would be put in place. However, it still remains a matter of fact that the bank has no legal means to intervene in the management of the current enterprise whilst it is being run by the agent-entrepreneur.

[106]Errico, Luca and Farahbaksh, op. cit., p. 13.

5.12 Assessment and Management of Investment Risks

As the above situation indicates, investment risk is the most critical operational risk affecting banks operating according to a paradigm version of Islamic banking because it is inherent in their core activities, namely those involving PLS modes of financing. Errico and Farahbaksh state that the assessment and management of investment risk is more difficult in an Islamic environment than in conventional banking because of the following four factors:

(i) In *mudarabah* contracts, the bank cannot exert control over the management of the investment project.
(ii) PLS modes of financing cannot systematically be made dependent on collateral or other guarantees.
(iii) The administration of the PLS modes of financing is more complicated compared with conventional financing and may involve several complex activities that are not normally performed by conventional banks. These activities include the determination of PLS ratios on investment projects in various sectors of the economy and the ongoing auditing of financed projects to ensure that Islamic banks' share of profits are fairly calculated.
(iv) The existing legal framework supporting bank-lending operations, which is relatively weak.

In order to safeguard invested funds and realise profits, Islamic banks are more dependent than conventional banks on the existence of an adequate and appropriate set of policies and infrastructure for portfolio diversification, monitoring and control. They also need a sufficient supply of trained banking staff skilled in investment and Islamic banking practices to implement these policies. Unfortunately, as the experiences of other developing and transition economics indicate, appropriate policies and infrastructure for risk-management and human technical expertise are difficult to establish and require a considerable amount of time to develop.[107] The regulatory framework for banking supervision should therefore be designed to specifically address these issues.

Information disclosure is also more important in an Islamic environment than it is in a conventional banking system. This is the case because the absence of protection for investment depositors is at the core of Islamic banking.[108] Indeed, the more depositors are left unprotected, the more public disclosure of information relating to the policy objectives and operational strategies of banks is necessary, in order to enable creditors and depositors to monitor their performance. Indeed, depositors have more incentives to monitor a bank's performance in the case of Islamic banking than in the case of conventional depositors. This is due to the fact that neither the capital value of investment deposits, nor their returns, are fixed and guaranteed, but, as noted previously, depend on a bank's performance in investment depositors' funds. Hence, depositors need to be able to monitor Islamic banks not only to protect the capital value of their funds, but also to seek to ensure that the rates of return paid to them reflect a fair application of the PLS principle on a bank's net profit.

By reducing information asymmetries, a clear and concise disclosure of key data and information allows depositors more flexibility in choosing a specific bank to which they can allocate their funds according to their risk preferences. This is the case in the paradigm

---

[107]Khan, Mohsin and Mirakhor, Abbas, "Islamic banking: Experiences in the Islamic Republic of Iran and Pakistan", 1989, argue that the shortage of expertise in PLS financing in commercial banking is one of the most important reasons explaining the slow growth of PLS modes of financing in Iran.

[108]It should be noted, however, that, in principle, a deposit insurance arrangement, whereby a third party (excluding the central bank, the government and the interested deposit bank) agrees, against the payment of a price, to ensure investment depositors is possible in an Islamic banking framework.

version of Islamic banking (where the relationship between banks and depositors is regulated according to an unrestricted *mudarabah* contract) because depositors would be able to choose among different banks disclosing different investment objectives and policies. It is even more the case if banking practices diverge from the paradigm version as, for instance, in the Islamic Republic of Iran, where banks are allowed to accept depositors' funds for investment in specific types of projects (in this case, a restricted *mudarabah* is also possible on the liabilities side). Additionally, appropriate information disclosure can provide the supervisory authorities with a better understanding of banks' strategies and their relevant risks. This places the supervisors in a better position to exercise effective prudential supervision, hence reducing systemic risks.

5.13 Proposals for a Regulatory Framework for Islamic Banking

Based on the above considerations, an appropriate regulatory framework for banking supervision in an Islamic environment should be designed to ensure that:

(i) Legal foundations for the supervision of Islamic banks are in place.

(ii) Investment and other risks are adequately dealt with, taking into account that financing through the PLS modes adds an element of complexity to the already difficult task of investment banking.

(iii) Adequate information is disclosed to allow supervisory authorities to exercise a more effective prudential supervision and to enable the public to make reasonably informed investment decisions.

Placing greater stress on these key issues, particularly during the licensing process, is likely to strengthen financial system surveillance in countries where Islamic banking is practised and this can only be a good thing for Islamic banking and finance generally.[109]

5.14   Conclusion

According to Dr Shahul Hameed M Ibrahim, accounting is coming full circle. Since the 1930s, accounting in the West has been narrowly focused within the economic domain, where it has been almost entirely identified with the growth of large corporations and the dominance of utilitarian economics. However, given the evident adverse effects of such a narrow world-view on both society and the environment generally, in terms of the depletion of natural resources, environmental pollutions and so forth, there have been increasing calls for a more holistic and sophisticated system of accounting, which will allow capitalism to coexist with conscience. Islamic accounting, in addition to meeting its own religious and cultural prescriptions, can be seen to be an answer to this call for a more holistic and accountable response on the part of global financial institutions in relation to the betterment of mankind and maintaining the world's natural resources and environmental balance for future generations.

Thus one can see accounting as increasingly broadening its scope, both in terms of the matters accounted for (which include not only economic activities, but also the physical and social environment in which they are enacted) and the units of measurement that are employed (which means breaking away from the existing framework which reduces everything to a monetary value). Unfortunately, globalisation and the Westernisation of the Islamic world may, in the short term, pull Muslim countries towards a more Western-style system of accounting in order to harmonise with global international accounting standards. But today, one lives in a neo-pluralist[110] world

---

[109]Errico, Luca and Farahbaksh, op. cit., pp. 11–15.

[110]Pluralist: a philosopher who believes that no single explanation can account for all the phenomena of nature.

where different power groups compete with one another to pull accounting into their grasp in order to use accounting to serve their own interests. At present, Dr Shahul Hameed M Ibrahim believes that it is the turn of multinational corporations, institutional investors and positivist academics to host the party, which is not to say that at other times other groups or stakeholders may gain power, for example, the trade unions, consumer groups, greenies and the like. They in their turn will seek to manipulate accounting for their own interests, until they too fade away. If, however, good sense prevails and Muslim societies do not forgo their Islamic legacy, Islamic banking does stand more than half a chance at competing professionally alongside conventional, capitalist-driven financial systems.[111]

At present, Islamic financial markets are highly segmented and differ considerably between nations. This has arisen out of divergent interpretations of the Shari'ah, differing legal systems and recourse to different financial instruments. However, globalisation is likely to bring about standardisation of financial products. Moreover, adherence to international regulations from designated Islamic institutions such as AAOIFI and IFSB, and, where relevant, secularist institutions such as the International Monetary Fund (IMF) and Bank of International Settlements (BIS), would place Islamic finance on par with conventional finance in the pursuit of best practices.

Islamic financial instruments add considerable variety and choice not only for Muslims but also for non-Muslims, giving Islamic finance a truly pluralist flavour. Religious orientations aside, all those who do care about the ethical content of their financial transactions are likely to be inclined towards Islamic finance in that there is much more to Islamic finance than the mere elimination of *riba* or interest. Islam prohibits transactions of a fraudulent nature, for it to be

---

[111]Bin Hj. Mohamed Ibrahim, Shahul Hameed, "From conventional accounting to Islamic accounting: A review of the development western accounting theory and its implications for the differences in the development of Islamic accounting", (http://vlib.unitarklj1.edu.my/htm/account1.htm) June 1997.

truly Islamic, financial instruments must be free from all forms of deceit, exploitation and ambiguity. Such universal values mean a lot to many people regardless of their religious backgrounds and the number of non-Muslims using Islamic financing is on the rise. Thus, for example, about one-fifth of the HSBC Amanah financing in Malaysia caters to non-Muslims.[112]

Globalisation is also likely to narrow differences in the yields of Islamic financial instruments between countries, due to a freer flow of funds. Competitive pressures and client expectations may push the rates of return on Islamic financial instruments closer to that of secular markets, notwithstanding the fact that the higher risks normally associated with Islamic finance would warrant higher returns.[113] And as Islamic banking plays an increasingly important role in mobilising deposits and providing financing, the development of an Islamic capital market allows the corporate sector to source their longterm financing needs based on Islamic principles. This, in turn, would increase the range of Islamic financial instruments available to meet the demands of the Islamic investors.

As Dr Zeti Akhtar Aziz, Governor of the Central Bank of Malaysia believes, at present, the absence of a truly global Islamic financial system based on Shari'ah principles, means that the continued growth and development of Islamic banking and finance is somewhat haphazard. In this last respect, governments could assume a more active role in promoting the development of Islamic financial systems. In particular, they need to provide the necessary infrastructure that will favour the growth of Islamic banking in their respective countries and this means putting in place, from the outset, a comprehensive, Shari'ah-compliant, legal and regulatory framework. Compliance with Shari'ah principles is not, however, in itself sufficient to guarantee the future success of Islamic banking and finance. In the

---

[112]Ibid.

[113]Ariff, Mohamed, "Islamic finance can benefit from globalisation", *The Malayan Institute of Economic Research* (www.mier.org.my), 29 August 2002.

long run, the sustainability of Islamic banking rests on satisfying the demand for quality in the products and services that Islamic finance can offer. This is the ultimate challenge for Islamic banking and finance, namely to be able to provide a comprehensive range of Islamic financial products and services that are not only Shari'ah compliant, but also innovative and competitive with conventional financial instruments.[114]

[114]Aziz, Zeti Akhtar, "Building a comprehensive Islamic financial system — New financial opportunities", Keynote address at the Institute of Islamic Banking and Insurance's International Conference on Islamic Insurance, London, 26 September 2003.

Chapter 6

Islam in South-east Asia

The great period of Islam in South-east Asia belongs to the distant
rather than the recent past and came about through commerce rather
than military conquest. Long before the advent of Islam, Arab merchants were trading with India for Eastern commodities — Arab
sailors were the first to exploit the seasonal monsoon winds of
the Indian Ocean — and it was commerce that first brought Arab
traders and Islam to South-east Asia. The financial incentive for
direct exchanges with the East was immense. The long journey to
the marketplace of most Oriental commodities was often hazardous
and there was a considerable mark-up in prices each time goods
exchanged hands. The closer to the source one got, the greater the
rewards.

6.1   The Coming of Islam to South-east Asia

In as far as South-east Asia is concerned, Arab ships were sailing
in Malay and Indonesian waters from the sixth century onwards.
Commerce with China was one reason for their presence there, but
perhaps even more of an incentive was the lucrative trade in spices —
mainly pepper, cloves and nutmeg — which were obtained from
Java, Sumatra and the Moluccas (Maluku) and Banda islands at
the eastern end of the archipelago. No doubt the first Arab traders
in the region were no more than seasonal visitors, swashbuckling
merchant adventurers who filled their holds with spices and other
exotic produce before sailing back with the north-east monsoon to

India and the Arabian Peninsula. In time, though, Muslim merchants began to establish permanent trading posts at various points along the maritime trade route between India and China, as well as at other strategic locations within the Malay and Indonesian Archipelago. By the fifteenth century, many of these trading posts, which initially were little more than a village at the mouth of a river, had grown into flourishing entrepôts, whose fortunes were built upon regional commerce (mainly in spices) and transhipment between East and West. City-states like Aceh in north Sumatra, Malacca on the Malay Peninsula, and Banten, Cirebon and Demak in Java, became mini-superpowers, in their own right fighting for control of the sea-lanes and waging war on their rivals. They were also cosmopolitan centres of learning and the arts, attracting writers, poets, scholars and artisans from as far away as China, Persia and the Arabian Peninsula. But diverse though they were in terms of the mingling of races and religions, by the middle of the sixteenth century the ruling elite of these entrepôt states was invariably a Muslim one and it was a Sultan who sat upon the throne (the ruler of Aceh was one of the first to convert to Islam in the thirteenth century).

In eastern Indonesia, Islamisation proceeded through the sixteenth and seventeenth centuries. According to the sixteenth-century Portuguese chronicler Tomé Pires, the island states of Ternate and Tidore, off the west coast of Halmahera in Maluku, had Muslim sultans, and Muslim merchants had settled in the Banda Islands. In 1605 the ruler of Gowa in southern Sulawesi (Celebes) converted to Islam and subsequently imposed Islam on neighbouring rulers. Muslim missionaries were sent from the north coast of Java to Lombok, Sulawesi and Kalimantan until the late seventeenth century.[115]

This commonality of culture and religion was itself an active ingredient in promoting trade and commerce, in the same way that

---

[115]The Library of Congress, Federal Research Division (USA), "Indonesia: The coming of Islam", (http://www.loc.gov/rr/frd/).

the spread of American popular culture — Hollywood, soft rock, Coca-Cola and Macdonald's — has helped American businesses to penetrate foreign markets today. As Jamil Jaroudi, head of Shamil Bank's investment banking, observes: "The Islamic economy once covered half the world," adding, "how do you think Islam reached Indonesia and Malaysia? It was through traders, not *jihad.*"[116]

6.2   European Rivalries and Colonisation

This era of Islamic greatness in South-east Asia lasted only a couple of hundred years and by the beginning of the seventeenth century these maritime sultanates found themselves in serious conflict with Christian rivals competing for control of the lucrative spice trade in nutmeg, cloves and pepper. The Portuguese were the first to arrive on the scene in the early sixteenth century, followed by the Spanish, English and Dutch; by the end of the seventeenth century the great days of the Sultanates was over and the Muslim initiative in South-east Asia was arrested.

The European colonisation of sizeable chunks of South-east Asia in the eighteenth and nineteenth centuries and the concomitant subjugation of regional Muslim politics to European rule was reflected in the eclipse of Islam as a military and political force worldwide, and the relegation of Islam to the status of just another religious belief system, alongside others. Seen from a South-east Asian perspective, the international order that had previously strengthened the position of local rulers in the region had floundered, while Islam itself had to face fierce competition from Christianity.

Western colonialism brought in new ideas, new institutions and a new world order. Secular ideals were embraced and new political frontiers were created which disregarded historical realities. Western concepts of government, justice and commerce were introduced and modern bureaucracies set up. Huge plantations were established in

---

[116]Useem, op. cit.

Java, Sumatra and the Malay Peninsula — coffee, sugar, tobacco and later rubber, were the principal crops — and immigrants were brought to the region from India and China to supply the labour. Steam navigation and the Suez Canal brought Europe that much closer, while the invention of telegraphy put South-east Asia in touch with the rest of the world. The sultans may still have sat in their palaces, but politically and economically they were on the sideline.

As a consequence, Muslims in South-east Asia retreated into their culture and their religion, this time in a very narrow sense. Religious education was emphasised, change was resisted and by and large they became immobilised. And while South-east Asian Muslims still continued to look towards the Middle East for inspiration and leadership, the Middle East at this time was also under serious threat from the West, a process that culminated, as we have seen, in the collapse and dismantling of the Ottoman Empire at the end of the First World War.

But just as the rubble of one empire provides the building blocks for a new beginning, so too with Islam at the turn of the last century. New ideas on how Islam should grapple with modern conditions began to evolve, giving birth to Islamic revivalism, which viewed the conventional and rigid approach to Islam as inapplicable.

From the sixteenth century onwards, Islam was in retreat, and falling under the domination of a Europe which was expanding at both ends. The process began with the reconquest of Russia and Spain. Western Europeans circumnavigated the African continent and began to establish a growing hegemony in South-east, southern and ultimately South-west Asia. Islam was, so to speak, caught in a pincers movement between Russia from the north and the Western European peoples from the south. These changes were for a while disguised or delayed by the imposing military might of the Ottoman, Persian and Mughul empires; but in time these also weakened and ceased to be able to resist the European advance.

Western domination continued until the aftermath of World War II, when the colonial empires of Britain, France, Holland

and Italy were dismantled and their former territories became independent.[117]

6.3   The Road to Independence

The war in the Pacific heralded the beginning of the end of the colonial era in South-east Asia, if only because it revealed that the Caucasian man was not as overwhelmingly superior in every respect as everyone had hitherto been led to believe. Churchill described the fall of Singapore as "the worst disaster . . . in British military history," but perhaps more significant in the long run was the huge loss of prestige on the part of the colonial rulers of Malaya and the Straits Settlements. The Dutch capitulation in the Netherlands East Indies and America's loss of the Philippines similarly dealt colonialism a fatal blow in those countries.

As it happened, the Japanese, who came as self-styled liberators, turned out to be far harsher masters than the colonial regimes they replaced, effectively turning their newly acquired territories into police states ruled by fear and suspicion. No one was sorry to see them go, but the victorious Allies, though welcomed in most of their former colonial territories — Java was a significant exception — returned to a very different world to the one they had fled back in 1942. They might have defeated Japan, but they could not escape the fact that the writing was on the wall as far as imperial possessions in South-east Asia were concerned.

The Philippines was the first to gain independence — General MacArthur did return, as he had promised, but it was only for a very short while and after not quite half a century of American rule the Philippines became an independent nation in July 1946. In the case of the Netherlands East Indies, despite a unilateral declaration of independence following the surrender of Japan on the part of

---

[117]Lewis, Bernard (ed), "The world of Islam", (http://www.islamia.com/History/history_of_islam.htm), as of 8 June 2004.

Indonesian nationalists, the Dutch hung on until 1950 before they too relinquished their claim to their former territories in South-east Asia. The British handover of Malaya was an altogether more orderly and seemly affair, though the colonial administration had to fight a bitter war against communist insurgents in the years leading up to full independence in 1957. Singapore gained her own independence six years later when she joined the newly constituted Malaysia but subsequently separated from Malaysia in 1965, to become a fully fledged nation in her own right. British North Borneo and Sarawak, which previously had been administered by the British, joined Malaysia in 1963, while Brunei, which had been a British protectorate since 1888, gained full independence in 1984.

6.4 Post-Independence: A New World Order

Post-independence, the phenomena of new nation-states, demanding new forms of loyalty and heavily influenced by Western political culture, has posed grave difficulties for Muslims in South-east Asia. To a large extent, they represented the old social order, which had managed to survive in spite of colonialism — indeed in the case of the Malay sultans, the colonial experience had arguably strengthened their position in terms of consolidating their territorial control and power base — but the realities before them had changed so much, particularly at the national, regional and global levels, that they found themselves marginalised. Compared to other religious communities in the region, Muslims probably had far greater difficulty in readjusting to the demands brought about by the emergence of the nation-state. New political institutions integral to the formation of the nation-state, such as a secular constitution, an independent judiciary, citizenship, political parties, elections and so on, were unfamiliar to them and the transition to modern nationhood, based to varying degrees on the idea of a Western-style liberal democracy, has been a difficult one.

Islam is the official religion in Brunei and Malaysia. Indonesia recognises five (Muslim, Protestant, Roman Catholic, Hindu and

Buddhist) official religions but with Islam dominating 88 per cent of its population. Islam is deeply rooted in the southern islands of Philippines though only an estimated 5 per cent of the population are Muslims. An estimated 14 per cent of the Singapore population is Muslim.

Brunei's legal system is based on English Common Law, with provision of Islamic law only on the Muslims. The legal system in Malaysia is based on English common law, with both Islamic law (Shari'ah) and customary law (*adat*) constituting significant sources of law, particularly in matters of personal status. The Indonesian legal system is extraordinarily complex, the independent state having inherited three sources of law: *adat* law, traditionally the basis for resolving interpersonal disputes in the traditional village environment; Islamic law which often applies to disputes between Muslims; and Dutch colonial law.[118] The Philippines legal system is heavily derived from the Spanish (e.g. family and property) and the United States (e.g. taxation, trade, government). Singapore's legal system is based on English Common Law, with the Muslim Law Act in 1966 establishing the Majlis Ugama Islam Singapore (Singapore Islamic Council) to advise the President on matters relating to the Islamic religion. As such, Islamic law is most prominent in the legal systems of Indonesia and Malaysia with the incorporation of Shari'ah law, whilst in Singapore and Brunei, the legislatives allow less involvement of the Islamic law and in Philippines it is virtually not included in its legal structure.

6.5   The Philippines

One response has been the emergence of so-called separatist movements initiated by Muslims who tried to isolate themselves from what were perceived as undesirable Western and Christian

---

[118]The Library of Congress, Federal Research Division (USA), "Indonesia: The judiciary" (http://www.loc.gov/rr/frd/).

influences. In the Philippines, for example, Islam has always been closely linked to an ideology of resistance against first, the Spanish-directed expansion of Christianity during the colonial era, and subsequently, after independence, the authority of the Christian-dominated Republic of the Philippines. After the Second World War, despite the Philippines' being granted almost-instant independence from the United States, the Muslim Moro people in the south still felt persecuted by the Christian majority in the north and resented the fact that southern Philippines was economically and politically inferior to the north. Beginning as early as the 1950s, they have managed to enlist the support of Muslims from all over the world, including Saudi Arabia, who have collectively objected to the perceived mistreatment, even persecution, of their coreligionists in the southern Philippines. Islamic governments have donated money they were earning from the petroleum trade to Muslim Filipinos and supported the study of Muslim Filipino students in Saudi Arabia. They have invited Muslim leaders to Middle-Eastern conferences to discuss their problems, and they have sent, and continue to send, Islamic missionaries to teach the Islamic religion in the southern Philippines.[119]

Today, Islam is strong in Mindanao and the other smaller islands of the southern part of the Philippines. The Bangsa Moro struggle for statehood in the southern islands of the Philippines dates back more than 300 years to the sixteenth century when Muslims first resisted Spanish colonisation and then American imperialism for almost half a century. In the contemporary period, resistance to the Philippine government persisted right through the 1950s till today. The most militant of the Islamic groups, Abu Sayyaf, has been linked to the Al-Qaeda and its more recent activities have occasioned American military intervention.[120]

---

[119]Vloeberghs, Isabelle, "Islam in the Southern Philippines", Northern Illinois University.

[120]Saravanamuttu, Johan, *Political and Civil Islam in South-east Asia*, as guest editor for *Global Change, Peace and Security*, Special Issue, Vol. 16, No. 2, June 2004.

6.6   Indonesia

The Islamic experience in colonial and modern Indonesia is a mass of internal contradictions. Although Sumatra was the area of initial acceptance in the thirteenth century, Islam has never succeeded in displacing indigenous customary law, or *adat*, and the two systems of jurisprudence coexist, side by side, if not in actual conflict, then as two competing perspectives for any given situation. In Java, on the other hand, Islam has been absorbed into a wider Javanese cultural setting and has thus acquired its own, peculiarly Javanese flavour. In both areas, Islam was important in the development of modern Indonesian resistance to colonial rule[121] and Muslim political parties continue to play an important part in contemporary Indonesian politics. Moreover, the religion is entrenched in institutions of State to a considerable extent; there is a (national) Department of Religion and a system of Shari'ah Courts as well as Islamic universities and institutions of higher learning.

We see that Muslims in Indonesia in the 1950s were very fragmented. Islam was represented by two big groups. The first one was the modernists, represented by the Muhammadiyah and also by the Masumi Party in the 1950s. The second group was the traditionalists, represented by the Nahdlatul Ulama. These two wings of Indonesian Islam rarely come to agreement amongst themselves, not only on religious matters but also in political matters.[122]

Indonesia is the world's most populous Muslim nation with 80 per cent of its 210 million population identified as Muslims, justifying the attention paid by the rest of the Muslim community on the Presidential elections in 2004.

---

[121]See Noer, Deliar, *The Modernist Muslim Movement in Indonesia 1900–1942*, 1973.

[122]ABC Australia, "Indonesia: Balancing the Secular State with Islam, post-September 11", http://www.abc.net.au/ra/asiapac/programs/s674845.htm, 13 September 2002.

6.7 Malaysia

In Malaysia, the transition to independence and the attainment of nationhood has been achieved relatively smoothly, though not without a certain amount of trouble along the way.

In 1826, the British settlements of Malacca, Penang and Singapore were combined to form the Colony of the Straits Settlements. From these territories, in the nineteenth and early twentieth centuries the British established protectorates over the Malay sultanates on the peninsula. Four of these states (Pahang, Perak, Selangor and Negri Sembilan) were consolidated in 1895 as the Federated Malay States.

During British control, a well-ordered system of public administration was established, public services were extended, and large-scale rubber and tin production was developed. This control was interrupted by the Japanese invasion and occupation from 1942 to 1945 during World War II.

After World War II, Britain tried to exert its previous authority and in October 1945, drew up a proposal to unite all the Federated and Unfederated Malay States, together with Penang and Melaka, under a centralised government known as the Malayan Union. Singapore, however, was excluded and considered to be a separate case on the grounds of its economy, racial structure and strategic importance, and was to remain a British colony.

However, the publication of the Malayan Union proposal incensed the Malays, especially as it eroded the power and status of the Sultans and the loss of rights for the Malays as a whole. They threw their support behind the United Malays National Organisation (UMNO) founded by Dato Onn bin Jaafar of Johor in March 1946. UMNO vehemently resisted the introduction of the Malayan Union, and Dato Onn toured the country leading demonstrations of national mourning. The issue aroused widespread political consciousness among the Malays. The stiff opposition in Malaya and informed criticism at home prompted the British Government to recall the idea altogether. In its place, a provisional kind of caretaker government was installed whilst the British set up a Working Committee comprising Malays, and later a Consultative Committee on which the other Malayan races were represented to submit reports.

Based on the reports from the two committees, the British Government formulated the Federation of Malaya Agreement, the terms of which were put into practice in February 1948. Its territories were identical with those of the abandoned Malayan Union. The chief official of the Federation was a British High Commissioner, whose appointment had to be endorsed by the Malay sultans. There were two councils: an Executive Council and a Legislative Council, whilst the sultans were members of the Conference of Rulers. The issue of citizenship of the Federation became much more restricted than under the Malayan Union.

Under the twin pressures of a communist rebellion and the development of a strong Malay nationalist movement, the British introduced elections, starting at the local level in 1951. Political cooperation amongst the three main ethnic groups in the country, that is the Malays, Chinese and Indians, was forged by the formation of the Alliance, which comprised UMNO, the Malayan Chinese Association (MCA) and the Malayan Indian Congress (MIC). In the first Federal elections of 1955, the Alliance won 51 out of the 52 seats contested. At a ceremony held in Kuala Lumpur on 31 August 1957, Malaya's Independence was proclaimed. Tunku Abdul Rahman became the first Prime Minister of Malaya, and held the post until 1970. The British colonies of Singapore, Sarawak and Sabah (called North Borneo) joined the Federation to form Malaysia on 16 September 1963.[123]

Singapore withdrew from the Federation on 9 August 1965 and became an independent republic. Neighbouring Indonesia objected to the formation of Malaysia and pursued a programme of economic,

---

[123] *Windows to Malaysia* (http://www.windowstomalaysia.com.my/nation/11_4_1.htm), as at 17 June 2004.

political, diplomatic and military "confrontation" against the new country, which ended only after the fall of Indonesia's President Sukarno in 1966.

Local communists, nearly all Chinese, launched a long, bitter insurgency, prompting the imposition of a state of emergency in 1948 (lifted in 1960). Small bands of guerrillas remained in bases along the rugged border with southern Thailand, occasionally entering northern Malaysia. These guerrillas finally signed a peace accord with the Malaysian Government in December 1989. A separate, small-scale communist insurgency that began in the mid-1960s in Sarawak also ended with the signing of a peace accord in October 1990.[124]

Under former Malaysian Prime Minister, Mahathir Mohamed's watch, Malaysia was transformed by twenty-first-century infrastructure and rapid growth. Yet race and religion remain flash points in a secular nation with a Muslim majority and elite Chinese and Indian minorities. For twenty-two years, Mahathir held radical Islam at bay without alienating the Muslim majority to build a prosperous, multiethnic nation.[125] Malaysia, a democratic nation of 25 million people, has a large non-Muslim population and does not enforce Shari'ah or strict Islamic law. Whilst Islam is Malaysia's official religion and Muslims make up more than 51 per cent of the population, the country is not an Islamic state.

The main opposition party of Malaysia, PAS, has been unsuccessful in the bid to push the country towards a stricter Islamic state with their failure to replace the main governing political party, UMNO, in the March 2004 elections. UMNO continues to lead Malaysia with their leader, Abdullah Ahmad Badawi, who took over the reins from Mahathir Mohamed on 31 October 2003.

---

[124]*Malaysia* (2003), U.S. Department of State (http://www.state.gov/r/pa/ei/bgn/2777.htm), 17 June 2004.

[125]Montlake, Simon, "Islam will test new Malaysia chief", *The Christian Science Monitor*, 30 October 2003.

6.8 Brunei

In 1888, Brunei became a protectorate of the British Government, retaining internal independence but with British control over external affairs. In 1906, Brunei accepted a further measure of British control when executive power was transferred to a British resident, who advised the ruler on all matters except those concerning local custom and religion.

The discovery of large oilfields in the 1920s brought economic prosperity to Brunei. The country was occupied by the Japanese in 1941 and liberated by the Australians in 1945, when it was returned to Britain. In 1950 Sir Omar Ali Saiffuddin Saadul Khairi Waddien (1916–86), popularly known as Sir Omar, became sultan.

In 1959, a new constitution was written declaring Brunei a self-governing state, whilst its foreign affairs, security and defence remained the responsibility of the United Kingdom. An attempt in 1962 to introduce a partially elected legislative body with limited powers was abandoned after the opposition political party, Partai Rakyat Brunei, launched an armed uprising, which the government put down with the help of British forces. In the late 1950s and early 1960s, the government also resisted pressures to join neighbouring Sabah and Sarawak in the newly formed Malaysia. The sultan Omar eventually decided that Brunei would remain an independent state.

On 4 January 1979, Brunei and the United Kingdom signed a new treaty of friendship and cooperation. On 1 January 1984, Brunei Darussalam became a fully independent state.[126] The current ruler of Brunei is Prince Al-Muhtadee Billah.

Governed by an Islamic monarchy, Islam is the official religion in Brunei, though religious freedom is guaranteed under the constitution. It holds membership in the United Nations, Association of Southeast Asian Nations (ASEAN), the Asia Pacific Economic

---

[126]*Brunei Darussalam* (2004), U.S. Department of State (http://www.state.gov/r/pa/ei/bgn/2700.htm), 17 June 2004.

Cooperation (APEC) forum and the Organisation of the Islamic Conference (OIC). In some quarters of society and government, there is also a vigorous interest in the implementation of a law code based on Islamic law. At present the Brunei legal system is a British colonial one, including much legislation of English origin, and it might be suggested that some questioning of this system is an inevitable part of the process of decolonisation. In this regard, it should be remembered that Brunei became fully independent only in the mid-1980s. Another consideration in explaining the current Islamic enthusiasm in political, legal and social areas is the role of religious influence from Malaysia, where there has occurred a strengthening of Islamic institutions since the 1970s. To replace the colonial-based law with a more Islamic-influenced system, however, raises two issues. First, Brunei is in many ways a moderate rather than a fundamentalist Muslim state: it is influenced by long-established traditions of Muslim kingship and the government is also concerned to promote a strong commitment to Malay ethnicity as well as a sense of Islamic brotherhood. Second, the Brunei Government is seeking to become a serious player in ASEAN, and particularly a major centre of commercial activity in the East Asian growth region, embracing Indonesia's Sulawesi, Moluccas and Kalimantan, Malaysia's Labuan, Sarawak and Sabah and the Southern Philippines. Demands to implement a more vigorously Islamic legal (and perhaps political) system will need to be balanced against the desire to present Brunei as a growing commercial entrepôt especially attractive and welcoming to the international business community.[127]

6.9   Islam in South-east Asia Today

The chronic problem of armed Muslim insurgence in South-east Asia in pursuit of the goal of secessionism is far from over, whilst

---

[127] *Asean Focus Group — Asian Analysis*, "Brunei — August 1998", in cooperation with the Faculty of Asian Studies at The Australian National University (1998), (http://www.aseanfocus.com/asiananalysis/article.cfm?articleID=51).

the post-Second World War experiment with nationhood is still going on. The shortcomings of liberal democracy are glaring and in the wake of a more general resurgence of Islam, worldwide, in the 1970s and the 1980s, many Muslims feel the need to reassess the whole range of Western ideas, values and institutions, which appear to have created tensions, dissatisfactions and even disillusionment amongst the people. There has been a demand for desecularisation and Islamisation. An Islamic resurgence is clearly evident in Malaysia, the Philippines and Indonesia. With the tremendous resources available in South-east Asia, in terms of manpower, raw materials, capital, markets, entrepreneurial skills, and a probably renewed and religiously inspired vigour to look for alternatives, the economic and religious future certainly looks brighter for the Muslims of South-east Asia.

Chapter 7

Colonial Legacies: Islam and State Law in South-east Asia

Colonialism made a great impact on the political constitution of the countries of South-east Asia, introducing ideas of a Western-style democracy, parliamentary government and an independent judiciary in place of the autocratic rule of an absolute sovereign and his court. This, of course, was more a legacy of the colonial era than a fact at the time, but today, every country in South-east Asia arguably owes something to the West if only in terms of the idea of a nation state with geographically delineated boundaries. The extent of this debt to the West varies from country to country — in Brunei there are no political parties and the Sultan still governs by decree; Myanmar (Burma) is ruled by a military junta — but everywhere one sees evidence of Western influence in the apparatus of government. Even Thailand, which of course was never colonised, not only has a constitutional monarch, but also an elected parliament.

The way by which the modern nation states of South-east Asia came by their present systems of government varies. In the case of Malaysia and Singapore, the British colonial administration actively sought to leave behind them a parliamentary system of government closely modelled on their own, albeit without the division between upper and lower chambers. In Indonesia, the introduction of a multi-party parliamentary democracy following a unilateral declaration of independence in August 1945, was one of choice. Brunei, which was a British protectorate from 1888 to 1984, remains a sultanate, but nevertheless has opted for a British-style judiciary and legal system.

7.1 Shari'ah vs. State Law

In as far as the application of Islamic law in modern South-east Asia is concerned, and in particular, the relationship of Shari'ah law to secular state legal systems, this has been very much a matter of individual state policy. In Myanmar (Burma), for example, Islam was the faith and personal law of an immigrant community, which came into being under (British) colonial auspices. However, in the half century of independence (Burma gained its independence in 1948), the policy of all Burmese governments has been to crack down on the freedoms of ethnic minorities which are seen as counteractive to the successful implementation of politico-economic programmes such as the "Burmese Way to Socialism". As a result, there has been a mass exodus of the immigrant trading community and the almost complete demise of Islam in Burma. In Southern Thailand, on the other hand, although ethnic Malay Muslims have always been a somewhat disadvantaged minority, Muslim law, though confined to family law, has remained relatively untouched. Even so, various Muslim "liberation" movements have made their appearances and there was even an attempt on the life of the King in 1977 which was ascribed to Muslim separatists.[128] Government policy has, therefore, concentrated upon an integration, perhaps even a forced integration, of the Muslim minority especially through education.[129] The result is that Muslim law, whilst formally available in the Thai legal system, is almost certainly informally administered.[130]

In Peninsula Malaysia, Islam is the received religion of the Malay people. During the colonial era, Britain recognised both the Islamic and the indigenous element in Malay sovereignty and it is from this recognition that the contemporary state administration of

---

[128]See *Times*, 11 October 1977.

[129]See Haemindra, (1997) and Suhrke, (1970).

[130]There are no hard data available, and fieldwork is not possible at the moment.

Islam derives. The religion is entrenched in the State and Federal Constitutions of Malaysia and this formal recognition has made it both a constitutional issue and has also given it a direct relevance in contemporary Malaysian politics. But Malaysia is a multi-ethnic society and its constitution is a secular one with a legal system and judiciary inherited from the British. Historically, this is an interesting situation in that just as English common law was adapted to meet the needs of governing peoples of differing religions and cultures in Malaya, so too was Shari'ah law modified by the colonial experience. In this last respect, Malaysia provides an appropriate case study to illustrate the impact of non-Islamic influences (mainly Western, it must be said) on Shari'ah law in South-east Asia.

7.2   British Malaya

The Portuguese conquest of Malacca in 1503, though of enormous importance in terms of regional geopolitics, had little direct impact on the lives of the peoples of the Malay Peninsula except those living in the immediate environs of Malacca. Nor did the replacement of the Portuguese by the Dutch in 1641, and it was not until the late eighteenth century, when the English East India Company acquired the island of Penang (Pulau Pinang), off Malaya's north-west coast, from the Rajah of Kedah that Western influences first began to infiltrate traditional Malay society.

This was in 1786 and before long Penang became a flourishing entrepôt. But it was not quite the perfect location, being a little too far to the north to take full advantage of the maritime trade between East and West — in those days, before the building of the Suez Canal, the preferred route to China from Europe was through the Sunda Straits that divide Sumatra from Java. Then in 1819, Stamford Raffles established a second trading post on the island of Singapore at the southern-most tip of the Malay Peninsula. Strategically located on both the sea route between India and China as well as between China and Europe, and blessed with a fine natural harbour, Singapore soon became the region's principal commercial centre. Britain acquired Malacca from the Dutch in 1824 and thereafter the three major ports of the Straits of Malacca collectively became known as the Straits Settlements. After the dissolution of East India Company by the British Government in 1858, the Straits Settlements were administered by the India Office before becoming a crown colony in their own right in 1867.

At that time, the whole of the Malay Peninsula (Malacca excepted) was governed by Malay sultans who were frequently at war with one another. This was a largely agrarian society; rivers formed the principal highways and most of the Peninsula was still virgin rainforest, unexplored even by the Malays themselves. By the middle of the nineteenth century, Chinese immigrants — who were being driven to emigrate by increasing poverty and instability in their homeland — began settling in large numbers on the west coast of the Malay Peninsula where they cooperated with local Malay rulers to mine tin. The Chinese organised themselves into clan-based communities whilst forming alliances with rival Malay chiefs, and this soon led to an endemic state of petty warfare and lawlessness as different Chinese factions competed for the control of mineral resources.

British investors were also attracted to Malaya's potential mineral wealth, but they were concerned about the anarchic state of Malay politics. For a long time the British Government was unwilling to become involved in the affairs of the sultans, but in the end the colonial authorities capitulated to the demands of the mercantile community of the Straits Settlements and on 20 January 1874, a treaty was signed on the west coast island of Pangkor between the British and Sultan Abdullah of Perak, formalising British involvement in the political affairs of the state in the form of a "resident", who was there ostensibly to advise the sultan, but in fact acted as plenipotentiary of the British.

Initial British intervention into Malayan internal affairs was insensitive and heavy-handed — the first British resident to Perak,

James W. W. Birch, was murdered by Malays outraged at his auto-cratic and unseemly behaviour — but the British refined their act, appointed more able representatives, and gradually the res-ident system was taken up by other Malay states. In 1896, Sir Frank Swettenham was appointed as the first resident-general of a Malay Federation comprising Perak, Selangor, Negeri Sembilan and Pahang, with Kuala Lumpur as the capital. By 1909 the British had pressured Siam into transferring sovereignty over the north-ern Malay states of Kedah, Trengganu, Kelantan and Perlis; Johor was compelled to accept a British resident in 1914. These sultanates remained outside the federation and were called the Unfederated Malay States. Britain had now achieved formal or informal colo-nial control over nine sultanates, but it pledged not to interfere in matters of religion, customs, and the symbolic political role of the sultans. The various states kept their separate identities but were increasingly integrated to create British Malaya.

7.3 The Introduction of English Common Law to Malaya

"Wherever an Englishman goes, he carries with him as much of English law and liberty as the situation will allow". So wrote the distinguished Singapore barrister, Sir Roland St John Braddell, in 1921. "When a Settlement is made by British subjects of country that is unoccupied or without settled institutions", he continued, "such newly settled country is to be governed by the law of England, but only so far as the law is of general and not merely local policy and modified in its application so as to suit the needs of the Set-tlement".[131] However, in the case of Penang and Singapore it was argued that since the islands were part of the territory of Muslim sovereigns — the Rajah of Kedah and the Sultan of Johor respec-tively — the law of the land should therefore be "Muhammadan

---

[131]Cited in Hooker, M. B., *Islamic Law in South-East Asia*, 1984, p. 160.

law", that is to say Shari'ah law. Naturally, this did not really suit the British, especially as from an early point in the development of both Penang and Singapore, the population had been a largely Chinese one, but it was not until 1872 that the issue was settled in favour of English common law by a ruling of the Privy Council of England.

7.4 Out of India

The British may have been responsible for the introduction of English common law to the Malay Peninsula, but from the outset, this was not quite the same institution as one would have found back in the England at that time. In the essentials, yes, but it was English common law which had been modified by the experience of India.

By the time the island of Penang was acquired from the Rajah of Kedah in 1786, the East India Company had already been established in India for over one hundred years and the principles of the Honourable Company's legal policy in respect of the territories and peoples under its jurisdiction there had been codified in an Act of Settlement of 1781. This proclaimed:

> English law is the law of general application, subject to the
> religions, manners and cultures of the natives, provided
> these exceptions are not repugnant to justice, equity and
> good conscience.[132]

Even a cursory reading of this passage indicates its very restrictive nature and the judicial precedent developed throughout the nineteenth and twentieth centuries confirms this. "Religions, manners and customs" came to be defined as family law and charitable trusts, and even within this narrow definition certain practices, valid in religion, were either restricted or forbidden under the "justice, equity

---

[132]Hooker, M. B., "Introduction: Islamic law in South-east Asia", *Australian Journal of Asian Law*, Vol. 4, No. 3, 2002, 213 and 217.

and good conscience provision" (e.g. child marriage and aspects of charitable trusts). In most other respects, English common law was to be upheld as the law of the land, which of course greatly restricted the traditional scope of Shari'ah law.

But quite apart from restricting the application of Shari'ah law there were even more fundamental changes occurring, namely the re-formulation of Shari'ah in terms of English legal processes. Those principles of Shari'ah that were permitted to exist now became described in precedent and their validity and meaning was decided in terms of English legal reasoning. English judicial method absorbed the few principles of Shari'ah permitted to continue and in the nineteenth century a new hybrid legal system had begun to emerge, namely "Anglo-Muhammadan", or "Anglo-Muslim" law. (NB much the same thing was to happen in the case of "Anglo-Hindu", "Burmese-Buddhist", "Anglo-Chinese", and "Malay-*adat*" laws in South and South-east Asia during the colonial era.)

One important consequence was the long-term impact of the English doctrine of precedent. If one wished to know what "Islamic" law was in British India, or subsequently in British Malaya, then one simply looked to the precedent; it was certainly not necessary to refer to the classical Arabic texts. In some instances, court decisions that were actually contrary to Muslim law became authoritative and one can even find cases from the highest level which actually rejected classical Arabic rulings because acceptance would have meant over-turning existing local precedent. Other changes were also taking place. For example, Islamic rules of evidence came to be increasingly ignored and marginalised. At the same time, the absence of high-quality training in Islamic law for British judicial personnel impeded recourse to the principles of that law. What this meant was that the twin maxims of "justice and right" and "justice, equality and good conscience", which originally were devised to fill lacunae in the existing legal framework, were all too frequently used to mask judicial ignorance of Muslim law, thus leading to further application, not only of English law, but also of Roman law and other legal prescriptions.[133] Lastly, the use of English as the court language of a hierarchical general court structure and subsequently of law reporting in the Indian justice system inevitably tended to favour decisions made in accordance with English law rather than local legal precepts.

As this British-formulated legislation, tailor-made for the sub-continent, rather than English law itself, gained in prominence, more and more areas of law were taken outside the ambit of "justice, equity and good conscience" and the scope for the application of that maxim, though never totally closed, was greatly curtailed. On the other hand, the scope for the application of Muslim law was gradually reduced, too, so that, ultimately mainly matters of family law, including succession law, came to comprise the South Asian Muslim personal law as it is known today. By 1900, a classically trained Islamic jurist would have been at a complete loss with this Anglo-Muslim law. Conversely, a common lawyer with no knowledge of Islam could have been perfectly comfortable.

7.5   Muslim Law in Malaysia

During the colonial era, when the Malay Peninsula was under British rule, Muslim law (Shari'ah) developed in a rather piece-meal fashion, state-by-state. In terms of the treaties and agreements, the Malay States were sovereign States and English law was not formally introduced as in the Straits Settlements (Malacca, Penang and Singapore). Instead, the law applying in any Malay State at the time when it became subject to British protection, remained in force subject only to legislative amendment. Naturally a good deal of English law came in by way of adoption of Indian or Straits legislation and, in addition, an extensive reception was also accomplished by judges in an effort to fill the gaps in the laws of each State. It was not, however, until 1937, when the Civil Law Enactment of that year came into

---

[133]Pearl, David and Menski, Werner, *Muslim Family Law*, 1998, p. 35.

force, that the Federated Malay States had English common law and rules of equity formally introduced en bloc. This Enactment was extended to the other States in 1951 and the matter is now governed by section 3 of the Civil Law Ordinance of 1956 as amended. In short, the formative period in the development of modern Muslim personal law in the Malaya Peninsula was thus a period of rather extensive legal uncertainty, and there was a variation of practice from State to State; Muslim law was generally accepted as a general law and this continued up to the Second World War.[134] From 1948, States granted jurisdiction over application and legislation of Shari'ah from 1952 to 1978 and new laws promulgated in 11 Muslim-majority States of Malaysia and Sabah (generally entitled Administration of Islamic/Muslim Law Enactments) covered the official determination of Islamic law, explanation of substantive law, and jurisdiction of Shari'ah courts. New laws relating to personal law were enacted in most States between 1983 and 1987.[135]

There is the existence of a three-tier system: at the bottom, the indigenous *adat*, which is as old as time itself and a kind of pan-archipelago cultural base, overlaid by Shari'ah law, with International law on top. This implies that in some areas of the law, a three-way tug of war between conflicting legal systems and requirements may be present.

7.6 Conflict between Muslim Law and English Common Law

The English Common Law does not take into consideration the customs and Shari'ah law as stated in the Quran. Thus for Muslims, it is lacking in guiding their way of life in the religious path. With the separation of courts for the English legal system and the Shari'ah

---

[134]See Hooker, op. cit., p. 135.

[135]Emory Law School (USA), "Malaysia", (http://www.law.emory.edu/ IFL/legal/malaysia.htm).

system, there is room for inconsistency and if so, a decision has to be made as to which system supersedes the other, according to circumstances.

The Shari'ah, which is at the heart of Islam, can be nothing other than exclusive and though Islam does acknowledge a legal consequence to such ascriptions as "Christian" or "Jew", or *kitabiyya* (person belonging to different religion, not Islam), for some purposes, this is a personal and limited recognition. Another problem is the emphasis in the Shari'ah on a personal relationship with Allah rather than via institutionalised religious structures. This is perhaps both the strength and weakness of Islam — a strength in the religious sense of providing an immediacy of communication and contact between man and God, and a weakness in the lack of a developed theory of law in relation to political authority. In particular, Islam has found difficulty in coming to terms with the idea of the "State" as developed in Western Europe and exported to the Muslim lands. The main focus of tension here, so far as the present analysis is concerned, has been the question of the validity of the law as practised in English courts in situations where there is a conflict with Muslim law.

According to Hooker, this is the most fundamental aspect of conflicts; in essence it asks: how does one ascertain the proper law to decide a conflict of principle between the tenets of Islam and the laws of the State? The main issue in attempting to answer this question is that neither Islam, nor secular legal systems, of themselves provide an answer. Each must insist on its own application, because each is exclusive, so that the answer to the question is at least partly, if not wholly, a policy matter. That being said, it should be noted that policy choices commonly take legal guises, sometimes quite technically complex ones.[136]

---

[136]See Hooker, op. cit., p. 119.

7.7 Maria Hertogh: A Case in Point

These general comments bring one to the celebrated Maria Hertogh case in Singapore in 1950 which perfectly illustrates all the issues just outlined. The background here is as follows: Maria Hertogh was a Dutch Eurasian girl who had been separated from her parents when they were interned in Java during the Japanese occupation and was cared for and brought up as a Muslim by a servant of her parents. Her father traced her whereabouts after the war and attempted to regain custody of his daughter. Although he succeeded in an action brought before the Singapore High Court, there was a complication in that the girl, though only aged fifteen at that time, was already married to a Muslim man. The Court was asked to decide on the validity of the marriage. In fact, it was found that the girl was a Muslim. It was decided, however, both at first instance and on appeal, that the marriage was invalid and a variety of different reasons were put forward, at both levels, to justify this decision. All jurisdictions started from the fundamental private international law (conflicts of law) principle that capacity to marry is determined by the law of the domicile at the time of marriage. In the case of a minor her domicile was that of the father, in this instance the Netherlands. According to this law, a girl had no capacity to marry at the age of fifteen unless certain permissions had been obtained. Naturally these permissions had not been obtained and the marriage was thus declared invalid. The Court's decision resulted in three days of violent rioting by certain elements of Singapore's Muslim community which left eighteen dead and 173 injured.

This is the sort of reasoning, based on an orthodox interpretation of the law in a situation where there was serious conflict of legal principles, that was criticised as being mechanical and unsuitable to the needs of a multi-ethnic society, such as Singapore, in which a variety of religious and racial groups live side by side and as we have seen, resulted in violent political confrontation between Muslims and the State authorities. From the Muslim point of view, the judgement was an unwarranted interference in what was a perfectly valid arrangement under Muslim law — after all, the Court had also found as a fact that the girl was "Muslim". This impasse could have been avoided by placing the social implications of a decision before the technical constraints of laws which are not designed to deal with the implications of *internal* conflicts involving personal laws. Such a solution may, however, be thought slightly too radical in that it tends to dispose of a major principle of common law conflicts of laws, viz. that domicile determines the right to decide the application of a personal law.

One of the judgements in the Hertogh case, however, consisted of an ingenious attempt to find a way round the criticisms just made, whilst simultaneously giving effect to English conflicts of laws principles. Justice J. Brown began from the proposition that because the girl was Muslim and the marriage was valid according to Muslim law, it was the latter which must determine validity. He then found that Muslim law required validity to be judged by the law of the place of contracting; this was taken to be a reference to English law and, by extension, to the English conflicts of laws. This view rests upon an equation of contracts of marriage with all other contracts under Muslim law. In the event, the domicile rule prevailed, despite the fact that dependent domicile — in this case the Netherlands — had nothing to do with the concept of one's home nor with the relevant religion.[137]

Countless other instances could be given of conflicts arising out of differences between English law and Shari'ah law in former British colonies, but they would do no more than underscore the point that has already been made by the Maria Hertogh case, namely that at a general level, the two systems of law are all too often incompatible making conflict inevitable and indeed endemic. The situation is complicated still further by the possibility of conflict

---

[137] Ibid, p. 120.

between statutory laws and legal precedents as well as the private international law aspect.

7.8   Post-Independence

In 1957, the newly independent Malaya opted for a continuation of the existing British legal system, but the recent history of Islamic legal administration in Malaysia has been one of a continuing development towards a more direct and exact implementation of Islamic precepts. In the colonial era, the legal administration was primarily concerned to implement only those precepts that were immediately required so as to avoid offending the religious sensitivities of the Malay peoples. In effect this limited Islamic law to "Muslim family law" and the latter was further restricted in some places and for some subjects by local customary law or *adat*.

Since Malaysian independence, however, there has been a move towards a more complete and comprehensive expression of Islamic legalism. The legislature and the Religious Courts have been an important element in this, as has the creation of the State Religious Departments. A significant move was the formation of the National Council for Islamic Affairs in 1968, which later was incorporated as Religious Affairs Division of the Prime Minister's Department in February 1974. From its inception the Council had a Fatwa Committee whose function was to make rulings for the Conference of Rulers. The membership consisted of the Mufti (an attorney in Islamic law) of each State plus a Muslim appointed by the Conference from among the officers of the (secular) Judicial and Legal Service. The Council also had a number of ad hoc committees which dealt, *inter alia*, with reviews of the polygamy and divorce laws, the Muslim calendar and the Shari'ah Courts. The Council has also sponsored the publication of a series of translations of *hadith*, a first volume of which (*Mukaddimah Mastika Hadith Rasulullah*) has been published. The Council also provided training courses for Muslim missionaries and lectures to State officers on religion.

No doubt, these developments can be seen as a reflection of a desire to demonstrate independence from the colonial past. At the same time, though, as this brief historical overview clearly demonstrates, despite the fact that the common South-east Asian Islamic experience of the past century and a half has been one of subjection to secular forces, Islam, as a religion, is more than the sum of individual experiences, hence present-day demands, which are usually expressed politically, for an increase in the "Islamic" as opposed to secular content of law.

Nevertheless, despite these measures, there still remains an inherent conflict between state law and Muslim law in contemporary Malaysia — the lasting legacy of the formative influence of English common law on Malaysia's legal system. To a large extent this situation is unavoidable given that Malaysia's secular constitution and multi-ethnic population militates against the adoption of Shari'ah as the state law. In this last respect it is interesting to note that although recent years have seen the more heavily Islamicised states within Malaysia — notably Trengganu and Kelantan — agitating for the adoption of Shari'ah law, the crushing defeat of the principal Islamicist parties in the 2004 general elections seems to indicate that the majority of modern Muslim Malaysians would prefer to continue with the present legal system despite the inevitable tensions and contradictions between English common law and Shari'ah. All the same, there can be no doubt that the gradual move towards a more complete and comprehensive expression of Islamic legalism since independence has helped to pave the way for the implementation of Islamic banking over the past twenty-five years as we shall see in the next chapter.

Chapter 8
Islamic Banking in Malaysia

Malaysia certainly has changed under Mahathir's administration, transformed by twenty-first-century infrastructure and rapid growth. Yet race and religion remain flash points in a secular nation with a Muslim majority and prominent Chinese and Indian minorities. For twenty-two years, Mahathir has held radical Islam at bay without alienating the Muslim majority to build a prosperous, multiethnic nation. Under Mahathir, Malays were given Islamic schools and told that Islamic values were central to government policies. On 31 October 2003, Abdullah Badawi took over from Mahathir.[138]

Among the countries in Asia with aspirations to become one of the region's financial centres, Malaysia is making considerable efforts to enhance its financial industry. A distinctive feature of Malaysia's economy is the fact that Islamic banking and financial services have been fully integrated into the country's existing financial system. In this last respect, Malaysia provides a good example of the banking industry's inventiveness and capacity for innovation.

Islamic banking was introduced to Malaysia through the Islamic Banking Act (IBA) of 1983 and the simultaneous establishment of the Bank Islam Malaysia Berhad. The move was part of the Malaysian Government's strategy to support Muslim Malays who were perceived to be losing out to the more commercially minded Chinese (although Malays make up the majority of the country's population nationwide, in the capital Kuala Lumpur, and also in

---

[138]Montlake, op. cit.

144

provincial Penang, it is the Chinese who dominate the business sector and who have played a leading role in the industrialisation and economic growth of Malaysia).[139] The first entirely Islamic bank to be established, Bank Islam Malaysia Berhad, operates through eighty-five branches in the country whilst the more recently-established Bank Muamalat Malaysia Berhad has forty-six branches. In addition to the Islamic banks, there are also thirteen commercial banks that offer products and services under the Islamic banking scheme.[140]

Today, Malaysia is believed to have one of the most developed interest-free financial systems in the world. Besides the Interest-free Banking Scheme, there is an Islamic debt securities market developed in 1990 and an Islamic equity market, operating since 1995; an Islamic Interbank Money Market was established in 1994.

In 30 June 2003, Islamic banking assets accounted for 9.4 per cent or RM75.5 billion of the banking system in Malaysia. Deposits and financing accounted for 10 per cent and 9 per cent respectively, whilst *takaful* assets accounted for 5.3 per cent.[141] The government wants that share to rise to 20 per cent by 2010 and plans to do this by opening the door to foreign Islamic banks as well as introducing new measures to help the country emerge as a regional hub for Islamic finance.[142]

8.1   Origins of Islamic Banking in Malaysia

In Malaysia, civil disturbances in the late 1960s by ethnic Malay Muslims protesting at the dominance of ethnic Chinese in the commercial sector prompted a government programme to redistribute

---

[139]Davies, Rod, "Malaysia capsule", *Orient Pacific Century*, 10 June 2002.

[140]Malaysia Industrial Development Authority, "Banking, Finance & Foreign Exchange Administration", (http://www.mida.gov.my/).

[141]The Star (Malaysia), "Islamic Banking Sector Sets Target", (http://www.neac.gov.my/index.php?ch=19&pg=30&ac=412), 19 August 2003.

[142]*The Financial Gazette* (South Africa), op. cit.

wealth and concentrate more political power in the hands of the Muslim Malays. This was at a time when Islamic traditionalists were also protesting against what they saw as decadent Western influences, which had taken root in Malaysia, corrupting the moral and cultural life of the nation. It was partly in order to placate these activists as well as to provide business opportunities specifically aimed at Muslim Malays that the government initiated Islamic banking in parallel with conventional banking on a trial basis. Ten years later, it made Islamic banking a permanent part of the financial structure, and increasingly takes pride in its Islamic banking sector.

A dual banking system was introduced by the IBA of 1983 which allowed Islamic banking and conventional banking to co-exist side by side. Today, almost all financial institutions in Malaysia have opened separate Islamic departments and there are Islamic securities and money markets.

The IBA of 1983 was introduced to govern the operations of Islamic banks in Malaysia. It provided Bank Negara — Malaysia's central bank — with powers to supervise and regulate Islamic banks, similar to the case of other licensed banks.

The Government Investment Act 1983 was enacted at the same time to empower the Government of Malaysia to issue Government Investment Certificates (GIC), which are government securities issued according to Shari'ah principles. As GICs are regarded as liquid assets, Islamic banks could invest in them as a means of meeting prescribed liquidity requirements. They could also invest in them as a way of deploying their surplus funds. The Government Investment Act 1983 was subsequently amended for both (Islamic) Statutory Reserves and the Liquidity Reserve Requirement purposes.

The Banking and Financial Institutions Act (BAFIA) 1989, which came into force on 1 October of that year, provided for the licensing and regulation of institutions carrying out banking, finance company, merchant banking, discount house and money-broking businesses. It also provided for the regulation of institutions carrying out scheduled businesses comprising non-bank sources of credit and finance, such as credit and charge card companies, building societies, factoring, leasing companies and development finance institutions.[143] In 1996, section 124 of the BAFIA was amended to allow banks licensed under this Act to introduce Islamic banking business (1996).

8.2 Bank Negara Guidelines on Islamic Banking

As part of the effort to streamline and harmonise the Shari'ah interpretations among banks and *takaful* companies, Bank Negara Malaysia (BNM, the central bank of Malaysia) established the National Shari'ah Advisory Council (NSAC) on Islamic Banking and *Takaful* on 1 May 1997 as the highest Shari'ah authority on Islamic banking and *takaful* in Malaysia. The primary objectives of the NSAC are to act as the sole authoritative body to advise BNM on Islamic banking and *takaful* operations; to co-ordinate Shari'ah issues with respect to Islamic banking and finance (including *takaful);* and to analyse and evaluate Shari'ah aspects of new products/schemes submitted by the banking institutions and *takaful* companies.

Guidelines pertaining to Islamic banking, issued by Bank Negara from time to time, are as good as a legal requirement because under the Bank Negara Ordinance, Malaysia's central bank is vested with some powers to regulate the market.

Some examples of these Guidelines include having the Central Bank instruct all conventional banks operating Islamic banking business and Islamic financial business to maintain separate current accounts and clearing accounts with the Central Bank of Malaysia as the Islamic accounts need to be used only for transactions which are

---

[143]Non-scheduled institutions, which are engaged in the provision of finance, may be subject to Part X and XI of the BAFIA as the Minister of Finance may decide.

halah and conducted according to Shari'ah law. The same reason is also behind the separate membership code for RENTAS (Real Time Electronic Transfer of Funds and Securities) to be maintained. In addition, there should be separate submission of statistical reports in FISS (Financial Institutions Submission System) on a monthly basis.

In 2004, Bank Negara brought forward the Islamic banking sector's liberalisation, initially scheduled for 2007, by issuing three new licences to Islamic financial institutions from the Middle East. They are Kuwait Finance House, Al-Rajhi Banking & Investment Corporation and a consortium of Islamic financial institutions represented by Qatar Islamic Bank, RUSD Investment Bank Inc, and Global Investment House.

This move to speed up the liberalisation programme stemmed from the rapid development and steady performance of the Islamic banking industry over the recent years. The presence of these foreign players will position Malaysia as an international Islamic financial centre.

Bank Negara also introduced a policy on *takaful* coverage for Islamic financing in October 2004, whereby Islamic banking institutions were required to offer *takaful* plans as the first choice to their customers in the offering of protection for Islamic financing that needs coverage.[144]

8.3   The Shari'ah Supervisory Council

In contrast to the Islamic banks that have been set up in Arab countries since the end of the 1970s, Malaysian financial institutions, with the support and encouragement of the government, have chosen their own approach in interpreting Islamic law and this has allowed

---

[144]"Fast forward for Islamic banking", *The Star* (Malaysia), (http://biz. thestar.com.my/news/story.asp? file =/2005/3/24/business/10495342 & sec=business), 24 March 2005.

them to develop a wide range of Islamic financial instruments. Of course they must still fulfil the requirements of Shari'ah law in this respect — Shari'ah compliance is a core component of the Islamic system of financial management and as noted previously, there can be no compromise. In Malaysia, the consistency and uniform application of Islamic rules is supervised by the NSAC.[145] Both the IBA and the BAFIA made the establishment of the Shari'ah Supervisory Council a statutory requirement. The IBA is imposed on a bank that wishes to conduct Islamic banking [section 3(5) b], whilst the BAFIA compels Malaysia's central bank, Bank Negara, to establish a National Shari'ah Supervisory Council at the national level to advise the central bank on matters pertaining to Islamic banking [section 124 (7) a]. Relatively speaking, this move to implement a Shari'ah regulatory body for financial matters (the second after Sudan) has proved to be successful in regulating Islamic banking business in terms of Shari'ah compliance as well as standardisation.

8.4 Making Islamic Banking Compatible with Conventional Banking

Changes were made precisely to recognise and address the need to reconcile the differences between Islamic and conventional banking. The Stamp Duty Act in 1989 was amended to avoid Double Stamp Duty and double taxation is prevented under the Real Property Gains Tax (RPGT) of 1979. Under the amended provision, any gain from the transaction if realised within five years from the date of disposal will be considered as a chargeable gain, and would be taxable. If the acquisition and disposal were affected in the same year (as in the case of *bai bithaman ajil* for house financing), the rate

---

[145]Sudan has a Shari'ah Supervisory Board at the central bank and in Iran they have a committee within the Council of Guardians, which sets the rules for the banking and finance sector. In other jurisdictions, individual Islamic financial institutions and the Islamic banking units at conventional financial institutions appoint their own Shari'ah supervisory boards or advisors.

of tax would be 30 per cent from the profit or gain generated from the transaction. Therefore, amendments in 1985 provided that in case of disposal of an asset by a person to an Islamic bank under a scheme wherein that person is financed by such bank in accordance with the Shari'ah, the disposal price shall be deemed to be equal to the acquisition price.

Other legal developments that encouraged adherence to Shari'ah law in financial transactions have included an amendment to the Hire Purchase Act 1967, which was "Islamicised" by the preparation of a Bill on Islamic Hire Purchase by a Technical Committee at the national level. The Islamic Hire Purchase Bill is scheduled to be tabled in Parliament by the end of 2004 to pave the way for Islamic hire purchase in the country. The move will provide an alternative to the conventional hire purchase system. The Bill would be similar to the Hire Purchase Act 1967 but with new elements incorporated, taking into account Islamic insurance (*takaful*) and the abolition of interest.[146] An Islamic Tribunal Panel was also established to solve disputes pertaining to Islamic banking outside the court following the procedures of the Code of Arbitration as laid down by NSAC and efforts were made to neutralise legal impediments towards allowing Islamic bank/Islamic windows to offer *musharakah* and *mudarabah* financing, for example issues pertaining to some provisions in BAFIA about acquiring shares and immoveable property as well as compliance with other relevant law such as the National Law Code.

8.5   Some Observations on the Malaysian Legal Framework

Despite ensuring that Shari'ah law is incorporated within the legal boundaries of banking and finance, there still exists the underlying gap between Islamic and conventional banking. The IBA and

---

[146] "Islamic hire purchase bill to be tabled in parliament this year", *New Straits Times (Malaysia) Berhad*, 30 April 2004, Nation, p. 14.

BAFIA are very brief and regulatory in nature; also they do not offer substantive law where the bankers or customers would be able to understand how it works for them. Ultimately, the jurisdiction of the courts to hear Islamic banking disputes still lies with the Civil Court due to a few provisions in the Federal Constitution of Malaysia.[147] Double taxation is presently under the Income Tax Act and *Zakat* Obligation. Currently, rebate from the taxable amount, is only given to individual Muslims who paid *zakat* under section 6A (3) of the Income Tax Act. No such rebate is given to an "Islamic" corporation or company who paid *zakat*.

An important question to be answered is, what extent have the provisions in IBA and BAFIA (Islamic Windows) prevailed over other legal requirements? Section 55 of IBA states that in case of conflict between the provisions of the Company Act 1965 and the provisions of IBA, the latter shall prevail. Does this mean, in all other conflicts, the provisions of IBA shall be put aside? (This principle referred to as "*espressio unius est exclusion alterius*" or "the express meaning of one thing implies the exclusion of another".) In comparison, Pakistan's Ordinance on *Mudarabah* Companies and *Mudarabah* (Flotation and Control), 1980 (XXXI of 1980), where section 42 provides that the provisions of this Ordinance shall have the effect notwithstanding anything contained in the Companies Act, 1913 or any other law for the time being in force.[148]

8.6   Islamic Financial Products in Malaysia: The Concept of an Islamic Window

Islamic financial products in Malaysia were introduced in a form of an Islamic Window where instead of establishing a number of

---

[147]Tinta Press vs. Bank Islam Malaysia Berhad; Bank Islam vs. Adnan b. Omar and Dato' Nik Haji Mahmud vs. Bank Islam Malaysia Berhad.

[148]Bakar, Mohd. Daud, "Legal issues: The Malaysia case", The International Islamic Financial Forum, International Institute of Research, Dubai, March 2002.

new Islamic banks, existing conventional banks were allowed to offer Islamic banking products to customers. It was the objective of the Malaysian Government to develop the Islamic banking system parallel to the conventional system. The concept of an Islamic Window was implemented in March 1993 when the central bank of Malaysia introduced an Interest-Free Banking Scheme. Twenty-one Islamic financial products were developed to cater for this scheme though it only involved three major banks initially. By July that same year, the scheme was extended to all financial institutions in Malaysia.[149] As of April 2004, the Islamic banking system was represented by two Islamic banks which provide banking services based on Islamic principles.[150]

8.7 The Malaysian Government Investment Certificate

The Malaysian Government Investment Certificate (MGIC) is an experiment by Malaysia to issue Treasury Bills or Government Bonds on a Shari'ah basis. It was created and introduced when Islamic banking came into operation following the establishment of Bank Islam in 1983. Conceptually, government bonds are certificates showing the borrowing by the government from the country's financial institutions, etc.; effectively they represent a loan taken by the government from its own citizens. The loan is usually required by the government to finance its recurrent expenditures or development expenditure for public projects. MGICs are issued by BNM on behalf of the Malaysian Government. These are issued according to the Islamic contract of *al-qardh al-hasan* and are of various maturities, both short-dated and long-dated. Each certificate carries a face value in multiples of RM10 000 and issued at par. It is also redeemable at maturity or on demand at BNM at par.

---

[149]See Ahmad, Norafifah and Haron, Sudin, "Perceptions of Malaysian corporate customers towards Islamic banking products and services", *International Journal of Islamic Financial Services*, March 2002.

[150]Malaysia Industrial Development Authority, "Banking, Finance and Foreign Exchange Administration".

Al-qard al-hasan is a benevolent debt-financing contract quite distinct from the strictly commercial deferred contract exchange. The benevolent nature of this contract is well suited to lending by the country's citizens to their government for financing its operation and development of social projects. Under *al-qard al-hasan*, the borrower is not obliged, but has the option, to reward the lender for his benevolent deed. The government thus has the absolute discretion whether to reward, and if so by how much, the holders of MGICs. It may also vary the rewards for the short-dated and the long-dated MGICs. The absolute discretion that the government has, in respect of the rewards that it can offer, means that MGICs are potentially a highly suitable instrument of monetary policy under the Islamic financial system.[151]

8.8   Debt Securities

In Malaysia, Islamic debt securities are traded in the interbank market and money market. Debt securities belonging to the category of loan stocks may be traded on the Kuala Lumpur Stock Exchange (KLSE).[152]

Islamic Debt Securities (IDS) is an evidence of debt issued by corporates and defined as an IOU with a commitment to pay the coupon over a fixed period of time or the selling price at the end of a specific period. Issuance of IDS can be based on the concepts of *murabahah/bai bithaman ajil, mudharabah* or *sukuk al ijarah* (certificates of leasing). It can be traded in the secondary market under the concept of *bai al dayn* or debt-trading and provides investors with an investment avenue for short- or long-term funds.[153]

---

[151]See Ismail, op. cit.

[152]Ibid.

[153]*Bai al dayn* is a short-term facility with a maturity of not more than a year. Only documents evidencing debts arising from bona fide commercial transactions can be traded.

The IDS is rated by Rating Agency Malaysia (RAM) or Malaysia Rating Corporation (MARC) and may either be bank guaranteed or stand-alone.

(i) Short Term Debt Securities are available for tenures (such as one, three, six or nine months), the customer may invest in these notes in denominations of RM500 000 or RM1000 000 and the notes will be issued at discount and redeemed at face value upon maturity.

(ii) Long Term Debt Securities are available for tenures of three years and above, the customer may invest in these notes in denominations of RM1 000 000 to RM5 000 000 and the bonds will earn an income semiannually (dividend) or will be issued at discount and redeemed at face value upon maturity.

As local Islamic investors in Malaysia have been deterred by the poor performance to date of the KLSE, three of the fund management groups have launched Islamic bond funds that aim at capital preservation and a regular non-interest-based income. The Islamic securities market in Malaysia developed in the 1980s, with the issue of government and then corporate notes based on *al bai bithamen ajil*, the sale of goods on a deferred payments basis. Usually the notes were issued to cover equipment financing, the client settling by instalments that provided the income stream on which the security could be based. Although there are objections in the Gulf amongst Shari'ah scholars to *bai al-dayn*, the sale of debt, as it is argued that those owing money should know their creditors, in Malaysia it is argued that as long as those being financed know in advance their debts will be traded, the issue of debt securities is legitimate.[154]

---

[154]See Wilson, Rodney, "The need for more risk taking products", The International Islamic Financial Forum, International Institute of Research, Dubai, March 2002.

8.9   Islamic Accepted Bills

Bank Negara has also introduced a new Islamic financial instrument known as the Islamic Accepted Bills (IAB). The concept of IAB is similar to bankers' acceptances (BAs), but is formulated on the basis of Islamic principles, namely *al-murabahah* (price mark-up) and *bai al-dayn* (debt-trading). There are two types of financing under the IAB facility, namely:

- Imports and domestic purchases; and
- Exports and domestic sales.

In order to provide consumer financing on the basis of Islamic principles, and to explore the possibilities of financing the consumer for the purchase of consumer good under the existing Hire Purchase Act, Bank Negara was actively involved in the drafting of the Islamic Hire and Purchase Bill, 1990 which was forwarded to the Ministry of Trade to be tabled at the Malaysian Parliament.

Bank Negara granted approval for a syndicate of banks in Malaysia to issue corporate bonds for a multinational company on the Islamic principle of *bai bithaman ajil* in 1990. To create an active market for this Islamic financial instrument, the syndicate was allowed to trade in the notes amongst institutions approved by Bank Negara under the Islamic concept of *bai' al-dayn* (debt-trading). Since then, Bank Negara has approved two more Islamic papers.[155]

8.10   *Takaful* Insurance in Malaysia

The *Takaful* Act introduced by the Malaysian Government in 1984, was enacted to provide for the registration and regulation of *takaful*

---

[155]Rahman, Azizan Abdul and Idris, Rustam Mohd, "Overview of the Malaysian financial system and the development of Islamic banking in Malaysia", *Bank Negara Malaysia* (http://faculty.unitarklj1.edu.my/home-page/coursewareweb/BEB2213/lesson12/note.htm).

businesses in Malaysia and for other purposes relating to or connected with *takaful*. *Takaful*, it will be recalled, is the term used to describe insurance schemes that are Shari'ah compliant. In this instance, section 2 of the *Takaful* Act defines *takaful* as "a scheme based on brotherhood, solidarity and mutual assistance which provides for mutual financial aid and assistance to the participants in case of need whereby the participants mutually agree to contribute for that purpose."[156]

In Malaysia, *takaful* insurance is not conducted through brokers or agents but directly by employees of *Syarikat Takaful Malaysia*, through desks at Bank Islam branches, and at sixteen *Tabung Haji* offices.[157]

In Malaysia, there are two forms of *takaful* insurance:

(i) General *Takaful* Insurance

Under general *takaful* insurance, the types of cover offered are fire, motor, accident, marine, personal accident, workers' compensation and employers' liability. The participant determines the amount for which he wishes to insure, and pays his *takaful* contribution to the company. The amount of contribution is assessed on the value of the asset to be covered. The contract runs for one year and specifies that any profit will be shared in a given ratio if the participant does not make any claims. The company pools all contributions and invests them in *halah* investments. The participants agree that the company shall pay compensation from the general fund to any fellow participant who might suffer a loss, and also operational costs.

(ii) Family *Takaful*

This is an investment programme to provide *halah* investment returns to the participant as well as mutual financial aid. Individuals participate to save regularly a sum of money to provide

---

[156] "What is Takaful", The Malaysian Insurance Institute.

[157] Hussain, op. cit., p. 191.

for dependants if they should die prematurely, or as a contingency savings if they survive to maturity of the plan. The plan may be taken for terms of ten, fifteen or twenty years. Participants must be between the ages of eighteen and fifty years, and the plan must mature before the participant reaches sixty years.

The contract is also based on the *mudarabah* principle. This is a partnership where one partner gives money to another to invest in a commercial enterprise: the investment comes from the first partner (the *rabb-ul-mal*), whilst the management and work is the exclusive responsibility of the other (the *mudarib*). The participant decides the amount of insurance required and the amount he wishes to pay and the company determines the minimum amount of installment (RM$15 per month in 1988). The company maintains two accounts, the Participant's Account (PA), into which as much as 95 per cent of the participant's contributions are paid as savings and investment, and a Participant's Special Account (PSA) where the balance of the contribution is credited as *tabarru'* (donation) for the payment out of compensation to claimants. The proportion credited to each account depends on the age group of the participant and the maturity period of the policy and is worked out by actuaries. The PA operates as a kind of savings account while PSA is a form of mutual fund.[158]

8.11 Conclusion

Islamic banking has been available in Malaysia since 1983 and to date, Islamic banking products are available at two full-pledge Islamic banks as well as at all commercial and merchant banks in Malaysia. Deputy Finance Minister Datuk Shafie Mohd Salleh regards the Financial Sector Masterplan's target for the Islamic Banking and *takaful* industry to achieve 20 per cent share of the total banking system by 2010 to be within reach.[159]

---

[158]Ibid.

[159]The Star (Malaysia), op. cit.

Could Malaysia become a role model for countries like Britain, which is looking to integrate Islamic banking with its conventional banking system? This is certainly the opinion of experts like David Vicary, the former director of financial services in Deloitte Kassim Chan, a professional services firm in Kuala Lumpur.[160]

"These countries are now looking at Malaysia," he says, noting that Kuala Lumpur is serious about setting up a proper Islamic banking framework in terms of products as well as legal and accounting infrastructure, "unlike the fragmented or ad hoc Islamic banking attempts in some Muslim countries."

Vicary notes that surveys show demand for Islamic banking is increasing globally at an estimated compounded annual growth rate of 15 per cent. He adds that there is strong desire to relocate Arab funds currently residing in New York, London, Frankfurt and Paris to Shari'ah-compliant financial centres such as Kuala Lumpur.

Malaysia, which has steadily developed integrated, or dual, banking systems has the potential to be one of the most suitable candidates for these migrating funds. "The Labuan International Offshore Financial Centre, under the guidance of the Labuan Offshore Financial Services Authority, is one of the attractive plays for these potential funds to reside in," adds Vicary.

Another plus point for Malaysia is the IFSB, an association of central banks, monetary authorities and other institutions that regulate the Islamic financial services industry. Established in Kuala Lumpur in November 2002, the board's members include a strong list of international players. "The presence of the IFSB in Malaysia could significantly raise the attractiveness of the marketplace in Malaysia," notes Vicary.

Bank Negara Malaysia has awarded the first foreign licence for a full-fledged Islamic bank in Malaysia to Kuwait Finance House

---

[160]"Dual Banking System Attracts Global Interest" (2003), *Malaysia Industrial Development Authority*. (http://www.mida.gov.my/beta/news/print_news.php?id=407), 13 June 2003.

(KFH) which will allow the Kuwait-based bank to open up a new foreign Islamic bank in Malaysia. The move, which is part of the overall efforts to strengthen the integration of Malaysia's Islamic banks into the global system, will effectively open up part of Malaysia's banking sector to foreign competition three years ahead of its World Trade Organisation deadline. A market leader in the Islamic banking industry in Kuwait, KFH provides a large spectrum of services that includes real estate financing, lease financing, trade finance and portfolio investing. The expedited liberalisation on licensing reflected the government's belief that Malaysia has already developed a competitive, world-class Islamic banking system. According to Bank Negara, the central bank, the decision to open up the industry to foreign players sooner than 2007 was made following the robust achievement of the Islamic financial industry in the country.[161]

In June 2003, Bank Negara said it would issue new Islamic banking licences to foreign banks active in the global Islamic banking sector. Governor Zeti Akhtar Aziz says the move "will promote greater competition and act as a bridge between Malaysia and other global Islamic financial markets."[162]

Malaysia's Islamic banking system enjoyed a bumper year in 2004 with total assets of the sector increasing to RM94.6 billion — 10.5 per cent of the total assets of the banking system. The market share of Islamic banking deposits and financing, according to Bank Negara Malaysia, the central bank, had increased to 11.2 per cent and 11.3 per cent respectively for the year ending 31 December 2004.

To date, the Malaysian Islamic banking sector is on course for Bank Negara's target for the sector to reach a market share of

---

[161]Saifuddin, Sadna, "Kuwait finance house secures Islamic banking licence" (2004), *New Straits Times (M) Berhad* (http://www.nst.com.my), 17 June 2004.

[162]"Role model: Malaysia is showing the world how to integrate conventional and Islamic banking systems", *The Asian Banker Journal*, Issue 41, 2003, p. 17.

20 per cent by the year 2010. Latest figures from the central bank suggest that the Malaysian Islamic banking sector has been growing rapidly over the last five years, averaging 19 per cent per annum.

The total capital base of the sector increased from RM6.8 billion in 2003 to RM7.8 billion in 2004; and as previously noted, the total assets of the Islamic banking system amounted to RM94.6 billion — up 15 per cent on the year; similarly risk-weighted assets of the sector increased by 20.4 per cent to RM62.5 billion for the same period. Total Islamic banking financing amounted to RM57.9 billion — some 61.2 per cent of total Islamic banking assets. Asset quality of the sector too improved in 2004 with gross and net non-performing loans (NPL) ratios decreasing from 8.5 per cent to 8.1 per cent and from 5.5 per cent to 5.3 per cent respectively.[163]

It is interesting to note that Malaysian Islamic banking assets are half the total Islamic banking assets in the Gulf Cooperation Council (consists of Bahrain, Kuwait, Qatar, Saudi Arabia and United Arab Emirates) in 2004 — quite a significant base for Islamic banking and finance in South-east Asia.

Also, approximately 82% of Islamic fixed income securities globally were issued out of Malaysia.[164]

Malaysia has now become the largest Islamic banking market in the world, with an Islamic money market monthly volume of RM30–40 billion.[165]

---

[163]Parker, Mushtak, "Malaysia's Islamic Banking Enjoys another Bumper Year", *Arab News*, (http://arabnews.com/?page=6&section=0&article=66788&d=11&m=7&y=2005), 11 July 2005.

[164]Report of the Islamic Capital Market Task Force of the IOSCO as of 31 December 2003 and ISI Emerging Markets as of 31 December 2005.

[165]Ghani, Badlisyah Abdul, "South East Asia: The Islamic Finance Growth Story", presented at the Islamic Finance Singapore 2006 conference held in Singapore from 21–22 February 2006.

Chapter 9

Islamic Banking in Indonesia

Indonesia has come to Islamic, or Shari'ah-compliant, banking fairly late. This is despite the fact that Indonesia, as a country, has the world's largest population of Muslims, 210 million[166] out of a global Muslim population of 1.254 billion[167] in 2004. The reasons for this are various, not least the fact that many of Indonesia's Muslim leaders do not believe that commercial interest, in its modern form, is prohibited. Such a view reflects, in part, the singular nature of Islamic belief in Indonesia. At the same time, it is also a reflection of Indonesia's secular constitution, which clearly separates religion from government. Modern Indonesians by and large subscribe to the five principles of *pancasila*, formulated by the country's first president, Sukarno, in 1945 as the basis of Indonesian public life. They are: belief in one God, national unity, humanitarianism, democracy based on consensus and representation, and social justice. Naturally, the inherent vagueness of the *pancasila* ideology has allowed for many interpretations over the years, but from the beginning, the newly independent Republic of Indonesia was conceived as a secular state despite an overwhelming Muslim majority. Which is not to say that Islam is an unimportant element in Indonesian politics, or that Islamic parties are absent from the political scene; far from it. From the very beginning of the post-war era there have been calls from Islamicists to make Indonesia an Islamic state, notably when the

---

[166]*The World Factbook 2004*, Central Intelligence Agency.

[167]*Encyclopædia Britannica Book of the Year 2004*.

constitution was first drawn up; following the abortive 1965 "communist" coup; and in the wake of the collapse of the Suharto regime in 1998.

Indeed, militant Islamicists, who at various times have called for the formation of an Islamic state have always been perceived as a threat to national security, especially on the part of the Western-educated elite who have dominated Indonesian politics ever since General Sukarno's unilateral declaration of independence in August 1945.

9.1   Islam and Government in Indonesia

Indonesia was one of the earliest parts of South-east Asia to receive Islam, though the actual process was sporadic and piecemeal. The earliest states in the region were Hindu-Buddhist kingdoms, with Hinduism and Buddhism having been introduced to South-east Asia by Indian merchant adventurers around the first century AD. Their conversion to Islam was a gradual one. Arab traders were doing business in various parts of the archipelago from the sixth century onwards but the actual process of Islamisation did not begin until the thirteenth century with the conversion of the ruler of Aceh in northern Sumatra. Gradually, Islam spread to other entrepôt city-states stretched out along the principle maritime trade routes of the Indonesian Archipelago, notably the northern coast of Java, and the spice islands of Maluku—Ternate, Tidore and Bandar. By the early part of the sixteenth century, the process was more or less complete, leaving only the island of Bali as the last bastion of Hindu-Buddhism in the archipelago.

But just as the reception of Hinduism and Buddhism in Indonesia had been coloured by local belief systems, so too in the case of Islam, and from the outset the Muslim faith in Indonesia diverged significantly from the orthodoxies of Islam in, say, the Arabian Peninsula. Elements of Hindu-Buddhism continued to flourish alongside more ancient animistic beliefs, while in-coming

Islamic traditions were given a distinctly Indonesian spin. This is a situation that has persisted until today, particularly in Java.

The highly syncretic nature of Islam in Indonesia has meant a more than relaxed attitude towards the Shari'ah, which may be one of the reasons why Islamic banking has been so slow in coming to the region. In the past, several well-respected Indonesian intellectuals, including former Vice President Hatta, have argued that the prohibition of *riba* is not the same as interest charged or offered by modern commercial banks. Whilst Islamic jurists in Indonesia have naturally opposed this view, the greater Muslim public seems somewhat indifferent to the issue.

Another important factor has been the de-politicising of Indonesian society during successive Sukarno and Suharto regimes. Although independent Indonesia was founded along the lines of liberal democracy, with a multi-party parliamentary system, a free press and freedom of organisation including the formation of trade unions, the country's first president, General Sukarno, was very much opposed to a Western style of governance, which he saw as at variance with Indonesian cultural values of harmony and consensus. A breakdown of parliamentary democracy in the mid-1950s as a result of widespread discontent with the government's failure to deliver the revolutionary promises of 1945 — mainly prosperity for all — gave Sukarno the opportunity to implement his programme of "Guided Democracy" with a balanced political party representation in parliament whose representatives were drawn from various "functional groups", which included peasants, workers, Muslim scholars and the military, as well as numerous minority groups. Perhaps inevitably, the armed forces group, known as Golka, quickly rose to the top — the army had always played a significant role in Indonesian political life from the earliest days of independence, riding high on its popular acclaim as a people's revolutionary army, which had ousted the Dutch colonialists from power.

The army's put down of the attempted communist coup of 1965 and the replacement of President Sukarno's "Old Order" regime by President Suharto's "New Order" government only served to strengthen the position of Golka in the scheme of things. Although regular elections were held every five years from 1971 onwards, Golka always enjoyed the benefits of government funding and the full support of Indonesia's extensive bureaucracy, while opposition parties were subject to rigorous vetting. Unsurprisingly, Golka invariably romped home with two-thirds or more of the vote in every election held between 1971 and 1997.

Having effectively disposed of the Indonesian Communist Party (PKI) in the bloodletting of 1965, Suharto's government saw militant Islam as its next-biggest threat — the 1970s and 1980s were of course a time of Islamic revival partly as a result of the Iranian revolution and partly reflecting a more general resurgence of Islam in the Middle East. Consequently, every effort was made to promote *pancasila* as the sole ideological basis for any form of political or social organisation in the country. The Golka-led political consensus was hailed as *pancasila* democracy, and school and university students were obliged to pass exams in *pancasila*, as did civil servants and members of the armed forces. Although the more fervent Islamicists never abandoned their hope for an Islamic state, the vast majority of Indonesians accepted the status quo vis-à-vis their religious beliefs, acknowledging the fact that Indonesia could never become one because of the religious diversity from one end of the archipelago to the other, and not least within the Muslim community.

The collapse of the Suharto regime in 1998 brought a possibility that things might change, especially with the success of the Party of National Awakening, a modernist Islamic party led by Abdurrahman Wahid, which was runner-up to the Indonesian Democratic Struggle party, led by Megawati Sukarnoputri, daughter of former president Sukarno (Golka finished a poor third). The subsequent election of Wahid as president in October that year further raised the profile of Islam-based parties in post-Suharto Indonesian politics — Wahid was a Muslim cleric, who was educated in Indonesia, Egypt, Iraq and Canada and had a reputation for religious tolerance and moderate politics. Unfortunately, after twenty months of weak and indecisive rule he was removed from office by the People's Consultive Assembly and Vice-President Megawati Sukarnoputri became the new president in his place.

After years of upheaval following the overthrow of former President Suharto, President Megawati presided over a period of relative stability. However in late 2004, she was replaced by Dr. Susilo Bambang Yudhoyono, the senior minister in charge of political and security affairs then. Corruption is still rife, problems associated with separatist movements in Aceh and Papua persist, and there is the ever-present threat of further terrorist violence.

9.2   Traditional Islamic Financial Institutions in Indonesia

After some false starts, Islamic financial institutions are developing rapidly and have the enthusiastic support of many young people and intellectuals. The work of the Shari'ah Bureau of Bank Indonesia demonstrates that Indonesia, especially in particular parts of the country, has considerable unmet demand for Islamic banking.

There are interest-free financial institutions operating in Indonesia. One form of traditional interest-free borrowing is the still widely prevalent form of informal rural credit known as *ijon*[168] because the loan is secured on the standing crop.[169] Another is the *arisan* system practised among consumers and small craftsmen and traders. In this system, each member contributes regularly a certain sum and obtains interest-free loans from the pool by drawing lots.

---

[168]This is the unjust system of sharecropping at plantations. Farmers grew food crops on unused land in the plantations, but were forced to sell the harvest to the plantation company cheaply before it was ready.

[169]For a description, see Partadireja, Ace, "Rural credit, the Ijon system", *Bulletin of Indonesian Economic Studies*, Vol. 10, No. 3, 1974, pp. 54–71.

9.3 Introduction of Measures to Permit Islamic Banking in Indonesia

The present government in Indonesia seems to associate Islamic banking with Islamic fundamentalism to which the regime is not at all sympathetic.

In order to accommodate the public demand for the existence of a new banking system, the Indonesian Government has implicitly allowed the Shari'ah banking operations in the Act No. 7 of 1992 concerning banking which is elucidated in the Government Decree No. 72 of 1992 concerning Bank Applying Share Base Principles. The set of regulations have served as legal foundations for Shari'ah banking operations in Indonesia (the new era of dual banking system).

In 1998, the Act No. 10 of 1998 on the amendment of the Act No. 7 of 1992 concerning banking came into force to give stronger legal foundation for the existence of Shari'ah banking system. The new Act No. 23 of 1999 concerning Bank Indonesia gives an authority to Bank Indonesia to also conduct its task according to Shari'ah principles.[170]

9.4 Contemporary Indonesian Islamic Financial Institutions

Indonesia has a small market and loyal customers of Islamic banks. Bank Indonesia ideally wants Islamic banks to reach a 5 per cent market share over the next ten years. Currently there are two fully Islamic banks and about eight Shari'ah branches of conventional banks. The trend of conventional banks opening Shari'ah branches started with the enactment of dual system banking by the government in 1998.[171]

---

[170]*Bank Indonesia*, op. cit.

[171]Aurora, Leony, "Shari'ah banks should invite foreign investors or go public" (2004), *Jakarta Post* (http://www.thejakartapost.com/), 17 June 2004.

Islamic financial institutions in Indonesia include: the Bank Muamallat Indonesia which has been functioning since 1992, several new Islamic branches of regular commercial banks and at least one bank just converted from the interest system, eighty Bank Perkreditan Rakyat Shariyah (BPRS — smaller banks limited to borrowing and lending in limited areas), and 2470 Bait Maal Wat Tamwil (BMT — Islamic Savings and Loan Cooperatives of which about 200 are reported to be registered with the Ministry of Cooperatives and Small Business). The Islamic commercial banks and BPRS file frequent and detailed reports with Bank Indonesia and thus produce reliable and current statistics. This is not yet the case with BMT.[172]

Bank Indonesia has established an Islamic Banking Development Committee comprising Oversight Committee, Expert Committee and Working Committee. It has also recorded and assessed the existing regulatory instruments in order to develop a more comprehensive set of rules and regulations. These measures are intended to foster a conducive environment for the development of Islamic banking.

Other than that, Bank Indonesia has also issued or is currently developing the issuance of decrees by the Board of Managing Directors concerning Islamic commercial and rural banks which have provided legal framework in developing and expanding the network of Islamic banks. In addition, there is the issuance of regulations on operational guidance for Islamic banks and conducting assessment on the development of prudential banking regulations and developing accounting standards for Islamic banks. Lastly, Bank Indonesia has been active in educating the public in the Islamic banking concept as an alternative interest-free system which is becoming popular around the world.

The response of the public has been overwhelming and with this, the industry is seeing some significant changes in the fate of the Islamic banking industry. Further research is taking place on

---

[172]Timberg, June 1999, op. cit.

the voice of the public to help in the further growth of Islamic banking in Indonesia. Recent surveys show that the public has a better understanding now and is in favour of the *riba*-free, Shari'ah-compliant system.[173]

9.5 The Introduction of Standard Accounting Procedures

As of today, there are a number of banks delivering Shari'ah banking in Indonesia, namely Bank Mandiri, Bank Danamon, Bank Muamalat Malaysia Berhad and Bank IFI. The Islamic banking sector continues to provide similar banking and finance facilities which conventional banks have been providing but in accordance with Shari'ah law.

PT Sigma Cipta Caraka (SCC) and Association Syariah Banks in Indonesia (ASBISINDO) is collaborating to support the application of Standard Accounting Procedure for Shari'ah Banking 59 (PSAK 59).

According to the chairman of ASBISINDO, Wahyu Dwi Agung, PSAK 59 stems from the development of Shari'ah banking in Indonesia. It is built on the principles of AAOIFI. PSAK is an interesting issue in Shari'ah banking, as it integrates the principles of accounting with the unique features of Shari'ah banking.

As previously discussed, absence of accounting (and auditing) standards pertinent to Islamic banks, causes uncertainty in accounting principles which involve revenue realisation, disclosures of accounting information, accounting bases, valuation, revenue and expense matching, etc. Thus the results of Islamic banking schemes may not be adequately defined, particularly in the profit and loss shares attributed to depositors.

---

[173] "Islamic banking: The Indonesian experience", www.halah.com.my, 15 December 2000.

Those Islamic banks which are audited by public accountants tend to disclose considerable information, but, not enough. For instance, due to the negative posture towards interest income, alternative sources of revenue probably should be disclosed, but may not be.[174]

9.6   Forms of Lending and Borrowing in Indonesia

The Indonesian Islamic institutions take a variety of funds from depositors on which they pay various sums connected with their profits. They lend on various bases in ways that involve sharing risks with their clients. The following list details the various borrowing and lending instruments used by Bank Muamallat (Indonesia), Indonesia's first Shari'ah commercial bank, as summarised in its 1998 Annual Report.

9.6.1   *Lending Forms*

Advance Purchase Forms

- Cost Plus Financing — *Murabaha*
  Murabaha is a sales contract made between the bank and the customer for the sale of goods at a price which includes a profit margin agreed to by both parties. As a financing technique it involves the purchase of goods by the bank as requested by the customer. Repayment is conducted by installments within a specified period.
- Purchase with Specification — *Istishna*
  Istishna is a sales contract between the bank and the customer where the customer specifies goods to be made. After the goods are made or shipped the bank sells them to the customer according to a pre-agreed arrangement.

---

[174]Haqiqi, Abdul Wassay and Pomeranz, Felix, "Accounting needs of Islamic banking" (2000), *IBFNet* (http://islamic-finance.net/islamicethics/article-12.html), 17 June 2004.

- Purchase with Deferred Delivery — *Bai al Salam*
  Bai al Salam is a sales contract where the price is paid in advance by the bank and the goods delivered later by the customer to a designee.
- Lease and Hire Purchase — *Ijarah Mutahia Bittamlik*
  Ijarah Mutahia Bittamlik is a contract under which the bank leases equipment to a customer for a rental fee. It is pre-agreed that at the end of the lease period the customer will buy the equipment at an agreed price from the bank, with the rental fees already paid being part of the price.

9.6.2 *Profit-Sharing Forms*

- Trust Financing/Trustee Profit Sharing — *Mudharabah/ Mudharabah Muqayyadah*
  In this instance, the bank provides the capital (*shahibul maal*) and the customer manages (*mudharib*) the project. The profit from the project is split according to a pre-agreed ratio.
- Partnership/Participation Financing — *Musyarakah*
  This is a partnership between a bank and its customer in which profits are shared on a pre-agreed basis, but losses are shared on the basis of equity contribution. Management of the partnership may be done either by the bank, the customer, jointly, or by a third party.
- Benevolent Loan — *Qard al Hasan*
  These are interest-free loans, generally with a charitable motivation.
- Collateral Agreement — *Rahn*
  In this instance an agreement is made to provide collateral to the bank, either in the bank's or the customer's custody as appropriate. This is connected with some other form of lending.
- Agency/Trust — *Wakalah*
  This is an agreement authorising another party to be an agent to conduct some business — in this case, an authorisation to the bank to conduct some business on the customer's behalf.

- Agency — *Havalah*

  This is an agreement made by the bank to undertake some of the liabilities of the customer. When the liabilities mature, the customer pays back the bank. The bank is paid a fee for undertaking the liabilities concerned.

9.6.3 Borrowing Forms

- *Ummat* Savings — *Tabungan Ummat*

  This comprises a savings account from which money can be withdrawn any time at any *muamalat temiz* or ATM. Customers share in the bank's revenue. The *Ummat* Savings customers also receive life insurance and the opportunity to win a free *Umrah* (pilgrimage) to Mecca.

- *Trendi* Savings — *Tabungan Trendi*

  These are savings accounts for teenagers and students. Besides accident insurance coverage, it offers special prizes for high-ranked students and one-year scholarships for fifty students.

- *Ukhuwah* Savings — *Tabungan Ukhuwah*

  This is a savings account which is conducted in cooperation with Dompet Dhuafa Republika for convenience in making regular and automatic *zakat*, *infaq* and *shadaqat* payments by means of a choice of three packages: Rp. 25 000, Rp. 50 000 and Rp. 100 000. This saving can also give the depositor an ATM, shopping discounts at certain shops and accident insurance coverage.

- *Arafah* Savings — *Tabungan Arafah*

  This is a savings account specifically designed for the Haj pilgrimage. The saving scheme helps customers to plan their Haj in accordance with their financial capability and intended Haj date. Life insurance is also provided. The depositors are also eligible for various prizes.

- *Fulinves* Deposits — *Deposito Fulinves*

  This is a time deposit with a revenue-sharing package. It is available for various terms and with a chance for various prizes. Life insurance is provided to those with long-term deposits.

- *Wadi'ah* Current Account — *Giro Wadi'ah*
  This is a current account which provides cheque facilities, whilst allowing some profit-sharing.
- Muamallat Financial Institution Pension Fund — Dana Pensiun Lembaga Keuangan
  This is a pension fund for those who make regular deposits. Bank Muamallat Indonesia soon intends to add a variant which will offer life insurance.

9.7   Conclusion

Islamic banking only became available in Indonesia in the mid-1990s. Previously former Presidents Sukarno and Suharto had been unwilling to support the introduction of Islamic law for banking, on the basis of the country's racial and religious diversity.

Whilst it is now a relatively small percentage of overall banking, it is growing rapidly as Indonesian Muslims embrace Islamic principles. In 2003, demand for Islamic banking grew by 85 per cent to seven and a half billion Rupia. Not to be left out, some established banks are now also offering Islamic financial products, with the emphasis on investments only being made in *Halal* goods and services.

The World Bank says special care needs to be taken in Indonesia given its recent banking fiascos.[175] The progress of Islamic banking in Indonesia is impeded by the lack of comprehensive and appropriate framework and instruments for regulation and supervision, limited market coverage, lack of knowledge and understanding by the public, lack of efficient institutional structure supporting efficient

---

[175]Robertson, Hamish, "Sharia banking grows in Indonesia" (2004), *ABC Online (Australia)* (http://www.abc.net.au/am/content/2004/s1130581.htm), 2004.

Shari'ah banking operations; operational inefficiency, domination of non-share base financing and limiting capability to comply with international Shari'ah financial standards.[176]

A blueprint was drawn in 2002 to develop Islamic banking and the Indonesian Capital Market Master Plan 2005–2009 was designed to develop Shari'ah-based capital market products.

The Shari'ah bond market was first introduced in 2002 with issuance amounting to Rp 175 billion (US$18.8 million) by PT Indosat Tbk.

Currently, Islamic banking assets have experienced rapid expansion to US$1.7 billion as compared to US$874.4 million in 2003, reflecting a 94.4 per cent growth. This resulted in an increase of Islamic banking assets from 0.7 per cent to 1.2 per cent in total banking assets. According to Burhanuddin Abdullah, Governor of Bank Indonesia:[177]

"Islamic banks reported a 79% increase year on year to Rp 8.76 trillion (US$1.36 billion) in business volume, and Islamic or syariah bank offices rose 50% in number to 349 units extending Rp 5.9 trillion in credits in January 2004."

Indonesia's central bank forecasts Islamic banking assets will expand by more than 12 folds by 2011 from $1.48 billion to $18.2 billion, or 2 per cent of total banking assets to between 5 to 9 per cent.

The authorities would like to see an aggressive development such that they are projecting that by 2011, Islamic assets will be 9 per cent of the total assets in the entire Indonesia banking system.

---

[176] *Bank Indonesia*, op. cit.

[177] 8 August 2006.

The future of Islamic banking and finance in Indonesia is huge considering that 85 per cent of its total population of 238 million people are Muslims.

As at June 2005, there were 15 Shari'ah fixed income securities issuances with a total value of Rp 1.95 trillion (US$200.2 million).[178]

---

[178]Ghani, op. cit.

Chapter 10

Labuan: A Niche in the Islamic Money Market

The 87-square-kilometre island of Labuan (population around 60 000), off the coast of Sabah, is geographically placed at the epicentre of the Asia Pacific region. Labuan originally came under the rule of the Brunei Sultanate. The British then officially declared Labuan a colony of the British Empire in 1849 and renamed it Victoria. The British lost its hold over Labuan in 1942 when the Japanese invaded the island. Britain resumed power over Labuan three years later and subsequently ceded the island to Sabah in 1963 when Sabah joined Malaysia. The administration of Labuan was handed over to the Federal Government of Malaysia in 1984. In 1990, Labuan was declared an International Offshore Financial Centre (IOFC). It is a tax-free or low-tax alternative environment for non-resident entities — there are no withholding, capital gains, transfer wealth, gift or income taxes.[179]

Major banks in Labuan include Standard Chartered Bank, Hongkong and Shanghai Banking Corp Ltd, Bank of Tokyo-Mitsubishi Ltd, Fuji Bank Ltd, BNP Paribas, Dresdner Bank AG and Deutsche Bank AG. Local players include Arab-Malaysian Merchant Bank Bhd, Public Bank Ltd, Maybank International Ltd, RHB Bank Ltd, Danaharta Managers Ltd, Bumiputra-Commerce Bank Ltd, Schroders Malaysia Bhd, Citibank Malaysia Ltd, AMMB International Ltd, Bank Islam Ltd and JP Morgan Malaysia Ltd.

---

[179] www.labuan.net.

After 1 October 1990, when Labuan was established as an IOFC, the Federal Government took steps to improve the island's infrastructure in order to help assist its development as an IOFC. It is also the Malaysian Government's intention that Labuan should expand its business activities in the area of offshore Islamic financing and fund management. The proposed establishment of the Islamic money market is expected to boost Islamic-based investments and mutual fund activities. The primary objectives here are to tap into the global pool of under-performing Islamic funds and to provide alternative investment opportunities and products. With many available Islamic products already developed in the domestic market in Peninsular Malaysia, Labuan is in the position to offer competitive Islamic offshore financial products such as Islamic financing, *takaful* and re-*takaful* (insurance and reinsurance), Islamic trusts, Islamic investment funds and Islamic capital market instruments. Other Islamic products are gradually being developed in response to market needs and requirements. These Islamic products may be participated in freely by non-Muslims, who are also welcome to tap into the capacity created.

10.1 Role of Labuan Financial Services Authority

The Labuan Financial Services Authority (LOFSA) which was established in 1996, is the single regulatory authority in Labuan, with responsibility for spearheading and co-coordinating the development of the island's offshore industry. LOFSA is also responsible for setting objectives, policies, promotional and developmental aspects of Labuan.

Labuan does have its own set of offshore legislation. Beginning in 1990, the Federal Government enacted a number of statutes with the aim of promoting Labuan as an IOFC:

- Offshore Companies Act, 1990
- Labuan Offshore Business Activity Tax Act, 1990

- Offshore Banking Act, 1990
- Offshore Insurance Act, 1990
- Labuan Trust Companies Act, 1990
- Labuan Offshore Trust Act, 1996
- Labuan Offshore Limited Partnership Act, 1997
- Labuan Offshore Securities Industry Act, 1998

10.2   Labuan Offshore Companies

The Labuan Offshore Companies Act, 1990 allows the incorporation of an offshore company (LOC) or registration of an existing foreign company (i.e. company incorporated outside Malaysia) with no prior government approval, except in the case of offshore banking, insurance and mutual fund companies where licenses under the applicable regulatory environment are required. An offshore company may issue shares of different classes and denomination of shares may be in any world currency other than the Malaysian Ringgit. Except for offshore banks and offshore insurance companies, there is no minimum capital requirement.

10.3   Currency and Exchange Control

The offshore transactions carried out in Labuan must be in any currency other than Malaysian Ringgit except for defraying any administrative and statutory expenses and certain allowable investments in Malaysian domestic companies. There are no exchange controls on any foreign currency.

10.4   Tax Incentives

Labuan offshore entities are exempted from withholding tax, stamp duty and any indirect taxes such as sales tax, import duties, surtax, excise duties and export duties. The Labuan Offshore Business Activity Tax Act, 1990 provides for special tax incentives for offshore companies carrying out offshore business activity such as banking, insurance or leasing in or from Labuan. An offshore company has the option of paying 3 per cent tax on net audited profits or a lump sum of RM20 000 per year of assessment. The election to pay at 3 per cent or RM20 000 is on an annual basis. On the other hand, an offshore company involved in offshore non-trading activity, such as investment holding, is exempt from tax.

10.5   Labuan International Financial Exchange

The establishment of the Labuan International Financial Exchange (LFX) is expected to further promote Labuan as a significant financial centre. The primary objective of LFX is to provide listing facilities for funds and other permitted financial instruments launched in Labuan and abroad.

The proposed activities of the LFX will include:

- Banking and investment banking
- Money broking
- Trusts
- Leasing and factoring business
- Fund management
- Insurance and reinsurance and other insurance-related activities
- Management companies
- Islamic financial services and instruments

The goal of LFX is to facilitate the influx of funds through the listing and trading of financial instruments. To achieve its stated goal, LFX will strive to be recognised as investor friendly, be market driven and transparent and to utilise international networking communication systems.

Its purpose is to cater for the changing needs of global investors and companies, the listing of a multitude of multi-currency financial instruments, companies wishing to raise capital effectively and efficiently in line with the concept of globalisation and liberalisation.

LFX aims at providing opportunities for global investors and companies by providing a funding mechanism for international companies operating in the Asia-Pacific region, the listing of conventional and Islamic instruments, the availability of multi-currency securities and instruments, flexibility of trading and free from selective controls for international investors.[180]

10.6 Moving Forward with Islamic Banking

The International Islamic Financial Market (IIFM) began operations in April 2002, arising from a cooperative agreement between the Islamic Development Bank, Bahrain Monetary Agency, the Central Bank of Indonesia, the LOFSA (representing Malaysia), the Central Bank of Sudan and the Ministry of Finance of Brunei Darussalam. The primary purpose of the IIFM is to provide a cooperative framework to ensure the continued growth of an Islamic financial market, based on Shari'ah rules and principles, as a viable alternative to the conventional banking system.

The roles of the IIFM are as follows:

(i) To promote the harmonisation and convergence of Shari'ah interpretations in developing Islamic banking products and practices which are universally acceptable.
(ii) To encourage a large number of Islamic financial institutions to participate in the market by introducing a wide range of Shari'ah-compliant products and the creation of an active secondary market thus providing liquidity to the instruments traded in the market.

It is designed to be a network of Islamic money markets which will be able to meet the liquidity needs of Islamic financial institutions worldwide engaged in international finance. It is anticipated

---

[180]http://lfxsys.lfx.com.my/.

that the establishment of IIFM will encourage the expansion of business and dealings between Islamic nations and generate spin-offs for the overall development of the Islamic capital market. The successful implementation of IIFM depends entirely on the concerted efforts between the governments of Islamic countries and the private Islamic bankers.

The IIFM will abide by Islamic Shari'ah rules and principles, which forbid investment in such sectors as alcohol, tobacco and gambling, as well as companies whose earnings are all or partly derived from interest, such as financial and insurance firms.

10.7   Conclusion

In May 2003, LFX signed a "Memorandum of Understanding" (MOU) with the Bahrain Stock Exchange (BSE) with the objective to further jointly promote and develop the Islamic capital market leading to the dual and/or secondary listing of instruments on both exchanges. A positive outcome of the MOU is the secondary listing of the Malaysian Government US$600 million Sukuk Al-Ijarah on the BSE in September 2003, following an earlier secondary listing on the LFX in September 2002. These secondary listings on BSE were expected to be reciprocated in the near future with listings of Bahraini Sukuk on the LFX.

LFX has also signed an MOU with the Bahrain-based IIFM on 19 January 2004. The objective of the MOU is to set a framework for greater co-operation between LFX and IIFM to pave the way for both organisations to jointly develop an Islamic Capital Market with an enhanced global reach. The MOU is set to promote development of channels of communications and exchange of information and collaboration in the listing and active secondary trading of Islamic financial instruments.

By playing a pivotal role in creating an environment that will encourage cross-border trading of Shari'ah-compliant instruments, the IIFM's principal objective is to develop an active international financial market based on Shari'ah rules and principles.[181]

To date, eleven offshore companies were incorporated in Labuan in 2005 to raise foreign debt. Of these, eight were listed on the Labuan International Financial Exchange (LFX) with a cumulative market capitalisation of US$2.4 billion, which brought the total number of listings on the LFX to 31 with an aggregate market capitalisation of US$12.5 billion. Listings for the year under review included debt and equity-linked instruments and Islamic debt certificates (Sukuk), as well as first preference shares. The Malaysian Government and domestic corporations, including Government-Linked Companies, formed the major group of issuers.

Efforts continued to be directed at further developing Islamic banking in Labuan IOFC, in line with the strategic move to promote Islamic finance in the Labuan IOFC to strengthen Malaysia's position as an international Islamic financial hub. In 2005, there were three full-fledged Islamic offshore banks and three Islamic investment banks operating in Labuan. As at end-2005, the total Islamic banking assets of the industry, including those of conventional offshore banks with Islamic windows, accounted to US$708.9 million (2004: US$678.7 million), and represented 3.9 per cent of the total assets of the offshore banking industry (2004: 3.4 per cent).[182]

---

[181]www.iifm.net.

[182]Labuan Offshore Financial Services Authority (LOFSA) Annual Report of the Members of the Authority for the Year Ended 31 December 2005, LOFSA.

Chapter 11

Islamic Banking in Brunei

11.1 Introduction

The Sultanate of Brunei Darussalam (the Abode of Peace) is situated on the north-west coast of the island of Borneo, at 5 degrees North of the equator. The total area of 5769 square kilometres borders Sarawak in Malaysia, and the South China Sea.

European presence in the south-east region grew around the mid-sixteenth century, and from the end of the sixteenth century to the nineteenth century, Brunei began to lose its grip on the empire, which was besieged by problems such as wars, internecine strife, insurrection and piracy. By 1904, Brunei which had become a British protected State in 1888, had shrunk to a small Sultanate surrounded on three sides by Sarawak and to the north by the South China Sea.

Sultan Omar Ali Saifuddien was the twenty-eighth Sultan of Brunei. His rule lasted from 1950 to 1967 during which period his vision and prudence propelled Brunei towards prosperity and modernity.

The early 1960s saw a series of talks taking place on Tunku Abdul Rahman's proposal to group the Federated Malay States, Singapore, Sarawak, Sabah and Brunei Darussalam into a federation called Malaysia, which was formed in 1963. It was a period of transition but the Sultan was keen to maintain a separate Bruneian identity and opposed all attempts made to merge Brunei with Sarawak and North Borneo.

Sultan Omar Ali Saifuddien abdicated in 1967, paving the way for his eldest son, the current sultan to ascend the throne as the twenty-ninth Sultan of Brunei. Brunei Darussalam resumed its international responsibilities as a fully independent and sovereign nation shortly after midnight on 31 December 1983, after almost one hundred years of British protection.

From 1984 onwards, Brunei Darussalam attained membership with ASEAN, OIC, the Commonwealth and the United Nations.

Islam was enshrined in the Brunei Constitution during its unique constitutional status of a British-protected Malay sultanate. In this instance, the law applicable to Muslims is contained in legislation which is a copy of the Kelantan (Peninsular Malaysia) Act. The advantage of this model for Brunei is that it gives scope to indigenous customary law (*adat-isiadat*) relating to the ranking and function of royal and semi-royal sets of traditional officials.

The tiny Sultanate of Brunei followed Malaysia's example in 1985 when the Sultan decreed an Islamic banking option. Although the government did not actually put an Islamic bank into operation until 1992, it has actively supported that bank and has provided subsidies that permit it to pay competitively attractive dividends to depositors. A profitable Islamic insurance sector has also been established.

Political stability and the vision of His Majesty the Sultan and Yang DiPertuan have made it possible for Brunei Darussalam to achieve sustainable economic prosperity and stability which has benefited the whole population. Brunei Darussalam continues to register reasonable growth despite the turmoil of oil prices and the financial crisis in Asia. Central to this economic achievement is the government's Five-Year National Development Plans, which provide strategic guidelines and direction for the economy. The country continues to pursue an economic diversification policy away from the traditional reliance on the oil and gas sector in order to enjoy rapid growth like that of its partners in the Asia-Pacific Region (APR).

11.2   Brunei International Financial Corporation (BIFC)

Brunei has for many years been a significant player in the ASEAN region. Its very strong ties with the United Kingdom, Singapore and regional countries have led to the build-up of considerable commercial activity. The economy has been dominated by the oil and liquefied natural gas industries and government expenditure patterns. Brunei Darussalam's exports consist of three major commodities, namely: crude oil, petroleum products and liquefied natural gas. Exports are destined mainly for Japan, the United States and ASEAN countries. Recently, however, the country has entered a new phase of development in its drive towards economic diversification and maturity.

Unlike many IFCs, Brunei has the advantage of already being an affluent society, which means that the country's motives in establishing an IFC regime are more subtle and socio-economic in nature than simply to generate an income-stream to supplement tourism.

The aims of establishing the IFC in Brunei include developing the capacity to

- Diversify, expand into and grow the value-added financial service sector of the economy of Brunei and the APR.
- Provide a secure, cost-effective, sensibly regulated IFC facility, which will offer a safe harbour for the conduct of significant regional and international business for corporate and private clients.
- Attract overseas professionals to assist in running the IFC to the highest standards.
- Encourage expatriate professionals to become involved in training and development of rewarding opportunities for professionally qualified and trained Bruneians in the International Business Sector.
- Increase returns for the hospitality, transport and amenity industries, including eco-tourism.

- Position Brunei as an equal partner in the globalisation of financial and commercial activity, and thereby to generate greater communication with and between other nations.

In order to achieve these goals, Brunei intends to deploy its sovereignty, wealth and human resources in a conservative but assertive manner so as to establish a jurisdictional environment which will be tax-free, and free from excessive government regulation. Brunei IFC offers a range of international legislation carefully crafted to permit flexible, cost-effective capabilities which are right up to date. Such capabilities include the full range of facilities necessary for the efficient conduct of global business.

11.3   The Exclusion of Money Laundering a First Priority

As a sovereign nation of high repute capable, for example, of hosting the September 2000 APEC Summit, Brunei is serving notice at the outset that criminal abuses of its financial systems will not be tolerated. The country is taking these steps voluntarily, rather than under pressure. This reflects responsible economic and social attitudes.

The first series of legislation enacted for the IFC regime therefore included the Money-Laundering and Proceeds of (serious) Crime measures implemented to international standards. Severe Drug Trafficking legislation has been in place for some time, whilst meaningful and enforceable regulation of the Trust, Company Administration, Insurance and Banking industries has already been legislated before these activities commence.

11.4   Parallel Jurisdictions

The consequence of this legislation means that Brunei now operates as a "dual jurisdiction" whereby the international legislation offers offshore facilities alongside the usual range of domestic legislation which is based on the English law owing to Brunei's status as a British protectorate. The jurisdictional distinction is thus jurisprudential rather than physical.

The judicial system is common to both domestic and international law and in this respect, Brunei is fortunate in His Majesty's choice of senior members of the judiciary, all of whom are highly respected judges drawn from Commonwealth countries. All the members of Brunei's Court of Appeal are distinguished Commonwealth judges, whilst final civil appeals are made to the Privy Council in London. In a recent judgement, Dato Sir Denys Roberts, KCMG, SPMP, a former Chief Justice of Hong Kong who for some years has held that office in Brunei had occasion to observe: "There has never been any interference by the executive with the judiciary, which has remained staunchly independent..." The importance of such a strong and experienced "British/Commonwealth" judiciary in an Asian regional context cannot be overstated.

11.5   Islamic Banking in Brunei

Banking in Brunei operates in a financial world where conventional capitalism sits side by side with an Islamic system that avoids usury or interest. The sultanate, where the majority of 250 000 inhabitants are Muslim, has ambitions to become an international financial centre. It plans to do so by excelling in both Islamic and conventional banking.

Brunei has been keenly promoting Islamic banking as an alternative to conventional banking during the past decade. There are three Islamic financial institutions in the country: the Islamic Bank of Brunei (IBB), Tabung Amanah Islam Brunei (TAIB or Islamic Trust Fund of Brunei) and Islamic Development Bank of Brunei (IDBB). The latter, wholly owned by the government, converted to the Islamic system in late 2000. At the time, Sultan Haji Hassanal

Bolkiah said: "It is a milestone for our country and will become much more significant in proportion to our status. We are confident that our way of doing business will be widely accepted by the world at large. This is not only because it brings profits but it also offers fairness and at the same time prevents exploitation."

In early 2001, a working capital credit fund was launched with the objective of injecting liquidity into Brunei's economy to stimulate industries, especially small and medium-sized enterprises (SMEs), which are considered the main plank for economic growth. In the past, SMEs complained that the banks were reluctant to give loans. Eight commercial banks — including the three Islamic banks — are supporting the fund in a joint effort with the government, which offers low interest not exceeding 4 per cent a year. The main principle of the scheme is that all of its loans are commercial ones, subject to terms and conditions of each participating bank.

Haji Abu Bakar, chairman of the IBB, says the number of Islamic banks has grown tremendously over the last thirty years but there are still questions and challenges to be resolved. "The greatest challenge is to demonstrate that the Islamic principles in banking and finance are practical and suitable in daily lives."

Established in 1993, when it replaced the International Bank of Brunei, the IBB conducts its savings and loans operations in accordance with Islamic law. The IBB comes under a group of companies known in *fiqh* (jurisprudence) as *al-'inan* companies. As previously noted, an *al-'inan* company refers to a partnership between two or more people in which their assets are used to trade and the profits obtained are distributed among themselves. As explained earlier, the majority of *"ulama"* (scholars) are of the opinion that *al-'inan* companies are both permissible and valid (*'sah*). According to the Shafie school, it is not a prerequisite that all members of the partnership in an *al-'inan* company be Muslims in order to make it *'sah*. All the other three schools also agree with this condition. This means that non-Muslims may own shares in the Islamic Bank of Brunei Berhad

Islamic Banking and Finance in South-east Asia

because an Islamic Bank is an *al-'inan* company and Islam does not require that all members of the partnership be Muslims.[183]

The world of banking is not excluded from the endeavour of establishing justice. There is no difference in the transactions of an Islamic Bank whether the customer is a Muslim or a non-Muslim. All customers are served equally on the basis of justice. IBB states that it is prepared to provide services and advice that may be required by its customers, regardless of their race or religion. Similarly, the distribution of dividends is done fairly in accordance with the customer's rate of investment and irrespective of whether they are a Muslim or a non-Muslim. The Islamic Bank does not and will not charge service fees that differ according to the different customers, for example Muslims are charged a lower fee whilst non-Muslims are charged a higher fee.[184]

Eighty per cent of the IBB's paid up capital is owned by Sultan Haji Hassanal Bolkiah and his family, with the balance held by Japan's Daiichi Kangyo Bank. Meanwhile, TAIB, which operates under a banking licence, is revamping its image. A new chairman recently took over and the focus is on customer service.

Prior to the formal establishment of the International Finance Corporation, several international conventional banks had already established their presence in Brunei. HSBC, Standard Chartered, Overseas Union Bank, Citibank, Maybank and Baiduri Bank, all operate in the Sultanate. The major accounting firms do business there, and around fifteen law firms practice in Brunei. Even with such advantages, the proximity of financial powerhouses such as Hong Kong and Singapore suggests that even a jurisdiction with tax burdens as low as Brunei's faces a challenge in establishing a global presence in international banking. Brunei is also investigating the possibility of establishing a "cyber park" to develop an indigenous

---

[183]See "Questions and answers on Islamic banking", *Islamic Bank of Brunei Berhad*, p. 15.

[184]Ibid, p. 13.

IT industry; again, such startup efforts face serious competition in the region.

11.6   *Takaful* in Brunei

It is not known for sure when the development of the insurance industry started in Brunei. The impetus was the need to protect foreign businesses, especially the British's, in the 1940s and in the 1950s. Insurance companies at that time operated through a network office or an insurance representative's desk. They were the agents in Brunei, carrying out insurance transactions with overseas insurance companies, most of which were stationed in Singapore. After the growth of the insurance identity in Brunei, overseas branches of insurance companies were established followed by the establishment of local insurance companies. Finally, in 1995, with the determined effort of the Islamic Bank of Brunei Berhad, an Islamic insurance company known as the IBB *takaful* Berhad was set up. Today, the IBB *takaful* is the largest Islamic insurance company in Brunei. It operates according to the Company Act, 1957, with the permission of the Ministry of Finance.

Non-Muslims are open to participate in the *takaful* plan of IBB — the situation is not much different from a Muslim buying retail products from shops and supermarkets owned by non-Muslims. However, *zakat* (charitable contributions) is not levied on non-Muslims; it is only levied on Muslims as clearly required by Islam.[185]

11.7   Latest Developments

Brunei and Bahrain have recently agreed to promote and encourage joint cooperation in investment and financial sectors. The two Muslim nations sealed their desire to deepen their friendship with

---

[185]Ibid, pp. 68–69.

a memorandum that would pave the way for them to strengthen bilateral economic relations as well as in other areas of cooperation. The two countries joined ranks by signing an MOU on 26 January 2003, aiming to make their relationships progress beyond the routine diplomatic and political domains. This historic move came as a highlight of the visit of Shaikh Khalifa Bin Salman Al Khalifa, the Prime Minister of Bahrain, to Brunei. Brunei and Bahrain lauded their move to strengthen their ties as significant as it reflected the wish of both Islamic nations to deepen their relationships through more economic co-operation and investment. Both countries have agreed to focus on joint efforts to promote and encourage cooperation in the investment and financial sectors. The fields of co-operation, amongst others, include co-operation in investment, banking and financial services including Islamic banking, financial information and relevant training activities. Also in the itinerary was an initiative to create joint venture schemes to promote investment and financial sectors. The event was also seen as a good sign for Brunei's renewed efforts to accelerate its economic diversification programmes. Under the so-called strategy to "kick-start" the economic diversification plan, Brunei hopes to bring in about US$4 billion foreign investment into the country to develop the special projects of Sungai Liang into a world class industrial zone and to develop Pulau Muara Besar as a first class global hub.[186]

In February 2006, the merger of two Islamic banks in Brunei were approved, Islamic Bank of Brunei Ltd and state-owned Brunei Islamic Development Bank Ltd were to become Islamic Bank of Brunei Darussalam Bhd.

According to Adrian Chee, the director of financial services ratings for South and South-East Asia at Standard & Poor's in

---

[186]"Historic Brunei-Bahrain MOU to boost Islamic banking", *Iran Trade Point*, 27 January 2003.

Singapore, the main reason for the merger was to create a much stronger entity, perhaps with a much wider business page.[187]

The sale of B$150 million (US$92 million) of 91-day commercial paper in March 2006 was the first of a series of planned sales from the Brunei government.

The government, which has no external debt, has said it has no fundamental need for the funds.

According to Aminuddin Taib, the acting special duties officer at the Brunei Monetary and Currency Board, the issuance was a move towards developing the commercial papers market and building Brunei as an Islamic market.

The Sultan Yan Di-Pertuan first said in November 2005 that Brunei planned to sell Islamic commercial paper in order to develop other areas of the economy, reduce the outflow of funds and encourage other local entities to sell Islamic debt.

As part of its issuance plans, Brunei launched an open-ended program that will allow for issuance of commercial paper with maturities of up to one year.

The debt will use the Ijarah — or sale and leaseback — principal and as such, the government has identified a swathe of government buildings and land, including hospitals, airports and ministry offices, to back the issuance.

In order to sell the paper, Brunei set up two special purpose vehicles, Sukuk Holding Properties Inc. and Sukuk (Brunei) Inc.

The Land Department — as an administrator rather than owner of the property — would first transfer the assets to Sukuk Holding Properties which would issue certificates to Sukuk (Brunei). The latter would, in turn, sell the certificates to five primary dealers; local banks Baiduri Bank Group and the Islamic Bank Brunei and foreign banks Citibank Inc., HSBC and Standard Chartered Bank.

---

[187] "Brunei agrees to merge 2 Islamic banks", *GlobalPro Training & Development (Malaysia)*, (http://www.globalpro.com.my/03jAN06-Brune-agrees-to-merge-2-Islamic-banks.htm), 3 February 2006.

The government would lease back the assets and the rental payments would be used to pay the dividends to the debt investors.

At first, the sales would be sold to the five primary dealers through a bookbuilding process although in the future, people familiar with the deal said the government is likely to adopt an auction process more commonly used in government debt sales globally.

As for now, the primary dealers would only be allowed to trade the paper among themselves.

Going forward, the government would likely consider alternative Islamic structures such as the Mudharabah or Musyrakah structures used elsewhere, but would need to set up alternative issuance programs.[188]

11.8   Conclusion

Brunei has about B$12 billion Islamic private deposit with the local banks. About 70 per cent of those funds are invested overseas because there are insufficient Islamic assets in the local market. The remaining 30 per cent is invested in Islamic instruments in the country.[189]

"We have made a lot of investments in Brunei over the past 54 years and I am glad to say that we are continuing to invest because we see this as a country that is going to grow," says Warner Manning, HSBC's chief executive in Brunei. "The new economy here has a long way to go. But then it is all relative and if you take a snapshot of the other ASEAN countries, Brunei is by no means at the bottom of the list." Manning believes that in some quarters, the idea of Brunei as an offshore centre is slowly beginning to grow. But the

---

[188]Lane, Karen, "Asia debt: Brunei prepares for debut Islamic debt sale", *Yahoo Finance*, (http://sg.biz.yahoo.com/060316/15/3zetu.html), 16 March 2006.

[189]Sidhu, B.K., "CIMB working on Sukuk in Brunei", *The Star* (Malaysia), (http://biz.thestar.com.my/news/story.asp?file=/2005/7/8/business/11431824&sec=business), 8 July 2006.

authorities are taking a cautious approach because they do not want the sultanate to be associated in the same category as some dubious tax havens elsewhere in the world. "The first message for Brunei is that they want to get on the best list," according to Manning. "The country has some good things going for it. First, they have done a great job putting together the legislation. Second, they have done a very good job in adopting best practices in the banking industry. So, they are doing all the right things here and now they need to sell it."[190]

---

[190]"ASEAN: Brunei and the Philippines", *Image World Ltd*, 16 September, 2001.

Chapter 12

Banking in Singapore

12.1 Introduction

Switzerland currently manages approximately US$2.2 trillion of offshore assets[191] due to its historic stable financial and political environment, which translates into a safe haven for investing money. Further, it also has long-standing expertise in multi-currency investments, with pro-investor banking secrecy laws, and discrete and well regarded personalised services. To many, Switzerland is a politically-neutral, tax-efficient and trustworthy financial centre.

But Switzerland's position as an offshore financial centre is set to weaken with the possibility of significant fund outflows to Asia and elsewhere. Switzerland will soon lose some of its tax competitiveness which is one of the main benefits for its past success in attracting offshore funds.

In June 2003, under pressure from G8 countries, Switzerland has agreed to repatriate income taxes on accounts held by citizens of the European Union, due to start in July 2005, but which may be delayed further until 2006. The tax rate will start at 15 per cent and increase to 35 per cent by 2011.[192]

---

[191]Cohn, Laura and Fairlamb, David, "Singapore and its growing effect on private banking. Swiss banks: Paradise lost", *eBrain Hosting* (http://www.ebrainhosting.biz/english/news/news-Singapore_ private.html), 2003.

[192]"EU Tax Deal Leaves Swiss Banking Secrecy Intact", *SwissInfo* (http://www.swissinfo.org/sen/Swissinfo.html?siteSect=105&sid=3900237), 2003.

Other EU countries have also adopted or will adopt the EU's Savings Tax Directive, which requires financial institutions to report financial information on their non-resident investors. This means that account holders will have to pay taxes on their investment income to their respective governments, which previously was not done.

In light of these developments, it is likely that the wealthy may decide to place their wealth away from Switzerland, and the other wealth management centres in Europe. The wealth management industry in Asia, especially Singapore, is poised to benefit from these recent developments in Europe over and above the growing amount of indigenous wealth in Asia.

Similar to Switzerland, Singapore has strong fundamentals. First, it has a good record of creating and maintaining sound economic policies and is politically stable. Its financial industry is regulated to the highest international standards. Second, it is the world's fourth largest foreign exchange centre with a large presence of public equity, private equity, and fixed income and hedge fund managers.[193]

Third, Singapore has an extremely favourable regulatory environment for the placement and investment of offshore funds. Its tax system allows offshore funds to compound tax free, as no taxes on interest and capital gains are imposed on non-residents. There are also no barriers to the entry and repatriation of funds.

Fourth, the Singapore government plays an active role at increasing transparency and minimising bureaucratic practices. Finally, it has stringent client confidentiality laws, comparable to those of Switzerland. With these advantageous factors measuring up to those offered by Switzerland, Singapore has positioned itself to being the benefiting party to the movement of offshore funds out of Europe.[194]

---

[193]Koh, Francis, Lee, Choon Li and Jindai, Parthsarthi, "Singapore as an emerging hub for wealth management", *Pulses, A monthly publication of Singapore Exchange Limited,* November 2003, p. 10.

[194]Ibid.

It can be seen that Singapore's development as an international financial centre began in the late 1960s. Since then, Singapore has implemented an economic blueprint that has encouraged inward investments of multinational corporations to Singapore. The inflows of foreign direct investment from the UK, US and Japan provided an impetus to the development of the financial sector. By the 1980s, many of the world's leading financial institutions had set up operations in Singapore.[195]

Over the years, its sound economic and financial fundamentals, conducive regulatory and business environment, strategic location, skilled and educated workforce, excellent telecommunications and infrastructure, and high living standards have attracted many reputable international financial institutions to set up operations in Singapore. On the back of growing prosperity in the region and support from the authorities, Singapore has developed into a regional, and subsequently, global foreign exchange trading centre. Today, only London, New York and Tokyo record higher foreign exchange trading volumes than Singapore. The Singapore International Monetary Exchange (SIMEX),[196] the first derivative exchange in Asia, also grew in stature to become a key Asian financial hub in the global chain of leading future markets. Today, financial services account for 11 per cent of Singapore's GDP.[197]

There is a large and diversified group of local and foreign financial institutions, numbering about 700, located in Singapore and offering a wide range of financial products and services. These include trade financing, foreign exchange, derivatives products, capital market activities, loan syndication, underwriting, mergers

---

[195]Economic Review Committee, Sub-Committee on Services Industries, Financial Services Working Group, "Positioning Singapore as a pre-eminent financial centre in Asia", *Channel News Asia* (http://www.channelnewsasia.com), 2002, p. 1.

[196]SIMEX and the Stock Exchange of Singapore (SES) have since merged to become the Singapore Exchange (SGX).

[197]Monetary Authority of Singapore (http://www.mas.gov.sg).

and acquisitions, asset management, securities trading, financial advisory services, and specialised insurance services. The presence of these leading institutions has contributed to the vibrancy and sophistication of Singapore's financial industry.[198]

Fund management companies in Singapore have expanded in terms of size, regional responsibility and capabilities, with 70 per cent of funds under management sourced from the US, Europe and Asia.[199]

Singapore's asset management industry has managed good growth since 1994. Assets under management (AUM) by Singapore-based financial institutions have grown steadily from S$66 billion in 1994 prior to the implementation of developmental measures to S$307 billion as at end of 2001. Singapore has evolved into a major regional asset management centre, hosting more than 200 asset management outfits, which employed 1114 professionals as at end of 2001. Almost three-quarters of discretionary AUM are sourced from overseas.[200]

Singapore's developmental objective is to become a centre for (a) managing the Asian investment portfolios of both Asian and Western clients and (b) managing global investments of clients in Asia. Today, 43 per cent of assets managed in Singapore were sourced from Europe and North America, with 30 per cent of assets invested in Singapore, 9 per cent in Japan and 18 per cent in the rest of the Asia Pacific. However, Singapore remains a predominantly Asian mandate centre, with funds mostly invested in Asia, although the amount of investment in the US and Europe carried out from Singapore has increased in recent years.[201]

---

[198]Ibid.

[199]Economic Review Committee, op. cit., p. 3. The major Swiss and European private banks such as USB, Credit Suisse and ABN-Amro all have regional headquarters in Singapore.

[200]Ibid.

[201]Ibid.

The offshore-banking business is now under pressure around the world. But as offshore participants (particularly the many institutions with businesses in Switzerland) review their business in light of unfavourable regulatory charges, they will find they have several options that will help them remain competitive.

One of the options is to grow beyond their home market. They can do so by building onshore presences in selected locations or by intensifying their efforts to grow in other key offshore locations such as Singapore. Thus there is the increasing need for Singapore to cement herself, in the minds of the offshore players, as the next best alternative.[202]

Singapore has responded accordingly to the directives and recommendations of the international bodies such as the OECD, FATF and IMF in terms of (a) harmful tax practices, (b) money laundering, (c) confidentiality and (d) exchange of information. The following analysis of Singapore's legal and regulatory systems will demonstrate how it has responded to these issues and why in totality this regional financial centre will continue to develop ahead of the other Offshore Financial Centres (OFCs), and in doing so, will become the new jurisdiction of choice for those seeking to use an OFC for future wealth management.

12.2   Legal Framework — Legislation Enacted by the Parliament of Singapore

Singapore, which is a republic, was a colony of the United Kingdom and briefly part of the Federation of Malaya. She has a unicameral parliament and a government patterned after the Westminister model, in which Parliament enacts laws and confers executive

---

[202]"Winning in a challenging market: Global wealth 2003", *The Boston Consulting Group*, July 2003.

powers thereunder upon ministers,[203] who form a cabinet headed by the Prime Minister.

The President is the constitutional Head of State. Although the President does not have executive powers, his assent is required before any legislation can have the force of law.[204] Local legislation comprises acts passed by Parliament and assented to by the President, and subsidiary legislation promulgated thereunder by ministers exercising their delegated authority.

Singapore's judicial system comprises three tiers of courts:

(i) The Subordinate Courts, consisting of the Coroners' Courts, the Juvenile Courts, the Magistrates' Courts, and the Small Claims Tribunal;

(ii) The Supreme Court, which comprises the High Court, the Court of Appeal, and the Criminal Court of Appeal, and

(iii) The Judicial Committee of the Privy Council, which traditionally has been the highest court of appeal for Britain's former colonies.

12.3 English Common Law and Statutes

The reception of English Common law in Singapore was effected by the Letters Patent issued on 27 November 1826, more commonly referred to as the Second Charter of Justice, which established the Court of Judicature of Prince of Wales Island, Singapore, and Malacca and required the court "to give and pass Judgement and Sentence according to Justice and Right". This phrase traditionally has been interpreted to mean that the English law and equity,

---

[203] The Ministers usually are empowered under their respective Acts to promulgate such subsidiary legislation as in necessary for the implementation of Acts.

[204] Article 58 of the Singapore Constitution provides that "the power of Legislature to make laws shall be exercised by Bills passed by Parliament and assented to by the President".

as it stood in England in 1826, was part of the law of the Straits Settlements.[205]

As a result of the foregoing, matters which have not been legislated upon by the Singapore Parliament are governed by English Common Law, embodied in decided cases of the English courts, with such adaptation as are required by local circumstances.[206]

The Common Law enjoys continuous reception in Singapore as "the Common Law was traditionally conceived of as having existed from time immemorial and was merely declared by the judges from time to time ...".[207] According to this interpretation of the Common Law, the courts in England deciding a case today simply would be declaring the law as it has always been (and, hence, as it was at the date of the Second Charter of Justice), and applying it to the facts before them.

12.4   Singapore — An Alternative to Switzerland

In June 2003, the EU agreement with Switzerland to claw back some tax revenue from income earned on assets of EU citizens that are held by Swiss banks opened the gates for the capital outflow of assets under management by its private banking industry.

Under the deal, in 2005, EU-based clients of Swiss banks will face a 15 per cent tax on income and/or dividends from assets — such as bonds — purchased from their Swiss bank accounts. The taxes will be passed on directly by the Swiss banks to the governments of the clients' home countries, without the clients' names being revealed. The deal allows Switzerland to maintain its banking

---

[205] *Regina v. Williams* (1858) 3 Kyshe 16; *Fatimah v. Logan* (1871) Kyshe 225.

[206] See Woon, Walter (ed.), *The Singapore Legal System*, 1989, p. 119, where he states modifications to "suit the customs, manners, usages and religions of the native inhabitants." An example, he cites, is the relaxation, in colonial days, of the common law concept of monogamous marriage in the case of the Chinese.

[207] See Bartholomew, G.W., "English law in Partibus Orientalium" in A J Harding (ed.), *The Common Law in Singapore and Malaysia*, 1985, p. 15.

secrecy laws, while permitting the governments of EU countries to collect tax revenue that has, thus far, eluded them. Over time, the tax rates will be raised, in stages, to a maximum of 35 per cent.

After 2005, therefore, private banking clients who keep assets in Switzerland will be faced with the prospect of lower — and progressively declining — post-tax rates of return on their holdings.

Many of them have already been induced to move their money elsewhere. Hence, many Swiss banks consider Singapore the best alternative, and are gearing up for the shift, since the regulatory and legal systems are in place, these global investors are voting with their feet; a clear vote of confidence in Singapore's compliance with the supranational directives.[208]

12.5 Singapore — Financial System Stability Assessment

Singapore has evolved into a major regional asset management centre over the past few years in response to the government's efforts to develop this industry and now hosts more than 200 asset management firms. Total assets managed by Singapore-based financial institutions increased from S$151 billion in 1998 to S$344 billion in 2002. This increase can be attributed to transfers of regional portfolios to Singapore for management and continued expansion of management and advisory activities for the pan-Asian region in light of Singapore's sound legal and tax environment and highly developed infrastructure. Some asset managers also centralised their regional trading and back office functions in Singapore. Of the S$183 billion of discretionary assets as of end 2002, 30 per cent came from Singapore and the rest from abroad — mainly Europe and the United States.

Although the regulatory systems and supervisory practices exhibit a high degree of observance of international standards and

[208]Khanna, Vikram, "S'pore an alternative to Switzerland?", *The Business Times* (Singapore), 5 November 2003.

codes, the IMF in 2004 made some specific recommendations to further enhance the risk-based regulatory and supervisory framework, to strengthen the accountability and independence on the MAS, and improve monetary and financial policy transparency.[209]

12.6   Singapore's Role as a Financial Centre

Singapore's sophisticated banking system, the transparent regulatory and the credible English Common law system have aided Singapore's development as a pre-eminent regional financial centre in Asia which is also underpinned by the existence of an attractive business environment for financial institutions and a desirable quality of life for professionals. Effective promotion to communicate Singapore's value proposition and financial sector opportunities has attracted financial institutions and talent to Singapore. A deep pool of financial sector expertise and pro-physical infrastructure are key components of an attractive business environment. This attractive business environment has been created by focusing on the promotion of Singapore's financial centre, education and training, taxation policies and business infrastructure.[210]

It has been noted that "Singapore is politically stable, it has the world's most competitive economy, the best rated legal system and is a leader in information technology. There are stringent client confidentiality laws, no taxation for non-residents, and robust anti-money laundering laws. Like Switzerland, Singapore is neutral and has an international reputation as a safe and secure environment."[211]

---

[209]International Monetary Fund, *Singapore: Financial System Stability Assessment, including Reports on the Observance of Standards and Codes on the following topics: Banking Supervision, Insurance Regulation, Securities Regulation, Payment and Settlement Systems, Monetary and Financial Policy Transparency, and Anti-Money Laundering* (IMF) 2004, p. 36.

[210]Economic Review Committee, op. cit., p. 28.

[211]Ibid.

Since, Switzerland has fallen in line with the EU's Savings Tax Directive, and as previously noted, with an estimated US$2 trillion in offshore assets held by EU citizens to be affected, it is not surprising that many of Europe's wealthy are reviewing other places to transfer their cash and the likely recipient of the outflow, it is now confirmed, is Singapore, which is not party to the EU directive.

Competition is limited. The global crackdown on terrorism financing means tax havens in the Caribbean and the South Pacific are blacklisted or otherwise seen as tainted. Singapore is among the few still passing the "sniff test". Hong Kong suffers "sovereignty risk" due to mainland China's increasing interference in the territory's affairs.

With these basic pillars in place, the city-state has now positioned itself to emerge as the major beneficiary of the flight of funds from Europe.

To date, Singapore has enjoyed only modest success as an offshore banking centre. Offshore assets are estimated at US$120 billion, a tenth that of Switzerland's, and most of that is held by overseas Chinese from South-east Asia. Assets held by EU citizens are easily under 5 per cent. That means there is room for growth.

Over the past five years, Singapore has stepped up its campaign to market the country as a financial centre, with bureaucrats on official trips to Europe holding meetings with private bankers to tout the charms of the South-east Asian nation.[212] This is further demonstrated by the number of major banks and financial institutions that have established a presence in Singapore and the subsequent flow of funds under wealth management in Singapore.

12.7   Islamic Banking in Singapore

Islamic Banking has become a priority for Singapore's central bank. As the Monetary Authority of Singapore's (MAS) new chairman,

---

[212] "Swiss tax decision could see Singapore shine as a haven", *Offshore Red: An OFC News Update*, Vol. 8, 2003, p. 175.

Senior Minister Goh Chok Tong has pledged to boost Singapore's status as a centre for Islamic financial services. Despite being a regional financial centre, Singapore is lagging behind Malaysia, now a key Islamic financial hub after it fast-tracked the liberalisation of this sector to attract rich Saudis following the 9/11 attacks.

According to Dr Zeti Akhtar, Malaysia's central bank governor, the Islamic banking sector remains largely untapped by South-east Asia, other than Malaysia, and the market out there is very large and greater activity will contribute to the development of Islamic banking and finance on a global basis. Singapore's efforts to become an international financial centre for Islamic services will not be threatened by Malaysia's ambitions in the same field. It will instead hasten global development of Islamic banking and finance in the region.

Singapore's efforts to develop Islamic finance should not be constrained by the fact that it is not a Muslim state as Islamic finance is already taking off in many non-Muslim countries. The Muslim Community Co-operative Australia (MCCA) was established in February 1989 to conduct financial dealings and transactions based on Islamic finance principles. The MCCA manages the Murabaha, Musharaka, Mudaraba, Qard-el-Hassan and Zakat funds. In July 2004, the former East German state of Saxony-Anhalt sold Europe's first Islamic sovereign bond. The first Islamic retail bank opened for business in the United Kingdom in September 2004.[213]

Compared to Malaysia, Islamic banking is in its early years in Singapore, due largely to a lack of awareness and a small domestic market. A local bank, OCBC is offering two Islamic deposit accounts in the consumer market in Singapore, but it has failed to replicate here the success it has had in Malaysia, where it is the second foreign player in the field with some RM457 million (S$204 million) in Islamic banking loans.[214]

---

[213]Siow, Li Sen, "S'pore can add value in developing Islamic finance", *The Business Times* (Singapore), 25 September 2004.

[214]Chua, Val, "Wooing the Islamic billion$", *Today* (Singapore), 24 September 2004.

On the other hand, the Islamic banking climate in Singapore is changing for the better. In 2005, OCBC became the first bank to appoint a full-time Shari'ah advisory council to provide guidance for OCBC's Islamic banking activities in Singapore and Brunei. The council will be the authority in determining the validity of such products and transactions conducted by the bank.[215] The first Shari'ah-compliant term deposit in Singapore was launched by OCBC Bank in February 2006. It will be sold wholesale to Muslim companies, financial institutions, mosques and non-profit organisations.[216]

Further, HSBC Insurance (Singapore) has S$220 million worth of assets under management for *takaful* products, which is about 80 per cent of the market in Singapore.[217] UOB's assets management unit, in partnership with Commerce International Merchant Bankers Bhd (CIMB), manages an Islamic fund called the Afdaal Asia Pacific Equity Fund, which invests in Asia-Pacific equity markets.[218]

In November 2005, Maybank, Malaysia's largest bank and also the leading Islamic operator in that country, started its Islamic banking in Singapore with a Shari'ah-compliant online savings account and Shari'ah-compliant savings cum checking account. As the leader in Islamic banking in Malaysia, Maybank has the expertise and is able to tailor products for the Singapore market. It will look into enlarging its offerings to loan products soon. Currently, Maybank's Islamic banking assets have grown to RM21.9 billion (S$9.8 billion).[219]

---

[215]Yee, Leslie, "OCBC appoints permanent Syariah council", *The Business Times* (Singapore), 17 December 2005.

[216]Yee, Leslie, "OCBC scores on 5-year risk-adjusted returns", *The Business Times* (Singapore), 9 February 2006.

[217]Yee, Leslie, "MAS looks into aiding Islamic finance", *The Business Times* (Singapore), 22 February 2006.

[218]Yee, 17 December 2005, op. cit.

[219]Siow, Li Sen, "Maybank launches Islamic banking", *The Business Times* (Singapore), 26 November 2005.

As well, Singapore largest motor insurer, NTUC Income has plans to introduce insurance policies (*takaful*) which are Shari'ah-compliant. A key issue is the possibility of premiums being 10 to 20 per cent higher than that of conventional insurance. This is due to the insurance operated being expected to manage claims and expenses and produce a profit which is to be shared among its insured parties. In Islamic banking, this is known as mudharabah. NTUC Income launched the Amanah Fund in 2005. It is the largest *takaful* fund in South-east Asia, investing in the burgeoning Islamic bond and equity market. Started at S$300 million, it is expected to expand to S$600 million by the end of 2006.[220]

Malaysian debt underwriter, CIMB Bhd had plans to introduce an Islamic unit trust fund in Singapore in 2006. CIMB was in talks with the MAS, intending to launch more Islamic banking products in the future as Singapore makes changes to its framework to accommodate Shari'ah-compliant products.

In September 2005, the MAS exempted murabaha transactions from the Banking Act restrictions as a step towards making Singapore an Islamic banking centre.[221] MAS executive director, Ng Nam Sin said, "The overall policy approach is to align the tax treatment of Islamic contracts with the treatment of conventional financing contracts that they are economically equivalent to." In the 2006 Singapore Budget, the Finance Ministry stated that changes would be made to facilitate Islamic transactions and remove any inequalities in the manner which they are officially treated.[222] Ng announced at the Islamic Finance Singapore Conference that MAS would be making regulatory changes to accommodate Islamic banking products. Tax policy surrounding Islamic contracts would also

---

[220]Chen, Gabriel, "Income may offer Syariah-compliant motor insurance", *The Straits Times* (Singapore), 27 February 2006.

[221]"CIMB to launch S'pore Islamic trust in 1st half", *The Business Times* (Singapore), 22 February 2006.

[222]Yee, 22 February 2006, op. cit.

be aligned with the treatment of the corresponding conventional financing contracts. Singapore has waived double stamp duties in Islamic transactions involving real estate and agreed to give concessionary tax treatment on income from Islamic bonds, making them comparable with conventional bonds.[223]

Besides the local banks increased involvement in Islamic banking, foreign investors have also shown interest in Islamic banking in Singapore. On 12 December 2005, Abu Dhabai Commercial Bank (ADCB) launched a S$80 million bond issue, the first Singapore dollar bond issue from the Middle East. A week before, the first Islamic financing deal was announced: a US$96 million murabaha facility from Baitak Asian Real Estate Fund I (Labuan) Ltd. Both transactions were undertaken by Standard Chartered Bank. The bond notes were rated Aa3 by the Moody's credit rating agency and A- by Standard & Poor's. According to Standard Chartered Bank, this is the highest rating given to any instrument from a bank in the Middle East.[224]

It was further reported in October 2005, that the Bahrain-based Islamic investment bank, Gulf Finance House (GFH) was looking to secure the relevant licences from the MAS to carry out Islamic banking activities. GFH was looking to conduct investment banking activities out of Singapore such as capital market fund raisings in a framework which is compliant with Islamic laws.[225]

On 21 February 2006, the Singapore Stock Exchange (SGX) in partnership with FTSE Group and Yasaar Research launched the FTSE SGX Asia Shari'ah 100 index, which tracks 100 Shari'ah-compliant stocks from Japan, Singapore, Taiwan, Korea and Hong Kong.[226] According to Majid Dawood, chief executive of

---

[223]Chen, Gabriel, "S'pore's financial skills can aid foray into Islamic banking", *The Straits Times* (Singapore), 22 February 2006.

[224]Siow, Li Sen, "Middle East bank launches $80 bond issue here", *The Business Times* (Singapore), 13 December 2005.

[225]Yee, Leslie, "Bahrain bank seeks licence for Islamic banking", *The Business Times* (Singapore), 25 October 2005.

[226]Yee, 22 February 2006, op. cit.

Yassar and president of Yassar Research, Islamic-compliant stocks include those that prohibit dealing in interest or speculation and certain products such as alcohol, pornography and non-halah food. That would rule out most hotel stocks, as they sell alcohol, and commercial banks because they charge interest. The market for such indexes is still in its early stages — outside the Middle East, the only Islamic stock indexes are in the United States, where Dow Jones compiles the DJ Islamic Market — but it is one with huge potential.[227]

Also, in June 2006, the MAS gave a clear encouraging signal to Islamic banking in Singapore as it gave its approval to banks to engage in non-financial activities, such as commodity trading, to facilitate a murabaha transaction for clients' investments. Prior to this, banks had been forbidden to engage in non-financial activities such as trading, which is not ordinarily associated with banking and finance. This move has shown that MAS recognises the fundamental characteristics of murabaha, a typical Islamic banking and finance tool.[228]

Another significant move in the development of Islamic banking in Singapore has been the announcement by the Singapore Islamic Scholars and Religious Teachers Association (Pergas) that 18 Islamic religious scholars would be trained in banking and finance to assist Singapore's aim of becoming a hub for Islamic finance. Pergas said in September 2006 that it would introduce a Shari'ah Advisers Training Programme, organized jointly with the Kuala Lumpur-based International Institute of Islamic Finance (IIIF). These religious teachers (asatizah) would be trained to strengthen the local expertise currently lacking in Singapore. More importantly, they are to be mentored by specialists from both Malaysia and the Middle East, thus overcoming, in part at least,

---

[227] Chen Gabriel, "S'pore bourse in deal to offer Islamic indexes", *The Straits Times* (Singapore), 6 January 2006.

[228] Asmani, Azrin, "Banks get light to offer another Islamic product", *The Straits Times* (Singapore), 13 June 2006.

the challenge of the different interpretations between the more traditional schools in the Middle East and those in South-east Asia.

12.8 Conclusion

From the above, it can be seen that Singapore has — due to the four pillars of: (a) strong political stability; (b) common law English legal system; (c) efficient regulatory regime; and (d) solid financial infrastructure — established a highly credible brand name which is of the utmost importance in the global banking and financial world, and is positioning itself to be the nexus for the convergence of both the conventional and Islamic banking and finance sectors in Asia.

At the "Islamic Banking Summit 2006 — Responding to the Challenges of Globalization", 3–4 October 2006, held at Grand Hyatt Singapore by the Asian Strategy & Leadership Institute (ASLI), the MAS Head of "Financial Centre Development" effectively annunciated the policy that they are implementing. It appears to be the intention of the MAS to position Singapore as a Global Financial Centre comparable to London & Bahrain (and to compliment KL) for such sectors as corporate banking, capital and fund administration markets by providing a regulatory regime that has a level playing field for Islamic Banking & Finance and to create market awareness through its membership of such bodies as the IFSB. Such a model is intended to accommodate the players in the Islamic Banking & Finance field, but not for the government to be a necessary player itself as in the case of the markets' successful and ongoing development in Malaysia.

As former prime-minister Goh has stated, this will complete Singapore's image as a true international financial centre, thanks to the stewardship of the government and the current generation of mandarins.

Singapore is where Dubai and Zurich, in terms of global wealth management, will come together.

Chapter 13

Conclusion

13.1 Introduction

According to the noted scholar, Mahmoud El-Gamal, it is becoming more widely accepted, that when one studies the economics of classical jurists (ibn Taymiyyah, 'ibn Rushd, ibn Al-Qyyim, Al-Ghazali ...), one should not look to import their thought into current times. Instead, one should look to replace their historical economic thought with the present state of the art knowledge, and replace their historical setting with the current legal technology. One would thus utilise their methods of understanding the Shari'ah in light of the best knowledge of their times.[229]

Islamic banking is presently still in a nascent stage of development. Nevertheless, practical applications of non-interest bearing modes of finance have clearly demonstrated the feasibility of interest-free banking. However, great circumspection has to be exercised to nurture it on truly Islamic lines and to consolidate it so as to meet any future challenges.

The practical implementation of the concept of profit-loss-sharing to serve as the basis of Islamic banking has opened the way for economy-wide Islamisation of the banking and financial system in Muslim countries such as Malaysia and Brunei. Progress in this direction will, however, depend on the circumstances of each

---

[229]See El-Gamal, Mahmoud, "Updating our understanding of Shari'ah rules", *The International Islamic Financial Forum*, International Institute of Research, Dubai, March 2002.

individual country. Islamic banks working in isolation in different countries are faced with a number of practical problems in the actual conduct of Islamic banking. In many countries where Islamic banks have been established, the legal framework is not suited for the growth of Islamic banking. Still, they have shown encouraging results. There is evidence that even in those Muslim countries such as Malaysia and Brunei where a decision to Islamise the entire banking and financial system has not yet been taken, awareness is growing for the need of taking suitable measures to provide support and assistance to the Islamic banks in order to nurture their growth and development.

Islamic banks have to work hard to build up the wealth of experience which has been developed by the conventional banks over hundreds of years. They have to develop their instruments of finance and also the nature of their funding. The short term nature of their funds with short term private depositors' money does not easily lend itself to ventures into long term finance. Despite this and the difficulties faced by Islamic banks trying to expand their medium and long term activities, one finds that the results are not as bad as expected. On the contrary these results, when compared with Islamic banks' age and experience, are far better than anticipated.

It is necessary to emphasise here that the top management of Islamic banks carries a very great responsibility for managing the affairs of these institutions so that all misgivings about the successful functioning of Islamic banks are removed and that an understanding of Islamic jurisprudence and the virtues of Shari'ah compliance for Islamic banking are fully demonstrated in practice.[230]

Listed below are some of the tasks involved in converting from a conventional banking system to one embracing Islamic principles. The acceptance and practice of Islamic banking is due to its rising importance beyond the Middle East and into the South-east Asia. In predominantly Muslim countries such as Malaysia, Indonesia and

---

[230]Al-Harran, op. cit., pp. 157–158.

Brunei, the Islamic resurgence cements the need to understand and cater to Islamic banking.

13.2 Conversion Project Plan

According to Hussain Hamed Hassan, for anyone wishing to enter the realm of Islamic banking, there are a number of critical issues that need to be addressed and strategies can then be implemented. They can be summarised as follows:

- Treatment of share-holders rights resulting from interest income.
- Treatment of loans and advances with interest.
- Treatment of deposits with interest.
- Training programs for senior management and all employees of the bank
- Modification/revision of computer systems (both hardware and software) to facilitate Islamic transactions.
- Introduction of Islamic products and modes of finance
- Implementation of a strategy to deal with mismatch in source and uses of funds
- Selective recruitment of personnel with Islamic banking experience
- Re-structuring the bank to facilitate new activities and assign employees according to the new structure
- Re-assignment of employees to function in the revised structure, with training needs where applicable
- Revision of Articles of Association byelaws of the bank[231]

Some of the banking problems specifically associated with Islamic banking involves moral hazard, the possibility of fraud, delay in payment, insolvency and prohibition of future contracts in Islamic banking.

---

[231] Hassan, op. cit.

13.3   Moral Hazard and the Risk of Fraud

The risk of fraud, which is especially worrisome to the regulators, seems to have two sources. One is the possibility of underreporting of profits earned by the firm via maintenance of two sets of books which is in turn motivated by tax-avoidance. The other source of risk of fraud is the perception that since in risk-return sharing arrangements, the banks will have to carry the burden of potential financial losses, there is an element of moral hazard involved in these transactions.[232] As discussed previously, most modern Islamic finance stems from *gharar* and the resolution of it through *mudarib* in the form of a profit and loss sharing partnership.

In the Islamic banking system, it is necessary to determine the exact amount of profits earned by the *mudarib* in order to calculate the bank's share. An Islamic bank therefore faces a dual risk:

(i) The moral risk which arises from the *mudarib* dishonestly declaring a loss, or a profit lower than the actual.

(ii) The business risk which arises from the behaviour of market forces being different from that expected.

Another factor increasing the degree of risk, is the lack of statistical data, such as profit distribution ratios among the parties involved in various trade, industrial, or service investment ventures. The contractual agreements do include a ratio for the distribution of profit. However, as the parties lack experience in such investment schemes, one or the other may feel either deprived of a due share, or taken advantage of, often after additional facts come to light.

There are at least three possible ways in which this residual risk can be minimised. First, is by implementing the Islamic law of contracts which requires that stipulations of agreements entered into must be faithfully observed, and which proposes well-defined retributive judicial measures to safeguard the terms of the contract.

---

[232]Mirakhor, A., "Analysis of short-term asset concentration in Islamic banking", IMF Working Paper, Washington, October 1987, p. 10.

Second, is the possibility of third-party insurance schemes with cost participation by the central bank and commercial banks. Third, is the maintenance of loss-compensating reserves by the banks. It must also be noted that hardly any bank can be expected to finance a risk-return-sharing project without sufficient information regarding the managerial ability, competence and character of the entrepreneur.

13.4 The Problem of Delays in Payment and Insolvency

Another challenge identified by Ahmed in 1985, which an Islamic bank faces is how to deal with delayed payment. Since Islamic banks do not charge interest, delays in due payments may cause a number of problems for them. There are three main elements which are germane to the possibility of defaults, viz:

(i) The nature of the party to whom finance is provided.
(ii) The purpose for which finance is provided.
(iii) The type of supervision exercised by the bank on the end-use of funds.

If sufficient care is not exercised in regard to these elements, defaults would arise irrespective of whether the bank concerned follow the traditional banking practices or the principles of Islamic banking.[233]

One way to solve this problem is to sell the collateral against which finance is provided by the Islamic bank. However, this may not solve the problem completely. The main difficulty is that it has to be done in a way that does not resemble the interest payment charged by conventional commercial banks in similar circumstances. It is therefore suggested that Islamic banks may impose some penalty on

---

[233]Ahmed, Z., "Some misgivings about Islamic free banking", *Faisal Islamic Bank of Sudan Publication, English Series 7*, 1985, pp. 17–19.

defaulters for delay in payment in accordance with the stipulations of agreement in one of the following ways:[234]

(i) Claiming part of the profit which customers might have made during the period of default.
(ii) Claiming the profit which a bank could have made if the held-up funds had been returned promptly.

It seems that the second course of action is more reasonable for an Islamic bank. Indeed, the first course of action could involve a situation in which a customer might not have made a profit during the period of default.

13.5   Problems with Futures Contracts

British academic Rodney Wilson's research found that there are two types of traders in futures markets.[235] The first are speculators who neither intend to sell or buy commodities, but merely wish to capitalise on the spread between sales and purchase prices. This is clearly an illegitimate objective of profiteering without true trade, and profits from non-guaranteed commodities, which is forbidden as far as Islamic banking is concerned.

The second type of futures trader tries to hedge what he already possesses — he deals in futures in order to avoid possible losses. However, such hedging is only needed for goods that the trader wishes to monopolise for a long period; if the commodities were sold a few days after they were acquired, it would not be necessary to hedge. The second kind of trader only deals in futures when they wish to monopolise some commodities for a longer period to increase their profits. Thus, it is clear that merchants only need futures to hold goods for a considerable period, which quite often is done out of the illegitimate objective of monopoly profiting.

---

[234]Ibid, p. 67.
[235]See Wilson, op. cit.

In the absence of a sophisticated legal system, named-contract rules of a *madhab* provided local followers of that school with the "legal fine print" for transactions known to be devoid of prohibition factors (e.g. *riba* or *gharar*) at the time of the ruling (e.g. *murabaha*, *ijarah*, *mudarabah*, *salam*, etc.). But it should be noted that a transaction satisfying that fine print need not be permissible today, and a permissible transaction today need not satisfy that fine print.

13.6   Moving Forward

Islamic finance is practised in over 60 countries across the world. The assets of Islamic banks and Islamic assets of window-based conventional banks are estimated to be worth over US$400 billion while Islamic mutual funds exceed US$300 billion.

Today, there are 266 Islamic financial institutions in the world with a capitalisation in excess of US$262 billion and financial investments of more than US$400 billion in many projects in the Arab states as well as in Britain, France and the United States.[236]

Some of the problems identified by academic commentators on Islamic finance are now being overcome. Vogel and Hayes saw the development of marketable instruments, organising financial markets and creating tools for risk management as key challenges.[237] Progress has been made on all of these fronts. The development of Islamic securities can reduce some categories of risks; yet at the same time encourage other types of desirable risk taking. The introduction of bills, bonds and notes that can be traded reduces the liquidity risk problems. Banks can move some liquidity from cash into Islamic securities, as the latter constitute an acceptable risk.

---

[236] "M'sia's move to set up Islamic finance education centre lauded", *Bernama.com*   (http://www.bernama.com/bernama/v3/news_lite.php?id=187096), 21 March 2006.

[237] Vogel and Hayes, op. cit., p. 295.

Islamic-managed funds consist of a portfolio of underlying equities and other securities, and the risks associated with a pooled fund should be lower than those associated with individual equities. Such funds have a proven track record in Islamic finance, dating back almost 20 years in some cases. Islamic managed fund investment has proved popular for middle-income bank clients, and not only those of high net worth. Nevertheless according to the British academia, Wilson, their contribution to equity financing in Muslim countries has been limited, largely because of perceived country risk and exchange rate uncertainties.[238]

Successful and beneficial innovations always share a few common features. They are more useful to users than existing forms; they allow users to retain many beliefs or practices they value; and they open the door to still greater possibilities. A mundane example of this is the computer-based word processor, an innovation in the development, manipulation, storage, and transmission of text and graphics. The word processor has a greater range of uses and capabilities than the typewriter but does not require the user to change valued existing protocols with respect to the content, form, or expressions of language; users can carry over acquired skills in typing, editing, and so forth. At the same time, the word processor has made many other things possible, such as desktop publishing, easy incorporation of illustrations, charts, graphs and even videos; and internet publication.

Successful innovation in Islamic banking and finance may have similar characteristics, namely to preserve what is essential about the Islamic heritage in law and economics, while also vastly improving on past commercial techniques, enabling Muslims to join in and effectively compete with world economic and commercial advances.

---

[238]See Wilson, op. cit.

13.7   Conclusion

This book has examined the development of the Islamic banking and finance in South-east Asia. Much of the introductory research came from the earlier scholars who were involved in religious and historical studies. The later work has relied on the analysis and reviews of modern academics such as Wilson, Hassan, Ahmed, Vogel and Hayes.

Islamic finance is now on the verge of either a major transformation, or a period of frustration and therefore possible decline. However, one would have to agree with that should this turning point be negotiated successfully, as the evidence in this book seems to be demonstrating, Islamic finance will enter a new and even more successful era. Until now, according to Vogel: "Islamic finance has largely been confined to the activities of Islamic banks which have tried to practice a Muslim version of conventional retail commercial banking. Elementary knowledge of Islamic law shows, however, that retail commercial banking is one of the most difficult commercial functions to perform in a religiously acceptable manner. Legal rules force Islamic banks to forego two basic features of conventional commercial banking — security for deposits against losses (achieved conventionally through the concepts of depositors seniority in banks' capital structures as well as supplemental deposit insurance) and stability and predictability of returns on the bank's assets (achieved through senior interest-bearing loans to a diversified portfolio of borrowers). Regardless of theory, Islamic banks have found that their competitive and regulatory context compels them to mimic conventional banks in both of these characteristics, pushing them into short-term, low-risk investments in an effort to offer their depositors returns similar in quantity and risk to those obtained by conventional depositors. This circumstance, and others, have prevented them from becoming the profit-and-loss investment intermediaries that Islamic economic theory demands. This in turn causes them both a legal and a financial embarrassments — a legal embarrassment because Islamic banks have survived not on profit-and-loss principles (*mudarabah*) but via markup (*murabaha*) transactions; and a financial embarrassment because the greater complexity of the transactions involved puts them at a disadvantage *vis à vis* conventional banks; some are saved only by the loyalty of their base of religious customers."

A crucial question asked by Vogel here is "Does Islamic jurisprudence (*fiqh*), as elaborated by the scholars and institutions devoted to it, have the potential to meet all the needs of modern Muslims in the commercial and financial sector, in the traditional sense of offering normative guidance for various aspects of daily life?" A success in this field would augur well for the law's extending its influence to other aspects of public life in Islamic societies now almost entirely unaffected by it, such as constitutional law, state economy (taxes, social services), public administration, or educational reform.

Contemporary *fiqh* has shown much capacity for development already, in permitting modern Islamic banking and finance to emerge in their present form. The solutions the scholars have reached have been generally accepted by participants as religiously sound. But much concern and even suspicion remain. Participants, both customers and practitioners, are lately demanding that the financial institutions achieve even higher degrees of religious legal compliance. For example, many now demand that the banks eliminate or reduce use of "synthetic" *murabaha* transactions. This new era or religious strictness now is combining with competitive pressures from the marketplace (such as the need to invest longer-term to improve returns on investments) to push banks and their religious-legal advisory boards into new and uncharted territory.

No doubt many of the legal challenges facing Islamic finance today are disquieting and difficult — such as creating derivatives or other risk-hedging devices or encouraging trade in financial products. If *fiqh* scholars take too cautious and literalist an approach, backing away from the deeper comparative and functional analysis and bolder legal reasoning or *ijtihad* which is not needed, Islamic finance could languish. Given the record to date, however, one can be optimistic about the future.

Finally, Islamic banking is facing another challenge: the lingering suspicion that it is connected to terrorism. So far, there is little evidence that its activities are any more suspect than those of conventional banks. (The US government's list of terrorist organisations included one small Islamic bank, Al-Aqsa Al-Islami in the West Bank.) Islamic finance has always had more to do with conservative, devout Islam than radical, political Islam. Nonetheless, 11 September has put the industry on the defensive, with some depositors withdrawing money for fear it would get caught in an anti-terrorism dragnet. "A lot of investors were frightened, to be honest," says Atif Abdulmalik, CEO of First Islamic Investment Bank in Bahrain.

As previously noted, amongst the optimists is Vogel, who believes, "It's very much in our interest that it succeed, yet I'm afraid that we're going to be against it, that we're going to make all these snotty remarks. Time is running out for healthy, happy experiments like this. The radicalisation, the desire to make yourself as ugly to the West as you can — that rage isn't only at us, it's at the secular forces in their own societies. We need Islamicisation, because they're not going to stop being Muslims overnight."

Oddly, Professor Samuel Hayes III, co-author with Vogel, of *Islamic Law and Finance: Religion, Risk and Return*, gives a different slant. In his view, literalist interpretations of the Quran threaten to choke off Muslim participation in the global economy. "Prophet Muhammad's teachings take very practical account of commerce in the seventh century," says Hayes. "It's not up to me to say, but if he were living today, I think he would find some accommodation. Otherwise, there's no way a business can operate competitively."[239]

Ultimately, even Islamic scholars concede that Hayes might have a point. "Once you face reality," Yaquby says, "it's not possible to isolate yourself from the whole economic system of the world."[240]

---

[239]Useem, op. cit.

[240]Ibid.

Glossary

The use of these terms, has developed over a period of time, dependent upon the school of law and geographical origins.

Adat	customary law
Aqd	binding, contract (plural uqud or uqad)
Amanat	trusts, safekeeping
Bai'	(also *bay*) a sale
Bai al dayn	sale of debt to another party
Bai' bithaman ajil	sales with advanced payment
Darura	overriding necessity
Eidul-Adha	festival of sacrifice, celebrated yearly on the tenth day of the last month of the Islamic lunar calendar
Fard	obligatory, omission is punishable
Fatwas	authoritative guidance, legal opinions from a jurist
Faqih	a Muslim jurist
Fiqh	(also *fikh*) Muslim jurisprudence
Furu	branches of law
Gharar	uncertainty, speculation
Hadith	communication or narrative, it is the record of an individual saying or action or approvals of Muhammad (s.a.w.) taken as a model of behaviour by Muslims.

Halah	Islamically permissible, that which is lawful according to the *Shari'ah*
Haj	the pilgrimage to the Mecca, obligatory once in a lifetime
Haram	forbidden
Haja	need
Havalah	contract of agency, with the bank acting as an agency
Hijrah	the Prophet's migration from Mecca to Medina, which marks the starting point of the Islamic calendar
hila	legal artifices, devices
Ijab	proposal, offer
Ijara	(also *ijarah*) leasing
Ijma	consensus of opinion
Ijtihad	reasoning and interpretation of the sources of law, which is the Quran and Sunnah
Ikhtiyar	choice
Inah	(A kind of Bai) double sale by which the borrower and the lender sell and then resell an object between them, once for cash and once for a higher price on credit, with the net result similar to a loan with interest.
'Inan	form of partnership in which each partner contributes both capital and work (using the Hanbali definition)
Infitah	open door policy
Istihsan	juristic preference
Istishab	presumption of continuity
Istisna'	kind of sale where a commodity is transacted before it comes into existence. It means to order a manufacturer to manufacture a specific commodity for the purchaser.
Jaiz	permitted, though the law is indifferent
Kitabiyya	person belonging to another religion, not Islam
Madhab	school of Islamic thought (plural: *Madhabib*)
Mandub	desirable and can be rewarded, though omission is not punishable

Mard al-mawt	sickness certain to cause death
Masjid	place of prostration, mosque
Maslaha	well-being, interest of the public
Maysir	games of chance, gambling
Mihrab	alcove in a mosque indicating the direction of Mecca
Minbar	pulpit
Maslahah Mursalah	public interest
Moulvis	Muslim expert advisers to British Indian courts
Mamalat	a secular transaction
Mubah	permitted, though the law is indifferent
Mudarib	trustee, agent
Mudarabah	(also *mudharabah*, also *mudaraba*) also called *Qirad*, a form of partnership to which some of the partners contribute only capital and the other partners only labour.
Mukruh	undesirable, disapproved of, though not always punishable but omission is rewarded
Muqarada	A technique which allows a bank to float what are effectively Islamic bonds to finance a specific project. Investors who buy muqarada bonds take not only a share of the profits of the project being financed, but also share the risk of unexpectedly low profits, or even losses. They have no say in the management of the project, but act as non-voting shareholders.
Musharakah	partnership or company; used in modern Islamic law for *'inan* and related forms of partnership
Murabaha	(also *Morabaha*, also *Murabahah*) similar to any fixed interest loan
Musalla	prayer hall
Mustahab	desirable and can be rewarded, though omission is not punishable

Qabul	acceptance
Qadi	judge
Qard	loan
Qard al-Hasan	(also *Qard al-hasanah*) benevolent loan
Qisas	retaliatory punishment
Qirad	dormant partnership
Qiyas	analogical deduction
Quran	Islam's holy book
Rahn	collateral agreement
Ra'y	discretion, juristic reasoning or speculation
Rabb-ul-mal	investor, capital provider
Riba	interest, usury as forbidden in the *Quran*
'Sah	valid
Sahabah	the companions of the Prophet
Sadaqat	gift
Salam	a form of sale where the price is paid in advance
Salema	peace, purity, submission and obedience
Shari'ah	(also *Syri'ah*) Islamic Law
Shirkah	partnership
Shirkah al-'Inan	limited partnership
Sunnah	practices and traditions of the Prophet Mohammed
Tabarru'	donation
Tabiun	successors of the companions of the Prophet Mohammed
Takaful	co-operative, joint guarantee
Taqlid	imitation
Ulama	qualified religious scholars
Ummah	community of Muslims
Uqud al-Muawadhat	contracts of exchange
Uqad al-Tabarruat	contracts of charity
'Urf	custom
Usul	foundation or principles
Usul al-fiqh	the science of Islamic jurisprudence
Wahy	divine revelation

Wakalah   (also *wakala*) the contract of agency
Wudu   ritually clean
Wajib   obligatory, omission is punishable
Zakat   a charity tax, equivalent to 2.5 per cent of a
              Muslim's savings given annually to the poor
              and needy

Bibliography

In researching a book of this nature, I have drawn on many important sources, and wish to acknowledge, in particular, authorities such as Vogel and Hayes, Hussain and Bakar.

ABC Australia, "Indonesia: Balancing the secular state with Islam, post-September 11", http://www.abc.net.au/ra/asiapac/programs/s674845.htm, 13 September 2002.

Ahmad, Norafifah & Haron, Sudin, "Perceptions of Malaysian corporate customers towards Islamic banking products and services", *International Journal of Islamic Financial Services*, Vol. 3 No. 4, March 2002.

Ahmed, Z., "Prohibition of interest in Islam", *Journal of Islamic Banking and Finance* (Karachi, Pakistan), Vol. 1 No. 1, 1984.

Ahmed, Z., "Some misgivings about Islamic free banking", *Faisal Islamic Bank of Sudan Publication, English Series 7*, 1985.

Al Jazeera (Qatar), "Global role seen for Islamic banking", 7 December 2003.

Al Tamimi & Company, "Islamic finance: A UAE legal perspective", The International Islamic Finance Forum, International Institute of Research, Dubai, March 2002.

Al-Harran, Saad Abdul Sattar, *Islamic Finance: Partnership Financing*, Pelanduk Publications (M) Sdn Bhd, Selangor, 1993.

Al-Suwailem, Sami, "Towards an objective measure of ghararin exchange", *Islamic Economic Studies*, Vol. 7 Nos. 1 & 2, 2000.

Ariff, Mohamed, "Islamic banking", IslamiCity.com, http://www.islamicity.com/finance/IslamicBanking_Evolution.asp.

Ariff, Mohamed, "Islamic banking", *Asian-Pacific Economic Literature*, Vol. 2 No. 2, pp. 46–62, September 1988.

Ariff, Mohamed (ed.), *Islamic Banking in Southeast Asia: Islam and the Economic Development of Southeast Asia*, Singapore: Institute of Southeast Asian Studies, 1988.

Ariff, Mohamed, "Islamic finance can benefit from globalisation", The Malayan Institute of Economic Research, http://www.mier.org.my/, 29 August 2002.

Asean Focus Group – Asian Analysis, "Brunei — August 1998", in cooperation with the Faculty of Asian Studies at The Australian National University, http://www.aseanfocus.com/asiananalysis/article.cfm?articleID = 51, 1998.

Asian Banker Journal, The "Role model: Malaysia is showing the world how to integrate conventional and Islamic banking systems", Issue 41, p. 17, 2003.

Asmani, Azrin, "Banks get green light to offer another Islamic product", *The Straits Times* (Singapore), 13 June 2006.

Aurora, Leony, "Shari'ah banks should invite foreign investors or go public", *Jakarta Post* (Indonesia), 2004.

AXCO Insurance Market Report on Brunei — Non-Life, 2003.

Aziz, Zeti Akhtar, "Building a comprehensive Islamic financial system — New financial opportunities", keynote address at the Institute of Islamic Banking and Insurance's International Conference on Islamic Insurance, London, 26 September 2003.

Bachmann, Helena, "Banking on faith", *Time Europe*, 16 December 2002.

Bakar, Mohd. Daud, "Shariah issues pertaining to Islamic banking", Labuan IOFC, 2001.

Bakar, Mohd. Daud, "Legal issues: The Malaysia case", The International Islamic Financial Forum, International Institute of Research, Dubai, March 2002.

Bakar, Mohd. Daud, "Pluralism of fatwas: Bridging the differences and disagreements", The International Islamic Financial Forum, International Institute of Research, Dubai, March 2002.

Bank Indonesia, "The blueprint of Islamic banking development in Indonesia", September 2002.

Bartholomew, G.W., "The application of Shari'a in Singapore", *American Journal of Comparative Law*, Vol. 13, pp. 385–413, 1964.

Bartholomew, G.W., "English law in Partibus Orientalium", in A.J. Harding (ed.), *The Common Law in Singapore and Malaysia*, Butterworth, Singapore, 1985.

Basle Committee on Banking Supervision, "Core principles for effective banking supervision", Bank for International Settlements, http://www.bis.org/publ/bcbs30a.pdf, September 1997.

Baydoun, Nabil and Blunt, Peter, "Notes on Islam, culture and organisational behaviour", Working Paper, Northern Territory University, 1997.

Bernama.com, "M'sia's move to set up Islamic finance education centre lauded", http://www.bernama.com/bernama/v3/news_lite.php?id = 187096, 21 March 2006.

Bin Hj. Mohamed Ibrahim, Shahul Hameed, "From conventional accounting to Islamic accounting: A review of the development western accounting theory and its implications for the differences in the development of Islamic accounting", http://vlib.unitarklj1.edu.my/htm/account1.htm, June 1997.

Bloy, Nicholas, "The challenge of an Islamic private equity fund", The International Islamic Finance Forum, International Institute of Research, Dubai, March 2002.

Boston Consulting Group, The "Winning in a challenging market: Global wealth 2003", July 2003.

Brown, Daniel, Rethinking Tradition in Modern Islamic Thought, Cambridge University Press, Cambridge, 1996.

Burton, John, The Collection of the Quran, Cambridge University Press, Cambridge, 1977.

Business Times (Singapore), The "CIMB to launch Singapore Islamic trust in 1st half", 22 February 2006.

Cairo Times (Egypt), "What is Islamic banking", http://www.cairotimes.com/, 3 April 1997.

Central Intelligence Agency, The World Factbook, 2004.

Chapra, M. Umer, "Money and banking in an Islamic economy", in M. Ariff (ed.), Monetary and Fiscal Economics of Islam (International Centre for Research in Islamic Economics, Jeddah), 1982.

Chen, Gabriel, "S'pore bourse in deal to offer Islamic indexes", The Straits Times (Singapore), 6 January 2006.

Chen, Gabriel, "S'pore's financial skills can aid foray into Islamic banking", The Straits Times (Singapore), 22 February 2006.

Chen, Gabriel, "Income may offer Syariah-compliant motor insurance", The Straits Times (Singapore), 27 February 2006.

Chua, Val, "Wooing the Islamic billion$", Today (Singapore), 24 September 2004.

ClariNet, "Assets in Islamic banking industry put at over 260 billion dollars", http://www.clari.net/, 25 September 2003.

Cohn, Laura and Fairlamb, David, Singapore and its Growing Effect on Private Banking. Swiss Banks: Paradise Lost, eBrain Hosting, http://www.ebrainhosting.biz/english/news/news-Singapore_private.html, 2003.

Coulson, N.J., A History of Islamic Law, Edinburgh University Press, Edinburgh, 1964.

Coulson, N.J., "Islamic law", in J.D.M. Derrett (ed.), An Introduction to Legal Systems, Sweet & Maxwell, London, 1968.

Davies, Rod, "Malaysia capsule", Orient Pacific Century, http://www.asiamarketresearch.com/malaysia/, 10 June 2002.

DeLorenzo, Yusuf, A Compendium of Legal Opinions on the Operations of Islamic Banks, Institute of Islamic Banking and Insurance, London, 1996.

Doi, Abdur Rahman I, Shari'ah: The Islamic Law, Ta Ha Publishers, London, 1989.

Ead, Hamed A., (ed.) "History of Islamic science", The Alchemy Web Site, http://www.alchemywebsite.com/, based on the book Introduction to the History of Science by George Sarton.

Economic Review Committee, Sub-Committee on Services Industries, Financial Services Working Group, "Positioning Singapore as a pre-eminent financial centre in Asia", Channel News Asia, http://www.channelnewsasia.com, 2002.

El-Badour, R.I., "The Islamic economic system: A theoretical and empirical analysis of money and banking in the Islamic economic framework", unpublished Ph.D. dissertation, Utah State University, USA, 1984.

El-Gamal, Mahmoud Amin, "Permissible investment vehicles", Islamic-World.net, http://islamic-world.net/economics/permissible_investment_vehicles.htm.

El-Gamal, Mahmoud, "Updating our understanding of Shari'ah rules", The International Islamic Financial Forum, International Institute of Research, Dubai, March 2002.

El-Gamal, Mahmoud, "Western regulatory concerns about Islamic banks", The International Islamic Financial Forum, International Institute of Research, Dubai, March 2002.

Elati, Mas, "The ethical responsibility of business: Islamic principles and implications", OIC Exchange, http://www.oicexchange.com, 2 May 2002.

Emory Law School (USA), "Malaysia", http://www.law.emory.edu/IFL/legal/malaysia.htm.

Encyclopaedia Britannica Book of the Year 2004.

Errico, Luca and Farahbaksh, Mitra, "Islamic banking: Issues in prudential regulations and supervision", International Monetary Fund, Monetary and Exchange Affairs Department, March 1998.

Euromoney Publications (Jersey) Ltd, "Asian law profiles 2002: Brunei Darussalam", http://www.asialaw.com/.

Europe Union Banking and Finance News Network, The "Labuan: A premier international jurisdiction", 2003.

Ferrara, Peter J. and Saffuri, Khaled, "Islam and the free market", Islamic Free Market Institute Foundation, http://www.islamicinstitute.org/freemrkt.htm.

Financial Gazette (South Africa), The "Malaysia to accept Islamic banks", http://www.fingaz.co.zw/fingaz/2003/June/June5/4052.shtml, 6 May 2003.

Ghani, Badlisyah Abdul, "South east Asia: The Islamic finance growth story", presented at the Islamic Finance Singapore 2006 conference held in Singapore from 21–22 February 2006.

GlobalPro Training & Development (Malaysia), "Brunei agrees to merge 2 Islamic banks", http://www.globalpro.com.my/03jAN06-Brune-agrees-to-merge-2-Islamic-banks.htm, 3 February 2006.

Haemindra, Nantawan, "The problem of the Thai-Muslims in the four southern provinces of Thailand (Part Two)", *Journal of Southeast Asian Studies*, Vol. 8 No. 1, pp. 85–105, 1977.

Halim, Shah Abdul, "Islam & Pluralism: A contemporary approach" IslamOnline.net, http://www.islamonline.net/english/Contemporary/2003/05/Article01a.shtml, 8 May 2003.

Haqiqi, Abdul Wassay and Pomeranz, Felix, "Accounting needs of Islamic banking", IBF Net, http://islamic-finance.net/islamic-ethics/article-12.html, 2000.

Hassan, Hussain Hamed, "Conversion of National Bank of Sharjah into an Islamic bank: A case study" The International Islamic Financial Forum, International Institute of Research, Dubai, March 2002.

Hathout, Maher, "Demystifying the fatwah", The Institute of Islamic Information and Education, http://www.iiie.net/.

Henry, Clement M., "Guest editor's introduction", *Thunderbird International Review of Business*, Special Issue on Islamic Finance, July 1999.

Hodkinson, Keith, *Muslim Family Law: A Sourcebook*, Croom Helm, London and Canberra, 1984.

Hooker, M.B., *Islamic Law in South-East Asia*, Oxford University Press, New York, 1984.

Hooker, M.B., "Introduction: Islamic law in south-east Asia", *Australian Journal of Asian Law*, Vol. 4 No. 3, pp. 213–231, 2002.

Hussain, Jamila, *Islamic Law and Society*, The Federation Press, Sydney, 1999.

Image World Ltd, "ASEAN: Brunei and the Philippines", http://www.images-words.com/, 16 September 2001.

Institute of Islamic Information and Education, The "The authenticity of the Qur'an", http://www.iiie.net/.

International Monetary Fund, "Singapore: Financial system stability assessment, including reports on the observance of standards and codes on the following topics: Banking supervision, insurance regulation, securities regulation, payment and settlement systems, monetary and financial policy transparency, and anti-money laundering" (IMF), 2004.

Iqbal, Zamir, "Islamic banking gains momentum", *Middle East Executive Reports*, January 1998.

Iran Trade Point, "Historic Brunei-Bahrain MOU to boost Islamic banking", http://www.irtp.com/, 27 January 2003.

Irfani, A. M. *Musharakah and its Modern Applications*, Islamabad, December 1984.

Islamic Bank of Brunei Berhad, The "Questions and answers on Islamic banking", 2001.

"Islamic banking: The Indonesian experience", http://www.halah.com.my, 15 December 2000.

Islamic Banking Practice, 1st ed., Bank Islam Malaysia Bhd, Malaysia, 1994.

Ismail, Abdul Halim Hj., "Overview of Islamic banking", Labuan IOFC 2001.

Jamall, Ashruff, "Role of western institution's with Islamic windows" The International Islamic Financial Forum, International Institute of Research, Dubai, March 2002.

Kamali, Mohammad Hashim, *Principles of Islamic Jurisprudence*, Pelanduk Publications (M) Sdn Bhd, Selangor, 1989.

Khalili, Sarah, "Unlocking Islamic finance", *Infrastructure Finance*, April 1997.

Khan, Mohsin and Mirakhor, Abbas, "Islamic banking: Experiences in the Islamic Republic of Iran and Pakistan", IFM Working Paper No. 89/12, International Monetary Fund, Washington, 1989.

Khan, Mohsin and Mirakhor, Abbas, "Monetary management in an Islamic economy", *Journal of Islamic Banking & Finance*, Vol. 10 (July–September), pp. 42–63, 1993.

Khanna, Vikram, "S'pore an alternative to Switzerland?", *The Business Times* (Singapore), 5 November 2003.

Koh, Francis, Lee, Choon Li and Jindai, Parthsarthi, "Singapore as an emerging hub for wealth management", *Pulses*, A monthly publication of Singapore Exchange Limited, p. 10, November 2003.

Kolesnikov, Sonia, "New Islamic financial market set-up", UPI Business, November 2001.

Labuan Offshore Financial Services Authority (LOFSA) Annual Report of the Members of the Authority for the Year Ended LOFSA, 31 December 2005.

Lane, Karen, "Asia debt: Brunei prepares for debut Islamic debt sale", *Yahoo Finance*, http://sg.biz.yahoo.com/060316/15/3zetu.html, 16 March 2006.

Lewis, Bernard (ed), "The world of Islam", http://www.islamia.com/History/history_of_islam.htm, 8 June 2004.

The Library of Congress, Federal Research Division (USA), "Indonesia: The coming of Islam", http://www.loc.gov/rr/frd/.

The Library of Congress, Federal Research Division (USA), "Indonesia: The judiciary", http://www.loc.gov/rr/frd/.

Lowtax.net, "Labuan offshore business sectors", http://www.lowtax.net/, 2003.

Malaysia Industrial Development Authority, "Banking, finance & foreign exchange administration", http://www.mida.gov.my/.

Malaysia Industrial Development Authority, "Dual banking system attracts global interest", http://www.mida.gov.my/beta/news/print_news.php?id=407, 13 June 2003.

"Malaysia to popularize Shariah compliant products and services", http://www.islamic-banking.com, 23 August 2002.

(The) Malaysian Insurance Institute, "What is takaful", http://www.insurance.com.my/.

Martin, Josh, "Islamic banking raises interest" The International Islamic Financial Forum, International Institute of Research, Dubai, March 2002.

Menski, Werner F., "South Asia Muslim law today: An overview", *Sharqiyyat*, Vol. 9 No. 1, pp. 16–36, July 1997.

Microsoft Encarta Online Encyclopaedia 2004, http://encarta.msn.com/, Microsoft Corporation, 2004.

Mirakhor, A., "Analysis of short-term asset concentration in Islamic banking", IMF Working Paper, Washington, October 1987.

Misys International Banking Systems (Dubai), "Islamic banking", http://www.misys.com, 2002.

Montlake, Simon, "Islam will test new Malaysia chief", The Christian Science Monitor, http://www.csmonitor.com/2003/1030/p06s02-woap.htm, 30 October 2003.

Muljawan, Dudang, Dar, Humayon A. and Hall, Maximilian J.B., "A capital adequacy framework for Islamic banks: The need to reconcile depositors' risk aversion with managers' risk taking", Economics Research Paper, no. 02–13, http://magpie.lboro.ac.uk/dspace/bitstream/2134/369/1/02-13.pdf, 2002.

Muslim World Book Review (Leicester), "Legal rationality vs. arbitrary judgement: Re-examining the tradition of Islamic law", http://www.algonet. se/~pmanzoor/ISL-LAW-MWBR-2000.htm, Vol. 21 No. 1, pp. 3–12, October–December 2000.

Nation (Pakistan), The "Government encouraging Islamic banking in country", http://www.nation.com.pk/, 8 November 2002.

Naqvi, Ghazanfar, "Islamic mortgages, including refinance" The International Islamic Financial Forum, International Institute of Research, Dubai, March 2002.

New Straits Times (Malaysia) Berhad, "Islamic hire purchase bill to be tabled in parliament this year", Nation section, p. 14, 30 April 2004.

Nida'ul Islam Magazine, "Principals of Islamic banking", http://www.islam. org.au/, November–December 1995.

Nienhaus, V., "Why Islamic banks need top management: Basic problems of Islamic banking in a capitalistic world and some implications", The International Institute of Islamic Banking, Cairo, August 1981.

Noblehouse International Trust Sdn Bhd, "A general overview of the current standing of Labuan as an international offshore financial centre", http://www. noblehouse-labuan.com.my/, 2003.

Noer, Deliar, The Modernist Muslim Movement in Indonesia 1900–1942, Oxford University Press, Kuala Lumpur, 1973.

O'Hanley, Stephanie, "How Islamic banking works: A selection of financial products", http://www.ofcpublications.com/, July / August 2001.

Offshore Red: An OFC News Update, "Swiss tax decision could see Singapore shine as a haven", Vol. 8, p. 175, 2003.

Parker, Mushtak "Malaysia's Islamic banking enjoys another bumper year", Arab News, http://arabnews.com/?page=6&section=0&article=66788&d=11&m=7&y=2005, 11 July 2005.

Partadireja, Ace, "Rural credit: The ijon system", Bulletin of Indonesian Economic Studies, Vol. 10 No. 3, pp. 54–71, 1974.

Pearl, David and Werner Menski, Muslim Family Law, 3rd ed, Sweet & Maxwell, London, 1998.

Pipes, Daniel, "Islam and Islamism — faith and ideology", National Interest, http://www.danielpipes.org/article/366, Spring 2000.

Radio Television Brunei, "IBB flourishing despite business slump due to SARS", http://www.rtb.gov.bn/, 6 May 2003.

Rahman, Azizan Abdul and Idris, Rustam Mohd, "Overview of the Malaysian financial system and the development of Islamic banking in Malaysia", Bank Negara Malaysia, http://faculty.unitarklj1.edu.my/homepage/coursewareweb/beb2213/lesson12/note.htm.

Rashid, Syed Khalid, *Muslim Law* (1990) "Insurance and Muslims", paper given in Public Lecture series at IIU Malaysia on 13 October 1992, quoting Siddiqi, Insurance in an Islamic Economy, 1985.

Reed, Stanley, "How the Islamic world lost its edge", http://www.businessweek.com/, 28 January 2002.

Reszat, Beate, "Islamic banking in Asia", Hamburg Institute of International Economics, http://www.hwwa.de/, March 2003.

Robertson, Hamish, "Sharia banking grows in Indonesia", ABC Online (Australia), http://www.abc.net.au/am/content/2004/s1130581.htm, 2004.

Rosenthal, E.I.J., *Islam in the Modern National State*, Cambridge University Press, London, 1965.

Ruhanie, Norzuhaira and Ismail, Maisara, "Govt opens Islamic banking to foreigners", *Business Times* (Malaysia), 19 September 2003.

Russell, Susan, "Islam: A worldwide religion and its impact in South-east Asia", http://www.seasite.niu.edu/crossroads/russell/islam.htm.

Saifuddin, Sadna, "Kuwait finance house secures Islamic banking licence", *New Straits Times (Malaysia) Berhad*, http://www.nst.com.my/, 2004.

Saleh, Nabil A, *Unlawful Gain and Legitimate Profit in Islamic Law*, Cambridge University Press, United Kingdom, 1986.

Sanusi, Mahmood M, "Gharar", *IIUM Law Journal* Vol. 3 No. 2, p. 87, 1993.

Saravanamuttu, Johan, "Political and civil Islam in southeast Asia", as guest editor for *Global Change, Peace and Security*, Special Issue, Vol. 16 No. 2, June 2004.

Schacht, J., *The Origins of Muhammadan Jurisprudence*, The Clarendon Press, Oxford, 1950.

Schirrmacher, Christine, "Islamic jurisprudence and its sources", http://www.steinigung.org/artikel/islamic_jurisprudence.htm, adapted from Christine Schirrmacher "Der Islam 1 — Geschichte, Lehre, Unterschiede zum Christentum" Hänssler-Verlag Neuhausen/Stuttgart, 1994.

Sheridan, L.A., *Malaya and Singapore, The Borneo Territories. The Development of their Laws and Constitutions*, Stevens and Sons Ltd, London, 1961.

Sidhu, B.K., "CIMB working on Sukuk in Brunei", *The Star* (Malaysia), http://biz.thestar.com.my/news/story.asp?file=/2005/7/8/business/11431824&sec = business, 8 July 2006.

Siow, Li Sen, "S'pore can add value in developing Islamic finance", *The Business Times* (Singapore), 25 September 2004.

Siow, Li Sen, "Maybank launches Islamic banking", *The Business Times* (Singapore), 26 November 2005.

Siow, Li Sen, "Middle East Bank launches $80 bond issue here", *The Business Times* (Singapore), 13 December 2005.

Star (Malaysia), The "Islamic banking sector sets target", http://www.neac. gov.my/index.php?ch=19&pg=30&ac=412, 19 August 2003.

Star (Malaysia), The "Fast forward for Islamic banking", http://biz.thestar. com.my/news/story.asp?file = /2005/3/24/business/10495342&sec = business, 24 March 2005.

Suhrke, Astri, "The Thai Muslims: Some aspects of minority integration", *Pacific Affairs* Vol. 43 No. 4, pp. 531–547, 1970.

Sundararajan, V. and Errico, Luca, "Islamic financial institutions and products in the global financial system: Key issues in risk management and challenges ahead", International Monetary Fund, November 2002.

Swire, Mary, "Labuan Banks doubled their profits in 2000", Tax-News.com, April 2001.

SwissInfo, EU Tax Deal Leaves Swiss Banking Secrecy Intact, http://www. swiss-info.org/sen/Swissinfo.html?siteSect=105&sid=3900237, 4 June 2003.

Takaful Malaysia, "Takaful: Basis of Islamic insurance" and "Difference between takaful and conventional insurance", http://www.takaful-malaysia.com/, January 2003.

Taylor, Lenore, "Muslim fund for Australia", *Australian Financial Review*, 20 October 2003.

Thani, Nik Norzrul, *Legal Aspects of the Malaysian Financial System*, Sweet & Maxwell Asia, Selangor, Hong Kong, 2001.

Timberg, Thomas A., "Islamic banking in Indonesia", Partnership for Economic Growth, Small Scale Credit Advisor, Bank Indonesia, http://www.pegasus. or.id/Reports/02)%20Islamic%20Banking%20in%20C72.pdf, June 1999.

Timberg, Thomas A., "What we know about small and medium enterprise (SME) finance in Indonesia", Partnership for Economic Growth, Small Scale Credit Advisor, Bank Indonesia, http://www.pegasus.or.id/ Reports/01)%20SME%20Finance.pdf, 29 August 1999.

Timberg, Thomas A., "Risk management: Islamic financial policies — Islamic banking and its potential impact", Case Study funded in part by US Agency for International Development. Virginia, USA: Nathan Associates, Inc., http://www.basis.wisc.edu/live/rfc/cs_06b.pdf, 2003.

Toan, Robert & Barakat, Monir, "Islamic equity/Leasing funds: Investment objectives and marketing", The International Islamic Financial Forum, International Institute of Research, Dubai, March 2002.

U.S. Department of State, "Brunei", http://www.state.gov/r/pa/ei/bgn/2700. htm.

U.S. Department of State, "Malaysia", http://www.state.gov/r/pa/ei/bgn/2777. htm.

Useem, Jerry, "Devout Muslims don't pay or receive interest. So how can their financial system work?", *Fortune*, 10 June 2002.

Vloeberghs, Isabelle, "Islam in the southern Philippines", Northern Illinois University, http://www.niu.edu/cseas/outreach/islamSPhil.htm, 17 June 2004.

Vogel, Frank E. and Hayes, Samuel L., *Islamic Law and Finance: Religion, Risk and Return*, Kluwer Law International, The Hague, 1998.

Wilson, Rodney, "The need for more risk taking products", The International Islamic Financial Forum, International Institute of Research, Dubai, March 2002.

"Windows to Malaysia", http://www.windowstomalaysia.com.my/nation/11_4_1.htm, 17 June 2004.

Woon, Walter (ed.), *The Singapore Legal System*, Longman, Singapore, 1989.

Yee, Leslie, "Bahrain bank seeks licence for Islamic banking", *The Business Times* (Singapore), 25 October 2005.

Yee, Leslie, "OCBC appoints permanent syariah council", *The Business Times* (Singapore), 17 December 2005.

Yee, Leslie, "OCBC scores on 5-year risk-adjusted returns", *The Business Times* (Singapore), 9 February 2006.

Yee, Leslie, "MAS looks into aiding Islamic finance", *The Business Times* (Singapore), 22 February 2006.

Websites

Accounting & Auditing Organization for Islamic Financial Institutions, http://www.aaoifi.com/
Bank Muamalat, http://www.muamalat.com.my/
Bank Negara Malaysia, http://www.bnm.gov.my/
Brunei Direct, http://www.bruneidirect.com/
(The) International Investor, http://www.tii.com/
International Islamic Financial Market, http://www.iifm.net/
Labuan International Financial Exchange, http://lfxsys.lfx.com.my/
Labuan Online Community, http://www.labuan.net/
Lawyerment, http://www.lawyerment.com.my/
Monetary Authority of Singapore, http://www.mas.gov.sg/
Muslim Population Worldwide, http://www. islamicpopulation.com/
Wikipedia, The Free Encyclopaedia, http://en.wikipedia.org/
Yasaar Limited, http://www.yasaar.org/

Index